Understanding and Applying The Bible

Understanding and Applying The Bible

Robertson McQuilkin

MOODY PRESS
CHICAGO

The use of selected references from various versions of the Bible in this publication does not necessarily imply publisher endorsement of the versions in their entirety.

A workbook, developed by the author, is available for use with this text. It provides application for each of the principles and guidelines considered in the text, and is suitable for either individual study or class assignments. Furthermore, a complete media learning package for individual or group study utilizing the textbook, workbook, fourteen cassettes, and a syllabus is also available. If this learning package is used under the auspices of the Columbia Bible College and Seminary Extension program, a student can earn either four hours of graduate credit or five hours of undergraduate credit. For information on materials and tuition costs, write to: Biblical Education by Extension, P. 0. Box 3122, Columbia, SC 29230.

ISBN: 0-8024-9091-3

13 15 17 19 20 18 16 14

Printed in the United States of America

Dedicated with gratitude to the one
who practiced the teaching
of this book more faithfully than
any other I have known: my father

Contents

Principles and Guidelines for Understanding and Applying the Bible

Principles

	PRINCIPLE	CHAPTER
1.	Since the Bible was written by human beings, it must be treated as any other human communication in determining the meaning intended by the writer.	7
2.	Since Scripture is God-breathed and true in all its parts, the unity of its teachings must be sought, and its supernatural elements recognized and understood.	15
3.	Since Scripture is God-breathed, it is absolute in its authority for doctrine and life.	19

Guidelines for Principle #1

1.	Base the study on the historical, physical, and cultural setting.	8
2.	Research each unclear and important word.	9
3.	Analyze the structure of the basic unit of thought, the sentence.	10

GUIDELINES FOR PRINCIPLE #2

GUIDELINES FOR PRINCIPLE #3

Preface

This book has been growing slowly for thirty-five years. I have not been writing it that long—just contemplating it. The desire for this book was born in undergraduate days when I sensed the crucial place of Bible interpretation in knowing God and His ways. The longing intensified in seminary, where I discovered a great vacuum, only slightly filled after Hebrew and Greek studies. Then, as I began teaching seminarians, college students, and lay people how to understand and apply the Bible, I became increasingly frustrated.

For several years I used a battery of texts simultaneously. But that proved to be a load too heavy to bear and, in the end, only confused the beginning student. Encouraged by students and colleagues, I finally concluded that one solution to the problem would be to produce a basic hermeneutics textbook that would combine the essential elements in one volume. To what extent that purpose has been accomplished, others will judge. My aim has been to include the following characteristics:

Completeness. Many books deal with certain principles or guidelines for interpreting Scripture but omit others that are equally important. I felt the need for a textbook that would be comprehensive in scope, introducing as many as possible of the tools necessary for understanding the Bible and applying it authentically.

Balance. Some textbooks are thorough—even exhaustive—on a few aspects of biblical interpretation, but quite weak on others. For example, one book might leave the impression that studying how past scholars have interpreted the Bible is what students need to handle Scripture properly today. Other books concentrate only on analysis of the language structure. *Understanding and Applying the Bible* deals with the various aspects of interpretation in proportion to their usefulness in understanding the Bible.

Simplicity. The purpose of this textbook is to introduce serious Bible students to the basic principles of interpretation.

Scholarship. A book with simplicity should nevertheless not shortchange the student who desires to master the Word of God. Beginning students want to move beyond simple Bible study methods. Even an introductory textbook on hermeneutics ought to be so thoroughly grounded in solid scholarship that no student who masters the principles and guidelines would need to revise or discard any of them after moving on to a study of the original languages or theology. In fact, a comprehensive, introductory study of hermeneutics is probably the best foundation for effectively using the original languages and building a theology.

Biblical authority. Students always seem to ask the questions that scholars bypass. For years I have been asked, "Where did you get that principle of hermeneutics?" "How do I know that is the correct approach?" "Did you get that from the Bible?" The basis for an authentic hermeneutic should be in Scripture itself, since the Bible is one's final authority. For that reason I have distinguished between *principles* and *guidelines.* I have sought to demonstrate principles from Scripture. In contrast, guidelines deal with approaches and skills that are usually called "principles of hermeneutics," and I do not claim the same authority for those. I simply recommend them as reasonable ways to implement the principles that are clearly Bible-based. I have attempted to build an approach directly on the way Bible authors viewed Scripture.

Application. Throughout church history there has been a grave omission in scholarly biblical hermeneutics—the development of guidelines for applying Scripture authentically. The effort given to understanding the meaning of Scripture has been immense, but few evangelicals have given themselves to developing principles for establishing the significance of Bible teaching for faith and obedience today. This textbook is one effort in that direction.

Biblical illustrations. Some textbooks illustrate principles and guidelines with easily understood examples that are not drawn from Scripture. The reader must make the leap to actual Bible texts. I have endeavored to use the Bible itself to illustrate each guideline.

Although throughout the book I have used biblical illustrations, I have not tried to find the solutions to all the problems contained in the texts used. Though that might be frustrating to those who would like firm conclusions, this book is not designed to be a commentary on selected passages of Scripture. It is designed to be a guidebook for creating one's own commentary. Therefore, the purpose of this book is to teach ways to interpret, not to do the interpretation.

Significant illustrations. Although many biblical examples might be noted to illustrate a guideline, I have endeavored to use only illustrations that make a difference. That is, I have chosen illustrations on the basis of whether the interpretation of that passage depends on the correct use of the guideline under study.

That approach can be dangerous, for it is possible to offend almost everyone. But to illustrate principles for interpreting Scripture from only noncontroversial passages would be an intolerable offense to the purpose of this book. So I trust each person will find enough interpretations with which he agrees to compensate for those he finds troublesome!

Because the eight characteristics just listed are important for the beginning student, I have worked at combining them all in this book. I have not done it as well as I had hoped. But I have done it better than I would have without the help of many people. Second only to the dozens of specialists who have written in the field of biblical interpretation, I owe a debt to hundreds of students who would not allow me to get by with invalid or unclear answers to their questions about understanding and applying the Bible. In the final stages, I was greatly helped by my colleagues at Columbia Bible College in several daylong sessions of interaction on those themes. Many went the extra mile and critiqued the entire work. Among those, a special word of appreciation is due William Larkin, professor of New Testament in the Columbia Biblical Seminary and Graduate School of Missions, and my wife, Muriel, my most helpful critic.

Credit for this revised edition goes primarily to Brad Mullen, professor of theology and hermeneutics at the Columbia Biblical

Seminary and Graduate School of Missions. For example, he provided the very helpful addition of chapter 4, "Existentialism," and the updated bibliographies.

I commend this effort to God for whatever benefit He may see fit to bring from it in helping some of His people to better understand and apply His Book.

Introduction

How important is it to understand the Bible? Is it possible?

Church history indicates that understanding the Bible is very important, yet very difficult to do. The enormous energies devoted to explaining the Bible from the pulpit, in the classrooms of theological schools, and through the research and writing of theologians show the great importance of understanding the Bible. On the other hand, the division of the church into so many denominations bears witness to the fact that scholars and churchmen are far from agreement on what the Bible means. If it is *God's* Word, revealing *His* will, nothing could be of greater importance than understanding it. If the Bible was given to reveal the truth and not to hide it, God must intend that we understand it. If we do not, the fault must lie with us, not with Him. If we are not understanding His communication, it is imperative that we determine the reason.

Some people do not understand the Bible because they do not believe it is true, or at least, they do not believe that all parts of it are true. Others do not understand it because they are unwilling to obey it. Still others misunderstand the communication because they are unwilling to work hard at searching out the meaning. For those people who go astray in their understanding of the Bible, there are several words from God:

> All Scripture is inspired by God and profitable for teaching, for reproof, for correction, for training in righteousness; that the man of God may be adequate, equipped for every good work. (2 Tim. 3:16-17)

God's Word is to be trusted and obeyed. The one who does not trust it, or is not prepared to obey it, cannot expect to fully understand what God is saying.

> Be diligent to present yourself approved to God as a workman who does not need to be ashamed, handling accurately the word of truth. (2 Tim. 2:15)

It is not enough simply to trust and obey; one must be prepared to work diligently to understand Scripture.

But the right attitude or approach to the Bible is not all that is necessary for understanding its meaning. Do a good attitude and a commitment to hard work alone enable a person to build a beautiful piece of furniture? No, for there is a right way and a wrong way to build. Furthermore, certain skills must be developed before a person, though using the right method, can build properly. So it is with understanding the Bible. One must not only have the right attitude and approach; he must also use good methods and develop skill in their use. To introduce those methods and to develop some skill in their use is the chief purpose of this study.

The methods one chooses for biblical interpretation will depend on his presuppositions about the nature of the Bible. For that reason, we will first study major presuppositions concerning the Bible, and then determine which presuppositions are biblical. Using those biblical presuppositions, we will determine the principles for interpreting Scripture demanded by the presuppositions. That will be the order of our study: first, presuppositions; then, principles built on those presuppositions. After that, we will turn to the major portion of the study: examining the practical skills necessary to put the principles into practice. Through that method of study the student should be able to gain the knowledge and develop the skills necessary for determining and applying the meaning of Scripture.

PART ONE

PRESUPPOSITIONS AND PRINCIPLES

1
Presuppositions of Biblical Interpretation

General Approaches

The basic presupposition about the Bible that distinguishes believers from unbelievers is that the Bible is God's revelation of Himself and of His will for man. Although Christians are united in that basic affirmation, the implications of the statement are viewed in very different ways. It is important to understand those different approaches, for a person's presuppositions will determine, to large extent, how he understands and interprets Scripture. One author has explained it this way:

> We must know ourselves. . . . Each of us approaches Scripture with his own, or her own presuppositions. These presuppositions are part of our world view, part of our personal theology. In the first instance they relate to the way we regard Scripture. Does it consist of infallible propositions? Is it the record of certain acts of God? Is it an inspired record? Is there revelation outside Scripture? Our views here will dictate how we handle the text. Our minds are not empty when we read or listen to Scripture; what we hear is already partly predetermined by what is already in them; our presuppositions shape what we understand. It is not necessary to argue here for any one particular set of presuppositions, but to insist that we become aware of our own so that when we understand and interpret we know how we are being influenced by them. It is also important

> that we see that our presuppositions are consistent, that we do not operate with one set at one time and with another at another.[1]

If the Bible is accepted in any sense as a communication from God, a logical place to begin would be to inquire if the Bible itself tells us what approach we should take in seeking to understand its meaning. Does the Bible in one part interpret the meaning of statements in another part? It could almost be said that the whole New Testament is an interpretation of the Old Testament. Whether or not the methods employed by Christ and the apostles in determining the meaning of Old Testament passages are models for us to follow, certainly the presuppositions they held should be a model for us. What presuppositions, then, did Christ and the apostles hold about interpreting the Old Testament?

Christ and the apostles viewed the Bible as a document written by men, to be sure, but at the same time as a document whose source was God Himself.[2] Let us examine the implications of those two basic presuppositions—that the Bible is both a divine book, the Word of God; and a human book, the Word through men to fellow human beings.

The Bible Is Supernatural in Character

AUTHORITATIVE

Since God is the author, the Bible is authoritative. It is absolute in its authority for human thought and behavior. "As the Scripture has said" is a recurring theme throughout the New Testament. In fact, the New Testament contains more than two hundred direct quotations of the Old Testament. In addition, the New Testament has a large and uncertain number of allusions to the Old. New Testament writers, following the example of Jesus Christ, built their theology on the Old Testament. For Christ and the apostles, to quote the Bible was to settle an issue.

1. Ernest Best, *From Text to Sermon: Responsible Use of the New Testament in Preaching* (Atlanta: John Knox, 1978), pp. 97-99.
2. A good study of how Christ and the apostles used the Old Testament may be found in Richard Longenecker, *Biblical Exegesis in the Apostolic Period* (Grand Rapids: Eerdmans, 1975).

TRUSTWORTHY

Since God is the author, all the Bible is *wholly trustworthy*. Nowhere does Jesus Christ or any New Testament writer leave room for error. To be sure, Christ and the apostles presented a revelation of God and His will that went far beyond what was revealed in the Old Testament. But there is not the slightest hint of error, even when the New Covenant is explained as setting aside the temporary, Old Covenant. Since the Bible is the Word of God, it is considered absolutely trustworthy in its overall message and in each part of the revelation.

Because its source is God, the Bible is trustworthy in all its parts so that all parts form a harmonious unity. Paul wrote that "*all* Scripture is given by inspiration of God" (2 Tim. 3:16; italics added). New Testament authors quoted from every section of the Old Testament and from almost every book of the Old Testament. Furthermore, the message of the Old Testament was seen by Christ and the apostles to be a single message—redemption.

Because of its divine authorship, the Old Testament is viewed as a Christian book. The apostles used the Old Testament as the basis for their teaching concerning Jesus Christ. Christ did things "that Scripture might be fulfilled." That formula was characteristic of Jesus' teaching. The gospel writers and the apostolic letter writers followed the same approach.

Many prophecies in the Old Testament were direct, such as that concerning the death of Jesus Christ in Isaiah 53.

> But such clear predictive prophecy and fulfillment is seldom found in the New Testament; it is the exception rather than the rule. Instead, . . . the New Testament writers looked for the meaning of the Old Testament as contained in its *sensus plenior* (full meaning). In so doing, they found varied correspondences, analogies, and suggestive similarities—some more substantial, some less substantial—but all based on the underlying presuppositions of the sovereignty of God in the affairs of history; the unique character of the Scriptures as divinely inspired; and the identity of Jesus as the *telos*, or goal, of the history of salvation.[3]

3. Donald A. Hagner, "The Old Testament in the New Testament," in *Interpreting the Word of God*, ed. Samuel J. Schultz and Morris A. Inch (Chicago: Moody, 1976), p. 103.

We will study later whether we should follow the example of Christ and the apostles in making allegorical interpretations of Old Testament history and teaching. At this point, it is enough to emphasize that the Old Testament was viewed as a supernatural, Christ-centered book by both the Lord Jesus Himself and by His apostles.

The Bible Is Natural in Character

The New Testament treats the Old Testament as a supernatural book. The Old is filled with prophecy concerning the Messiah and the New Covenant. Those prophecies are explicit and found by Christ and the New Testament authors hidden within the events and words of the Old Testament. However, the New Testament does not treat the Old Testament as exclusively supernatural, or as a "magical" book. It treats the Old Testament as a human communication, using language in its common sense. The authors of the Old Testament are often designated. Moses, David, and Isaiah are constantly quoted, and lesser-known prophets are named as a source of revelation. Peter expressed it clearly: "Men moved by the Holy Spirit spoke from God" (2 Pet. 1:21).

Richard Longenecker writes concerning Jesus' method of interpreting the Old Testament:

> A number of times in the Gospels, Jesus is portrayed as interpreting the Old Testament in a literalist manner, particularly in matters concerned with basic religious and moral values. . . . In his teachings on human relationships, Jesus is represented as employing the Scriptures in a straightforward manner as well, with only minor variations in the texts cited. In rebuke of the Pharisees, for example, he quoted Exodus 20:12, "Honor your father and your mother," and 21:17, "Whoever curses father or mother, let him die the death." In support of the indissolubility of marriage he quoted Genesis 2:24, "For this reason shall a man leave his father and mother and be faithfully devoted to his wife, and the two shall be one flesh." . . . Like Judaism generally—whether pharisaic, nonconformist, or even Hellenistic—on matters having to do with man's basic orientation to God, man's basic moral values, and man's basic human relations, Jesus interpreted the Scriptures quite literally. These are matters of foundational importance upon which God had spoken plainly, and

therefore they were taken by Jesus and his contemporaries in Judaism without further elaboration.[4]

Inasmuch as the subject of his letter was basically ethical, James used the Old Testament in a direct, literalistic way. Stephen's recitation of Jewish history (Acts 7) may be the longest of that nature in the New Testament, but it is typical of New Testament handling of Old Testament history. Stephen was not using the stories of history to draw out a secret message. The real meaning upon which he based his argument is not hidden beneath the historic facts; the historic facts themselves are the real point.

Not only are biblical moral teachings and history taken by biblical writers in their ordinary sense, but even in theological teaching, both Paul and the author of Hebrews in most instances adhered to the original sense of the passage. Christ and the apostles often found meanings in the Old Testament that the ordinary reader would not suspect were there, and thus treated the Old Testament as a supernatural book. But their overwhelming use of the Old Testament was in the original, manifest sense of the passage.

In other words, the teaching of the Bible is to be accepted as straightforward, human communication to be taken in its natural sense.

Before we examine the principles based on the two presuppositions held by Christ and the apostles—that the Bible is both divine and human—we should note several ways those presuppositions have been distorted and misapplied. Four faulty approaches to biblical interpretation predominate today. First, *the naturalistic approach* limits the meaning and significance of Scripture to those elements that conform to natural processes and human insight. The possibility of divine authorship and supernatural events are ruled out from the start. Second, *the supernaturalistic approach* interprets all Scripture from a supernatural point of view. The interpreter's task, consequently, is to seek several meanings or hidden meanings, which are to be uncovered through intuition and spiritual experience. The "natural" meaning of the text is downgraded or totally ignored. Third, *the existential approach* is an

4. Longenecker, pp. 66-68.

attempt to combine the first two. It accepts the naturalistic approach, yet goes beyond it by locating the truth of Scripture in the encounter between the interpreter's response and the witness of the biblical author to a similar religious experience.

The final approach is *the dogmatic*. All specific interpretation is made to conform to a predetermined system of doctrine or external authority. This approach often is used by those who advocate one of the first three approaches. In addition, some believers, with otherwise sound approaches, may err in dogmatically setting aside the plain meaning of the text to make it conform to a system of doctrine, some human authority, or even a personal experience. Few would admit to espousing this approach, yet it is all too common. All of us are subject to the temptation.

Obviously, these approaches to understanding Scripture differ so basically that the meaning one finds in Scripture will be radically different. For example, take the story of Joshua's conquest of Jericho (Joshua 6). The naturalist may see the account as an ancient story that was made up (since walls do not normally tumble before trumpet blasts) to teach the victory of good over evil against great odds. Since the supernaturalist is looking for a hidden meaning, he may see the marching around Jericho in silence as a mandate for Christians to witness by their "walk" in silence six days a week until the leader (preacher) on Sunday proclaims the gospel, and the walls of unbelief come tumbling down and people are converted. Existentialists might focus on the call to personal religious faith that was at the writer's center of attention. The story for the existentialist might be only a legend, the details of which hold no importance. Some dogmatists will have a problem with the slaughter of the citizens of Jericho at God's command—a loving God would never order the death of innocent people. Others might have no problem at all, believing that the people of Jericho were created for the purpose of damnation anyway.

Chapters 2 through 5 of this book discuss in order the subtle, and not so subtle, elements of interpreting Scripture using the naturalistic, supernaturalistic, existential, and dogmatic approaches. It is important to begin with this overview since many interpreters today tend toward one of those approaches.

The balance of the book outlines a basic approach for understanding and applying the Bible in a way that gives full value to both its human and divine authorship. Some have called this the "grammatical-historical" approach, but that term suggests only a few of the many principles necessary for understanding human communication. And it does not include at all the dimension of divine communication that will modify, at certain points, the normative approach for understanding human language. Perhaps we could call the approach the Bible has for itself, and which we will seek to follow, "the human/divine communication analysis" approach. But first, let us consider those approaches that err in understanding and applying the Bible through an overemphasis on one characteristic of Scripture at the expense of another.

2
Naturalistic Approaches

A strict naturalist allows for nothing supernatural in the Bible or anywhere else. Some interpreters take that position. Others are less rigid and recognize some supernatural elements in Scripture. Those who approach the Bible naturalistically believe they must minimize or eliminate elements unacceptable to their reasoning because the Bible is of human authorship. Although there are many naturalistic approaches, we will consider the three most widely influential: (1) rationalism, which became dominant in the seventeenth century; (2) literary criticism, which rose to prominence in the nineteenth century; and (3) cultural relativism, which has become increasingly influential in the latter half of the twentieth century.

Rationalism

The Bible is rational because it appeals to the mind. In fact, its purpose is to "transform" minds from the mind-set that prevails in the world (Rom. 12:2). The Bible is rational in that it is perfectly truthful, never contradicting itself. The Christian approaches the Bible rationally rather than irrationally. Rationalism, however, denotes a system of interpretation that springs from a naturalistic worldview. A rationalist relies on his own reasoning as the ultimate authority. That view is reflected in the rationalist's presupposition: that which cannot be verified in terms of contemporary experience or rational thought cannot be accepted as true, and therefore cannot be God's Word. The rationalist's ultimate criterion for deciding whether or not a teaching is trustworthy is the individual's autonomous reasoning.

To the rationalist, three kinds of problems in the Bible have been a stumbling block to accepting it as wholly trustworthy, and thus an authoritative Word from God. First, some teachings in the Bible have been considered morally unworthy of God. David's prayers for vengeance on his enemies (the imprecatory psalms), and the commands to destroy the people of Canaan are examples of such unacceptable elements. The rationalist does not seek to reconcile those elements with the more acceptable (to him) teachings of Scripture, but simply affirms that they are not the Word of God. In recent years many other teachings of Scripture have been assigned to the same category by the rationalists. The biblical teachings on divorce, the role of women in marriage, acceptance of civil authority, and many others have been rejected on so-called moral grounds.

Two other elements in the Scriptures have been rejected by rationalists: the miraculous, and statements of Scripture that seem to contradict other scriptural statements (such as historical references that do not agree).

Following the Reformation, the spread of rationalistic interpretation was accelerated by the advances of science. There suddenly appeared a far larger number of problems in Scripture than had been considered previously. Any theory of physical or biological science could be accepted by the rationalist as a closer approximation of the truth than anything Scripture might say on the subject. That precipitated the great conflict between evolution and the teaching of Scripture concerning creation. As science advanced, a number of long-accepted interpretations of Scripture appeared to be in conflict with newly emerging scientific theory. The rationalists tended to side with the scientific theories.

Since the physical world is not the chief focus of biblical revelation, the conflict over physical and biological theories, though intense, was limited. Upon the birth of the behavioral sciences in the nineteenth century, however, the number of teachings of Scripture that became unacceptable to the rationalists expanded rapidly. Psychology and sociology were moving directly into the heartland of biblical revelation by dealing with a common subject, man—his nature, his relationships, and what makes him whole. The battlefield widened quickly to encompass most of the Bible.

Those were the secular rationalists. But when we speak of a rationalistic presupposition of interpretation, we do not refer primarily to the confrontation between the believer, who wishes to understand Scripture, and the unbelieving rationalist, who attacks from without. Rather, we speak of those who, in seeking to understand the Bible, adopt the presuppositions of rationalism. They rely exclusively on reason or a "scientific" approach to discern the meaning of the text and the message of God that may be found there.

The rationalist sets his own understanding (or that of another) as the authority whereby elements in Scripture are evaluated. If there is error in Scripture, someone must decide what is in error and what is true. According to the rationalist, that is decided by human reasoning. On that basis, the rationalist cannot accept the miraculous in Scripture because he has not personally experienced the miraculous, and also because reports of miracles cannot be verified by experimentation. Therefore, they must be explained either as a misapprehension of natural events or as myth growing up around some historical or imagined event.

For example, according to the rationalist, the crossing of the Red Sea was actually the crossing of the Reed Sea, a shallow swampland, through which the fleeing Israelites could walk. Also, the prophecies of Daniel were not written by Daniel, but by someone else after the events had taken place. And Christ did not feed 5,000 people; rather, using the generosity of the lad with the lunch, He inspired the others to share their own lunches generously. The presupposition is that the miraculous is impossible. Therefore, rather than resorting to the normal rules used by historians to verify historical events, the rationalist simply rules them out as unacceptable. That same approach is used to dismiss what is considered morally unacceptable teaching, and with passages that seem to contradict other historical evidences or contemporary scientific theory.

The end result of the rationalistic approach to Scripture is simply this: there is no sure word from God. That is, Scripture has no independent authority, for human reasoning is the final authority for judging anything that presents itself as a word from God.

Biblical Criticism

One of the significant features of the sixteenth-century Protestant Reformation was the insistence of its leaders upon *sola Scriptura*—Scripture alone. The Reformers' rejection of Scripture and tradition as equal authorities was influenced by discoveries that the Roman Catholic church's position was based on forgeries and altered documents. Protestants, consequently, became very interested in questions regarding the literary character of religious documents, particularly the Bible. Thus critical judgment was needed to discern truth from error. "Biblical criticism" is a technical term that does not imply sitting in judgment on the Bible as would an art critic sit in judgment on a work of art, or negativism as one with a "critical spirit." Rather, the term refers to skillful evaluation of the data to determine the truth about Scripture.

Biblical criticism took two forms. First, textual, or "lower," critics sought to determine the original text of Scripture. Many ancient copies of Scripture have been preserved in part or in whole. These exhibit varying degrees of compatibility. Textual criticism is the science of comparing text with text in order to determine the original text. Though we do not have any of the original manuscripts today, because of the great number of ancient copies and translations available (more than 5,000) we can be virtually certain of the original text. In those very few instances where questions remain, no significant doctrinal issue is at stake. Virtually all the early textual critics were motivated by the conviction that the original text was divinely inspired and thus that an accurate text was of utmost importance. Textual criticism seeks to establish the original text with the greatest possible accuracy.

The second type of biblical criticism, sometimes called "higher" criticism, examines the historical context of the document and the literary features of the book itself. This kind of analysis attempts to answer such questions as the date and author of a book and the type of literature in any passage. Such study is not inherently rationalistic. Knowing the difference between a law and a proverb, or poetry and an epistle, is helpful in properly understanding the author's meaning. Noting the theological purpose of any biblical writer also has its value. In the hands of the rationalists, however, the historical-critical method has typically become what has been called "destructive higher criticism"—a criticism whose end result, if not purpose, has been to destroy confidence in Scripture as being trustworthy and, ultimately, as being authoritative.

Historical criticism of this kind became a very useful alternative for those who dismissed the notion of a divinely inspired book but still saw some value in the Bible as a record of a religious quest. Israel's quest for God, the critic claims, is subject to all the limitations and errors of any religious pilgrimage. Israel's history, reconstructed by the critic, was made to conform to, and in most cases become totally explained by, the religious life of the peoples around it. This view is naturalistic because it rejects any possibility that God could have singled out Israel for His special purposes and could have inspired writers to accurately record their spiritual pilgrimage.

A typical example of the use of the historical critical method in a way that undermined confidence in the trustworthiness and authority of Scripture was the much debated JEDP theory. The theory held that the Pentateuch, or the five books of Moses, was actually a compilation of material from four different authors over many centuries. Using a similar technique, others have argued that the book of Isaiah was the work of two or three "Isaiahs," and that Paul could not have written the pastoral epistles that claim his authorship. This approach affirms error in Scripture to begin with and undermines the authority of Scripture to end with, making it easy to "interpret" the text in ways that conform to one's own reason as to what is possible or acceptable. Thus supernatural elements in Scripture or teaching that does not conform to one's modern biases are no longer true or authoritative.

All biblical critics, if they have done their homework, operate from the same evidence. If this evidence seems to undermine the trustworthiness of Scripture, one's presuppositions come into play. Those who believe the text is true will search for a solution that reinforces confidence in the trustworthiness of Scripture—and believing scholars have been remarkably successful in solving those problems. But those who believe that the Scripture, like any other book by human authors, may err, have no need to pursue further analysis. They solve the problem by concluding that the statement of Scripture is in error. Thus one's presuppositions about the character of the Bible precede and control interpretation.

For example, an interpreter holding naturalistic presuppositions might argue against the claimed authorship of a book, such as Moses or Paul, simply because the content of the book does not conform to assumptions about vocabulary and style. This undermines the authority of major portions of Scripture. The interpreter who accepts the Bible's statements concerning authorship, on the other hand, will argue the possibility—indeed the probability—that an author may use different styles at different periods in his life when dealing with different subject matter or when quoting from different authors. Similarly, a naturalistic interpreter may argue against the unity of Isaiah because the elements in one part of the book disturb a presupposition about the impossibility of anyone's predicting the future. In both cases, the Scripture is deprived ahead of time of exercising any independent authority. The whole design of the Bible is to challenge presuppositions, not to be controlled by them. And if the Bible is not supernatural, it is not merely the miraculous that is lost; the entire concept of a divine, authoritative revelation is eliminated. Thus destructive historical criticism chooses to acknowledge only the human authorship of Scripture. To be true to what Scripture affirms of itself, all critical analysis—textual, historical, and literary—must operate on the presupposition that it is both human and divine in origin.

Cultural Relativism

The task of bridging the gap between the distant world of biblical writers and the contemporary world is not new. Studying the context in which a passage was written has always been of importance for any who would understand the meaning of the Bible. With the exception of many who seek a "spiritual" meaning other than the natural meaning of the text, all interpreters seek for a clear understanding of the Bible by studying the historical, cultural, and religious context of the author.

On this side of the gap between ancient and modern, authentic interpreters of Scripture have sought to apply the meaning to the present situation. To do that effectively, the interpreters must understand the context of the reader or hearer. For the one who seeks to communicate biblical truth to people in a culture other than his own, a study of the culture of the recipient is of the utmost importance. The work of "contextualizing" the truth of God into the life of the hearer is what the incarnation is all about. Jesus Christ translated the truth of heaven into words and activities that human beings could understand. The apostles followed by applying the truth of God quite differently to Jewish and Gentile audiences.

Those two contexts, the author's and the contemporary reader's, are so important for understanding the meaning and applying the truth of Scripture that several chapters in this book will deal with developing skills in those two areas. But presuppositions must first be settled. What does one mean by "contextualizing"? In practice, contextualizers range all the way from those who study the cultural context of a passage simply as a method of clarifying the meaning of the text, to those who emphasize "context" so much that they become naturalistic in their approach.

The crucial questions are these: Does the validity of a biblical passage depend on a present-day understanding of ancient culture? Does the authority of Scripture depend on its compatibility with present-day cultural standards?

"Culture" is the way a group of people views things or does things. Cultural relativism holds that the value or truth of any idea depends on the culture in which it is found. Since the rationalist views culture as morally neutral, what produces desirable outcomes in one culture may not work in others, and is therefore not good in other cultures. The approach is legitimate in issues that are morally neutral. But to make that approach apply to everything in culture dethrones Scripture from its position of independent authority standing in judgment over all human thought and ways of behavior. In fact, it is not too much to say that Scripture was given precisely to change human culture and create a divine way of thinking and behaving.

Consider the implications of cultural relativism at both ends of the "understanding gap" between the ancient text and the present-day believer. What does cultural relativism do to the author's intended meaning on the one hand, and to the application of Scripture to present-day faith and life on the other?

When a present-day view of the context of the original writing differs from the clear meaning of the text, which interpretation prevails? If present-day understanding of the ancient culture—imprecise at best—is allowed to alter the plain sense of the text, the approach has become naturalistic.

Many teachings of the Bible prove troublesome for contemporary culture. A number of interpreters who consider themselves evangelical have handled those problems through a process variously called "contextualization," "dynamic equivalence interpretation," or "ethno-linguistics." That position holds that a Bible statement is merely a cultural "hull" that is temporary. It is authoritative only for the original hearers and may be set aside as nonbinding on other peoples with other cultures. But the "kernel" of truth hidden in the hull of culture is the enduring principle that is God's will for all peoples of all ages. At what point does such an approach become naturalistic? It becomes so when any teaching of Scripture is discarded as a dispensable cultural hull in favor of the kernel, or enduring principle, it is judged to contain, unless the Bible itself provides the basis for such a distinction.

The Bible nowhere authorizes a "hull and kernel" distinction. So on what basis is it made? Who judges? For example, which of the following commands are cultural hulls to be discarded?

> Wives, be subject to your own husbands as to the Lord. (Eph. 5:22)
>
> Children, obey your parents. (Eph. 6:11)
>
> Obey God. (Acts 5:29)

The person who evaluates which teaching to treat as enduring principle and which to treat as dispensable culture has become an authority above the authority of Scripture. If a marriage is deemed "dead" in the eyes of the marriage counselor, he should advise divorce, we are told. What of Christ's command against divorce? Well, Christ gave those commands in the context of first-century Jewish culture. Therefore, the principle behind that command is what should be obeyed, not the command itself. The principle is loving concern for one's partner. In some instances, it is held, loving concern will release the other partner from the legalistic bonds of marriage. The interpreter must not be bound by a simplistic, literalistic legalism, such contextualizers often say.

Consider biblical teaching on homosexual behavior. The prohibition in Scripture against homosexual relationships was made because of the reputation that homosexual people had in the Roman world, a reputation that would bring disrepute to the church if Christians condoned the practice. The principle behind the prohibition was one of fidelity. So, it is taught that a homosexual relationship should be condemned only if it is promiscuous. Ultimately, the interpreter's understanding of ancient culture becomes the authority for acceptance or rejection of biblical teaching. And since all Scripture was given in the context of a culture, virtually any teaching of Scripture is subject to that kind of contextual manipulation.

The presupposition for cultural relativists is the same as that for rationalists: naturalism. For the naturalist, when a clear teaching of Scripture is found in conflict with some human way of thinking, revelation must give way. For the cultural relativist, if one's understanding of the author's cultural setting or the contemporary cultural setting renders an interpretation that is contrary to the natural meaning of the text itself, the presupposition is that the contextualizer has greater authority in determining truth than the Bible itself. And that is naturalistic. (The question of contextualization is the crucial issue among evangelical interpreters. Therefore this subject will receive more thorough treatment in subsequent chapters.)

Selected Bibliography for Further Study

Aland, Kurt, and Barbara Aland. *The Text of the New Testament: An Introduction to the Critical Editions and to the Theory and Practice of Modern Textual Criticism.* Translated by Erroll F. Rhodes. Grand Rapids: Eerdmans, 1989.

Bruce, F. F. *The New Testament Documents: Are They Reliable?* Downers Grove, Ill.: InterVarsity, 1973.

Greenlee, J. Harold. *Introduction to New Testament Textual Criticism*. Grand Rapids: Eerdmans, 1964.

Krentz, Edgar. *The Historical-Critical Method.* Philadelphia: Fortress, 1975.

Soulen, Richard N. *Handbook of Biblical Criticism.* Atlanta: John Knox, 1981.

Stein, Robert H. *The Synoptic Problem: An Introduction.* Grand Rapids: Baker, 1987.

Stuhlmacher, Peter. *Historical Criticism and Theological Interpretation of Scripture: Toward a Hermeneutic of Consent.* Translated by Roy A. Harrisville. Philadelphia: Fortress 1977.

3
Supernaturalistic Approaches

As we have seen, Jesus set the example, which was followed by the New Testament writers, in treating the Bible as a supernatural book. Objects in the Bible such as a brass snake; events such as the exodus from Egypt; words such as the prediction that the prophet Isaiah would have a son; persons such as Melchizedek —all are understood as referring to Jesus Christ. Some of the references are clear enough that Jewish interpreters of the Old Testament—before the time of Christ—consistently saw references to the Messiah. But many references, like those noted above, would not have occurred to one who was in search of the meaning intended by the author. Unbelievers might say that a meaning was imposed on the text. Believers would say that a meaning lay hidden until revealed by Christ or His apostles. In any event, the Bible is viewed as a supernatural book, for future events could not be accurately predicted, in minute detail, many years in advance, merely by unaided human wisdom.

Jewish Interpreters and the Church Fathers

The way Jesus understood and interpreted the Scriptures was not a strange method to His Jewish listeners. Although some Jewish interpreters treated the Old Testament as a document to be understood in its plain meaning, the majority of interpreters at the time of Christ took it as their responsibility to discover subtle nuances and hidden meanings in Scripture.

> The central concept in rabbinic exegesis, and presumably that of the earlier Pharisees as well, was "Midrash." . . . "Midrash" designates "an exegesis which, going more deeply than the mere literal sense, attempts to penetrate in the spirit of the Scriptures, to examine the text from all sides and thereby to derive interpretations which are not immediately obvious."[1]

Some similarities exist between Jewish allegorizing (which holds that beneath the "letter," or the obvious, is the real meaning) and the way New Testament writers treated the Old Testament. But the New Testament does not treat every passage in the Old Testament in that way, as we have seen. Furthermore, the extreme and fanciful conclusions typical of rabbinic interpretations are not found in the New Testament.

Biblical scholars in the post-apostolic church tended to follow the example of the Jewish and, indeed, the Greek allegorizers more than the example of the New Testament writers. Although there was a group of scholars in Antioch (Chrysostom, Theodore of Mopsuestia, and Theodoret) who sought to determine the literal meaning intended by the authors, that school of thought did not prevail in the church. Clement, one of the great early North African Fathers of the church, and his disciple Origen of Alexandria set the pace for understanding Scripture throughout the early centuries of the church until the Reformation.

Origen held that the spiritual meaning of Rebekah's coming to draw water for Abraham's servants and cattle is that we must come to the wells of Scripture to meet Christ. Clement taught that the five barley loaves with which Christ fed the multitudes indicated the preparatory training of the Greeks and Jews that preceded the wheat harvest. The two fish indicate the Hellenistic philosophy: the curriculum of study and the philosophy itself. In the story of the triumphal entry the ass represents the letter of the Old Testament, and the colt, upon which Christ rode, the New Testament. The two apostles who brought the animals to Jesus are the moral and spiritual senses. Although Clement held that there could be both a literal and a spiritual meaning in a text, Origen held that everything in the Bible had a figurative meaning.

1. S. Horovitz, "Midrash," *Jewish Encyclopedia*, 12 vols. (New York: Ktav, 1904), 8:548.

That approach to Scripture, called the *quadriga*, or the four-fold method of interpretation, was firmly established from the fourth until the sixteenth century. The method examined each text for four meanings: literal, moral (tropologic), mystical (allegoric), and prophetic (anagogic). That approach was taught by means of a popular jingle:

> The letter shows us what God and our Fathers did;
> The allegory shows us where our faith is hid;
> The moral meaning gives us rules of daily life;
> The anagogy shows us where we end our strife.

A stock example is connected with the word "Jerusalem." Literally, it represents a city of that name. Allegorically it means the church. Anagogically it is the heavenly city. Tropologically (morally) it is the human soul.[2]

The Reformers took a firm stand against that kind of interpretation. The concern of Luther, Calvin, and Zwingli was to find the meaning intended by the authors and make that the authority for faith and practice. Those three Reformers were united in rejecting the claim of the church to be the interpreter. They affirmed the freedom, ability, and responsibility of the individual to understand the meaning of Scripture. All three were agreed on the authority of the Word of God as over all other authorities. They agreed that the entire Bible was trustworthy and, therefore, that Scripture could and should interpret itself. Furthermore, they agreed that the illumination of the Holy Spirit was needed for understanding Scripture, and that hard, solid work was also necessary. But they did not agree in every respect on how Scripture should be interpreted.

The Reformers differed in that Calvin was more consistent in following those principles. He held strictly to the one obvious meaning of a Scripture text. Luther was less precise and sometimes would use allegorization to interpret a passage in a way to reinforce his own theology. His interpretation was dogmatic, controlled by the system of theology to which he was committed—salvation by grace through faith alone. Furthermore, his interpre-

2. James D. Wood, *The Interpretation of the Bible: A Historical Introduction* (London: Duckworth, 1958), p. 72.

tation, at times, was subjectively rooted or was claimed to be received by direct illumination from the Holy Spirit.[3]

Although the Reformers differed in those ways, they were united in their commitment to the presuppositions held by the New Testament writers: (1) that the Bible is from God and through men; (2) that it is a straightforward communication of God's will for men; and (3) that it can be understood in terms of ordinary human language.

The Reformers provided a bridge from the often fanciful and always unpredictable interpretive efforts of the early and middle centuries of the church into the Protestant era, in which the meaning of the author became the object of search for those who would understand the Word of God. As the Reformers broke the stranglehold of allegorical interpretation, there was one other consequence: rationalists were now free to express their viewpoints. Immediately there were those who began to view Scripture as a purely natural book. In the end, the naturalistic approach became dominant in Protestant biblical interpretation.

Contemporary Spiritualizers

In saying that the Reformers endeavored to return the church more nearly to the view held by Scripture itself, and that the Reformers liberated the church from those who would view the Bible as purely supernaturalistic or even magical, it would be a great error to assume that allegorical interpretation ceased.

Indeed, this approach to Scripture is alive and thriving, particularly in evangelical circles. Consider the following use of Scripture by a prominent and widely read commentator:

> Third, the silence required of "the people" on this occasion supplied another important line in the typical picture furnished by this incident—though one which certainly will not appeal to many in present-day Christendom. Israel's capture of Jericho unmistakably pre-figured the victories achieved, under God, by the Gospel. The priests blowing with the trumpets of rams' horns pictured the servants of God preaching his Word. The forbidding of "the people" to

3. Ibid., p. 87f. See also Bemard Ramm, *Protestant Biblical Interpretation* (Grand Rapids: Baker, 1970), p. 54.

> open their mouths signified that the rank and file of Christians are to have no part in the oral proclamation of the Truth—they are neither qualified for nor called to the ministration of the Word. Nowhere in the Epistles is there a single exhortation for the saints as such to engage in *public* evangelism, nor even to do "personal work" and seek to be "soul winners." Rather are they required to "witness for Christ" by their *daily conduct* in business and in the home. They are to "show forth" God's praises, rather than tell them forth. They are to let their light shine. The testimony of the life is far more effectual than glib utterances of the lips. Actions speak louder than words.[4]

It will not do to excuse that way of handling the Bible by saying that there is only one meaning but many applications. It is true that a passage may be applied in many ways to contemporary settings. But to handle Scripture in that way, deriving a message that is far from the intention of the author, provides a model for interpretation that does not take the author and his intent seriously. In such an approach, the Bible is not its own authority, free to make its own point and to demand obedience to its own teaching. Rather, it is used to make some other point the commentator has in mind through the process of spiritualizing—finding a hidden meaning in the text.

The ingenuity of the Bible student is the only limitation to the exciting "interpretations" of Scripture in such an approach. When straightforward history is taken by the preacher to have hidden implications and exciting spiritual truths, it is no wonder that many evangelical Christians treat the Bible in the same way for devotional use and in seeking guidance. Many Christians who are faithful in reading the Bible devotionally feel "blessed" only when they find a surprising thought suggested to them by the text, a thought that bears no direct relationship to the intent of the author. To them, seeking to know God's will through careful study to understand the intended meaning of the author seems dry and boring.

In the same way, many Christians use Scripture in a "magical" way to give specific direction to decisions they must make. Where to go, what to buy, what employment to accept—all of

4. Arthur W. Pink, *Gleanings in Joshua* (Chicago: Moody, 1978), p. 102.

those are discovered through Scripture passages that, by marvelous coincidence, have a double meaning. First, there is the message intended by the author, and then the unrelated coincidental parallel to their own current experience. For example, a young couple may be seeking the mind of the Lord concerning their present employment in a mountainous area in the United States and their desire to go overseas for missionary service in an island nation. In their Bible reading they discover the injunction "Ye have compassed this mountain long enough" (Deut. 2:3, KJV*). Subsequently, they discover another biblical prophecy, "The isles shall wait for his law" (Isa.42:4, KJV). What could be clearer direction for their own lives than those words having the authority of the Bible? It does not matter that the message they received has nothing in common with the message the author intended to communicate.

I do not say that God has never given direction through such fortuitous coincidence. He may, as He does in circumstances of life such as the "chance" meeting of a person that becomes an integral part of God's guidance. But Scripture was not given for that purpose and to use it in that way, claiming biblical authority or God's endorsement of one's decision, is to abuse Scripture. The coincidence could just as well have occurred at God's providential arrangement through the daily newspaper, suggesting a course of action to the seeker after God's will. But one cannot claim, in either case, an infallible revelation of God's will as he could for the teaching of the passage intended by the author.

An even greater abuse occurs if this private "message" from God is used to set aside the plain teaching of Scripture—some biblical principle, for example, that forbids the proposed course of action. The Holy Spirit will never say something through the biblical writer, then contradict or change it for the reader. In other words, God will never enlighten the Christian through some understanding or application of Scripture that would in any way depart from what is written. If He did this, there would be no way to know if our interpretation was from the Spirit, from our sinful inclinations, from Satan, or from some psychological or physical stimuli.

*King James Version.

It should be clear that subjective impressions cannot run counter to the teaching of Scripture, if the Bible is to be the functional authority for our thinking and behavior. But the chief danger of relying on subjective impressions stimulated by Scripture is not to contradict Scripture. Rather it is to go beyond Scripture, finding meanings never intended by the author, especially in regard to personal guidance, and then to invest that impression with divine authority as if it were an infallible word from God. That is, the use of Scripture as a normal means of private guidance promotes the illusion of revealed truth with a higher level of authority than other providential circumstances of life because this "guidance" was found in the Bible.

The Bible should be used for guiding in "right paths." The right paths consist of the revealed will of God for human conduct, in line with the author's intended meaning. When a text has some coincidental relationship to present personal circumstances and a decision is based on such a "revelation," the individual should claim only his or her own subjective impression of the Holy Spirit's direction through an unusual circumstance, not the authority of scriptural revelation.

The essential error in all four faulty approaches to Scripture is subjectivism. In subjectivism, the interpreter becomes the ultimate authority for all interpretation. We have seen that the naturalistic approach to Scripture is subjective because the interpreter decides ahead of time what in Scripture is acceptable, given his or her naturalistic presuppositions. A less obvious kind of subjectivism, especially for those influenced by it, is spiritualistic subjectivism.

Evangelicals are prone to this error, perhaps because they take seriously the relationship between the Holy Spirit and the Word. The role of the Spirit is indispensable to proper biblical interpretation. The Holy Spirit inspired the writers of the Bible and He illumines Christians who read the words centuries later. Inspiration means that God superintended the writing of Scripture down to the last "jot and tittle." Illumination means that the Holy Spirit is now at work in the Christian to help him understand what is already there and to assist in applying the Word authentically.

Inspiration gave us a revelation of God's will without error, according to the Bible itself. But the Bible makes no such promise concerning illumination or Spirit-assisted understanding and application. Just as the Holy Spirit works to make us holy and we are not yet perfect, so He works to illumine our minds through Scripture, but the outcome of that illumination is not perfect understanding. If it were, all godly interpreters would agree. When an interpreter treats illumination as infallible, just as he would the text of Scripture, he has fallen to subjectivism. When such authority is claimed for one's interpretation of the meaning of Scripture it is bad enough, but when one claims that level of authority for his subjective impression of personal guidance, he errs even more, for he is bypassing the meaning of the inspired text.

Does this mean that sound hermeneutics and subjective "blessing" are mutually exclusive? By no means! Using hermeneutical principles to understand and apply Scripture authentically, recognizing the meaning God intended, will please God, to be sure, but it will also bring personal blessing. Scripture must be subjectively relevant or its purpose to transform our lives would not be accomplished. Christlikeness is not accomplished, however, by making God and His Word relevant to us, but by making us relevant to God and His Word.

Is There More Than One Meaning?

Does each Scripture passage have a single meaning, or are there hidden meanings to be derived through following special rules of interpretation or through the direct intuition of the Holy Spirit? The Bible gives examples of words revealed to one person, and the meaning of those words revealed to another. For example, in the experience of both Joseph and Daniel, the verbal message or vision was given to one person, whereas the interpretation was given to another (Gen. 41; Dan. 2). Is that what happened in the case of New Testament writers and Jesus Himself? Did the Old Testament author have one meaning in mind while the Author behind that author intended another or an additional meaning that He revealed to another New Testament person?

There are at least two views on that question. Some hold that there can be only one meaning for a passage if language is to be reliable and communication possible. Those people do not deny the possibility of many applications of a single meaning. Furthermore, they do not deny that there is a possible fuller meaning included in the original revelation. For example, in the difficult problem of Matthew's quotation concerning the calling of God's son from Egypt (Matt. 2:14-15), the quotation clearly referred to Israel's Exodus from Egypt (Hos. 11:1). How, then, does Matthew refer that to the sojourn of Mary, Joseph, and the infant Jesus in Egypt? Was there not a double meaning? Those who hold that there is only one meaning, and that that meaning was in the conscious intent of the author, understand the passage to be a statement of God's intent toward the Lord Jesus from the very beginning. In preparation for and as a symbol of the fact that Jesus Christ was to come from Egypt, God allowed His people Israel to have their own sojourn in Egypt. Indeed, at the very beginning He called the first of the chosen people, Abraham, from his sojourn in Egypt. Therefore, from the beginning only one meaning was intended. But the most complete fulfillment of that meaning awaited the advent of the One who brought that fulfillment.

Others have difficulty with such an approach. They believe that certain passages in Scripture cannot be explained as having a single meaning; such passages may have more than one intended meaning. The second (hidden or less apparent) meaning might have been in the mind of the author or it might have been only in the mind of the Holy Spirit, who inspired the author. In either case, they hold that additional meanings are there by divine intent. The Holy Spirit encoded a message and later revealed the secondary meaning through another inspired spokesman. (Most Scriptures about which there is sharp debate involve prophecy.) The approach to that problem will be considered in greater detail in chapter 18.

It must be granted, however, that it is legitimate for an author to have a secondary, or hidden, meaning. If Oliver Wendell Holmes, the writer of "The One-Hoss Shay," intended to write verse not only about a horse-drawn buggy that eventually fell apart, but to ridicule the system of Calvinism, that was his prerogative. If a comic strip writer intends to hide a political message in his comic strip, he has every right to do so. In fact, that is a common literary technique. One rule must be observed, however. If the author disclaims a hidden meaning, another person cannot with certainty or authority ascribe such a hidden meaning to it. In other words, the author himself is the only one who can legitimately identify the secondary meaning. That is the case with Scripture, if it is granted that there are secondary meanings in certain passages. And it is the Holy Spirit who inspired the author and who later inspired the interpretation of that author.

The question of whether the author had both an immediate and a fuller meaning in mind is complex and very important. For our purposes of establishing a basic presupposition for understanding Scripture, I suggest that that question need not be resolved. Even if one holds that there is only a single meaning in each passage, and that the author was aware of that meaning in its initial import and final implication, one must, nevertheless, agree that not just anyone can discern that fuller or final implication. On the other hand, if one holds that certain passages in Scripture were deliberately encoded with a dual meaning—one obvious and one to be identified at a later time—once again, it is not just anyone who can "break the code" or find that hidden meaning.

This point is important. Whatever position a person takes on the question of a hidden, secondary meaning in prophetic utterances or a fuller meaning intended from the beginning, Jesus Christ or the inspired writers are the only ones who can designate that secondary or fuller meaning. When Christ spoke, He had every right to interpret the author. The same may be said of those apostles He authorized to reveal God's will through the New Testament.

To ascribe hidden meanings to Scripture, a person assumes an authority equivalent to or superseding that of the author. The interpreter, whether an individual or the church, actually purports to be the authority standing above Scripture. But Scripture is to be the independent, final authority on what God says to His people.

It is true that revelation is supernatural in its content and in the way it was given. Scripture has supernatural effects in the lives of those who read and hear it. But the vehicle for that supernatural message is natural, human language that communicates in understandable words what God has on His mind. If there is a hidden meaning, the human author or God Himself are the only ones with the authority to so affirm. The child of God who desires to know and do His will must study diligently that he may handle properly the Word of Truth. He will give himself to identify the *single intended meaning of the author*, not to search for hidden meanings.

When the Lord Jesus Himself or an author of Scripture has disclosed a hidden meaning in a biblical text, in that we rejoice. And we are not surprised, for the Bible is a supernatural Book, and there is one Author behind the authors. But we must leave that kind of interpretation to the biblical authors, as we have not been authorized by God to be His infallible spokesmen of additional revelation.

Selected Bibliography for Further Study

Ackroyd, P. R., and C. F. Evans, eds. *The Cambridge History of the Bible*. Cambridge: U. Press, 1970.

Farrar, Frederic W. *History of Interpretation*. 1886 reprint. Grand Rapids: Baker, 1961.

Grant, Robert M. *A Short History of the Interpretation of the Bible*. With David Tracy. 2d ed., rev. and enl. Philadelphia: Fortress, 1984.

The Interpreter's Bible. "History of the Interpretation of the Bible," 1:106-41. New York: Abingdon-Cokesbury, 1952.

Smalley, Beryl. *The Study of the Bible in the Middle Ages*. Notre Dame: U. of Notre Dame, 1964.

Wood, James D. *The Interpretation of the Bible: A Historical Introduction*. London: Duckworth, 1958.

4
Existential Approaches

Rationalism did not provide the answers about the meaning and goal of life that its proponents anticipated. It ignored aspects of life beyond the rational. Existentialism, emphasizing the place of the will and emotions, arose early in the twentieth century as a reaction to rationalism. The existentialist proposed starting from the reality of human existence in order to interpret life more passionately and comprehensively.

In a sense, existentialism is actually an anti-philosophy. Its adherents reject the imposition of external forms or systems as restraining the free expression of human existence. Thus, unlike the naturalistic and supernaturalistic approaches, which might be characterized as "closet subjectivism," often unconscious of its subjective approach to interpretation, existentialism is openly and deliberately subjective as a basic operating principle.

Existentialism has its secular and Christian expressions. Secular existentialists, such as Jean Paul Sarte (1905-1980) and Albert Camus (1913-1960), believed that life has no objective meaning apart from the present experience. Without an objective reference point, secular existentialism led to nihilism, despair that life has any meaning. Christian existentialists also derive meaning and truth from personal experience but claim that the most fundamental experience of life is encounter with God. God's revelation to human beings, they claim, is personal, internal, and experiential. Theological liberalism, which was dominated by a rationalistic approach, was challenged and largely displaced by existentialism in the years following World War I. Among mainline Protestant theologians during the second half of the twentieth century, the predominant approach to understanding the Bible has been "existential."

The Existential Theologians

KARL BARTH

Søren Kierkegaard (1813-1855), the Danish philosopher, is credited with being the father of Christian existentialism. However, Karl Barth (1886-1968) was probably the most influential person in the movement. Barth was clearly supernaturalistic in that he strongly affirmed miraculous elements, such as the resurrection of Christ (although he did not view the resurrection as an event empirically verifiable in space and time, as classical orthodoxy did). Barth's approach recognized the supernatural; however, it was also thoroughly naturalistic.

Combining the supernatural and the natural in this way, the movement was called "neoorthodox"—"orthodox" in affirming the supernatural, "new" in adhering to naturalistic presuppositions in interpreting Scripture. Barth was able to combine these incompatible approaches by divorcing biblical truth from reason and history. Barth taught that the supernatural elements of Scripture could not really be true until, by faith, they were accepted by the interpreter as a word from God. An irrational "leap of faith" becomes necessary to personally experience a word from God.

Thus Christian existentialism is an attempt to be a halfway house between orthodoxy and liberalism, between supernaturalism and naturalism. An existential approach to the Bible holds that the Bible is, indeed, a vehicle of God's revelation to humankind. God gets His message through by means of the Bible. But the Bible, on its own, cannot be called the revelation of God. For the Bible to become fully God's Word, it must be received by someone; much like glue that is made up of epoxy and hardener, it becomes glue only when the two elements are properly mixed. So the Bible becomes revelation only when properly mixed with faith by the reader or hearer. The Word by itself will not hold. Until some human mind responds to the words of Scripture, it is only potentially a word from God, so the "mix" really determines the truth and authority of the text. For that reason, existentialist interpreters do not like to speak of the Bible as "the Word of God," but rather as "becoming" the Word of God.

Although the existential approach to the Bible claims to be first and foremost supernatural, its basic approach is naturalistic from two angles. First, existentialist interpreters generally adopt the historical-critical method, which, as we have seen, is based on naturalistic presuppositions. Second, the interpreter, by claiming authority for the significance of his own situation, ultimately controls meaning. Scripture alone is not revelation. It becomes revelation in the process of the interpreter's encounter with it. However, with their naturalistic presuppositions, the existentialists hold a view of Scripture unlike the view Scripture holds of itself. To them, the Bible is not an independent authority, but is subject to the judgment of the interpreter as to whether any element of Scripture is true, and therefore an authoritative word from God.

RUDOLF BULTMANN

Interpreters who approach the Bible existentially usually attempt to purge the Bible of all elements that do not conform to the conclusions of naturalistic historical criticism. If there were any doubt about the naturalistic base of existential interpretation, such doubt was thoroughly eliminated by the ascendancy in the movement of Rudolf Bultmann (1884-1976) and his disciples. Bultmann's "demythologizing" approach went far beyond the earlier existentialists in denying the historical trustworthiness of all the supernatural elements of Scripture, including the resurrection of Christ. Bultmann argued that in spite of the wholly natural quality of Scripture, those natural elements pointed to a higher reality, which was hidden in myth. Certain elements in Scripture could not to be taken as sober history. To strip away the myth and determine enduring significance was the task of the interpreter, Bultmann maintained, and demythologizing the Scriptures became the dominant theme of the existentialists after World War II.

It is not always apparent when a Bible commentator or preacher is using an existential approach. One characteristic of the approach is to use traditional words with nontraditional meanings. Such a person may teach about the new birth but have in mind spiritual insights that recur over and over. He may speak of the demonic, yet he does not refer to any supernatural being but rather to evil forces in society.

The Worldview of the Interpreter

More recently, leaders in the existential approach have moved into analyzing how human communication operates. This follows the general tendency of moderns to deflect attention from the ancient text and its author and to increase emphasis on the interpreter; to emphasize the role of the receiver of communication more than the role of the sender. Certainly God desires that His Word penetrate the twentieth-century interpreter in profound, life-transforming ways. The application of the Bible, however, must follow a faithful interpretation of the text's meaning, not determine it. The existential approach errs in giving as much, if not more, authority to the interpreter as to the text. In this view, the interpreter's input is an authoritative part of the mix that constitutes the word from God.

Those who study the phenomenon of understanding the mind of another person recognize that the recipient of any communication hears with a set of presuppositions that form a worldview. That worldview is a lens through which a person sees all of reality. It channels thought, explains experiences, and directs behavior. The lens is always functioning, but is rarely noticed. Furthermore, the language one uses makes sense only to one who understands the worldview of the speaker or writer. Effective communication, therefore, does not occur when the language employed by the sender (the Bible author, in this case) is plugged directly into the receiver's (the Bible interpreter's) worldview. Language is meaningful only as the receiver is able to understand the worldview of the sender and thus hear the words in the context of the sender's worldview.

Because the influence of one's worldview is so profound and pervasive, some have despaired of the possibility of meaningful communication between people of different epochs and cultures. In fact, the more extreme theoreticians have despaired of the possibility of accurate communication between male and female in the same culture or indeed between any two people. The religious existentialist believes that the problem is solved when the student of the ancient biblical text brings his own life-situation to the process of understanding so that the "mix" of ancient text and contemporary personal response yields a valid word from God.

Thus the existential approach claims that the life-situation of the interpreter plays a formative role in the meaning of any communication. The interpreter always arrives at an interpretation that is to some degree a composite of his or her ideas and the ideas of the original author. Because the interpreter has interacted with the text, it has reshaped the interpreter's thinking. But because the text has interacted with the interpreter, the interpreter has reshaped the message of the text. According to this existential approach, the gap between text and interpreter is not a regrettable feature, but rather constitutes the dynamic that enlivens all interpretation. The reason for this is that the new, presumably broader, perspective gained from interaction of text and interpreter becomes the basis on which the next encounter with the text occurs.

The New Hermeneutic and the Hermeneutical Circle

The name "the New Hermeneutic" has been given to the application of the existential approach to the phenomenon of human understanding. It is called "new" because it brings the interpreter into a formative role in the interpretive process. It is called "hermeneutic" (singular) because it is not interested in guidelines or methods by which one determines the meaning of the text, the traditional task of hermeneutics (plural), but rather in this one approach or theory of understanding human thought.

The New Hermeneutic has highlighted the problem of the "hermeneutical circle." The circular aspect of interpretation is evident when one asks, "Which comes first, the text or the interpreter's context, the ideas of the ancient author or the interpreter's ideas?" This is a legitimate question. It can alert the interpreter to the error of assuming the Bible can be read so objectively as to make that interpretation free from bias or blind spots.

There is a fundamental difference, however, between the perspective of the New Hermeneutic and the historic approach to understanding Scripture, as represented in this book. The New Hermeneutic says there is no way out of the circle. There is no objectivity in interpretation, no abiding meaning in a text apart from the interpreter's input. The Bible, however, is a communication from God, and the inspired human language of the text is backed up by His truthfulness and unchangeableness. It is objectively true, independent of anyone's interpretation of it. Thus, for those who accept the independent authority of the Bible, the interpreter does not attempt to create new meaning, though he or she may attempt to understand and apply the objective meaning of a passage more authentically than has been done in the past. There may in this way be a valid new interpretation, but never new authoritative revelation of God's truth.

The acceptance of the independent and objective truth of the Bible does not completely solve the problem raised by the "hermeneutical circle," however. How can any interpreter, holding a host of conscious and unconscious presuppositions, know that he or she is viewing the text from God's perspective, unencumbered by personal prejudices? The New Hermeneutic is correct when it claims that the text is not passive. That is, the text is not merely an object of understanding. The Bible is alive, examining and interpreting the interpreter. Also, the New Hermeneutic is right when it contends that the text and the interpreter are engaged in a process. Just as the new Christian is not born into the family full-grown, but grows in godliness for a lifetime, so growth in understanding and applying the Bible continues throughout the Christian's pilgrimage. The New Hermeneutic is seriously flawed, however, because it denies the objectivity of truth and rejects the independent authority of the Bible.

Though the ancient part of the hermeneutical process (the inspired text) and the modern element (the interpreter's role) cannot be separated, they can and must be distinguished. God's authority stands behind the word spoken in the ancient context; it does not stand behind what the interpreter brings to the text. The Bible is true and authoritative; the interpretation may or may not be. According to the New Hermeneutic, the interpreter jumps into the ever-spinning process of interpretation and is moved along by the uncertainties and complexities of the present context influenced by the ancient text. According to the method advocated by this book, the interpreter acknowledges the truthfulness and authoritativeness of the Bible given in the ancient context and employs guidelines for interpretation suited to let the text speak for itself. Though never free from the influence of the present context, the meaning of the authoritative text is there to be discovered. The Christian can be certain of his or her advance toward a proper understanding and application of the Bible because the Christian is moving toward a fixed point, not a moving target of existential interpretation.

Furthermore, the Christian interpreter can be quite certain of the meaning of the great, fundamental teachings of Scripture —such is the clarity of God's revelation. This certainty does not require an exhaustive knowledge of all God's truth. In other words, the Christian can apprehend God's truth and live in the light of it without claiming to comprehend fully all of God's truth. This distinction helps the Christian avoid unrelenting doubt on the one hand and uncompromising dogmatism in disputed interpretations on the other.

Several insights and warnings emerge from an evaluation of the New Hermeneutic. First, the interpreter must guard the independent integrity and authority of the biblical text at all cost. Second, interpretation of the Bible cannot be made with perfect objectivity. Third, the interpreter must approach the text with humility. Fourth, because the interpreter is not the only one interpreting the Bible, he or she should recognize the value of the church in the interpretation. Fifth, interpreting the Bible is a lifelong activity whereby God moves us along from one degree of knowledge to another. Sixth, the church can have certainty without needing to know it all. And seventh, dogmatism on matters not made clear by Scripture must be avoided.

Existentialist thinking, dominated by Barth, then Bultmann, and finally the New Hermeneutic, no longer has a dominant approach. Instead, the field of historical criticism is divided among many approaches, not all existential. In the search for new paradigms for bridging the gap from an ancient document to contemporary naturalistic thought, scholars are looking to literary criticism, linguistics, philosophy of language, and the social sciences. But no approach has come to a dominant position. On the other hand, many erstwhile evangelical scholars are moving toward the old Barthian approach.

Though twentieth-century existentialists set out to reclaim God's Word from the destruction of the rationalists, by the end of the century they had become just as destructive of any objective, true, and authoritative word from God. Perhaps this is the inevitable result when finite and fallen men look to themselves for the answers, which is the fatal flaw of the existential approach. In the end it cannot escape subjectivism, specifically naturalistic subjectivism.

Selected Bibliography for Further Study

Achtemeier, Paul J. *An Introduction to the New Hermeneutic*. Philadelphia: Westminister, 1974.

Barth, Karl. *Church Dogmatics*. Vol. 1, *The Doctrine of the Word of God*. Translated by G. T. Thomson. New York: Scribners, 1936.

Brunner, Emil. *Truth as Encounter*. Translated by A. W. Loos and D. Cairns. Philadelphia: Westminster, 1964.

Bultmann, Rudolf. "The Problem of Hermeneutics." In *Essays Philosophical and Theological*. Translated by J. C. G. Greig, pp. 234-61. London: SCM, 1955.

Gruenler, Royce Gordon. *Meaning and Understanding: The Philosophical Framework for Biblical Interpretation*. Grand Rapids: Zondervan, 1990.

Silva, Moises. *Has the Church Misread the Bible? The History of Interpretation in the Light of Contemporary Issues*. Grand Rapids: Zondervan, 1987.

Robinson, James M., and John B. Cobb, Jr., eds. *The New Hermeneutic*. New York: Harper & Row, 1964.

Thiselton, Anthony. *The Two Horizons: New Testament Hermeneutics and Philosophical Description*. Grand Rapids: Eerdmans, 1980.

5
Dogmatic Approaches

God cannot lie. Therefore, contradictions do not exist in the mind of God. And since all Scripture is inspired by God, all of it is trustworthy. In light of that basic presupposition, attempts to harmonize all the teaching of Scripture on a given subject or to compose a comprehensive systematic arrangement of all the teachings of the Bible are valid.

Not only is the systematic study of Scripture valid, it is necessary. For example, it is essential for the theologian to study all Scriptures that describe the way of salvation. Should he take a particular passage, isolate it from all other passages dealing with how a person may be saved, and construct a doctrine of salvation, the result would distort God's truth concerning salvation. Thus, the theologian's systematic work is not only valid and necessary but of great importance for understanding the meaning of Scripture. Efforts to harmonize or find the underlying unity of the various passages dealing with a particular theme are valid for the teacher and preacher as well as for the theologian.

The synthesizing of biblical teaching is not only valid, necessary, and important; it is inevitable. Each person approaches any written document with a set of presuppositions. Similarly, the Christian approaches the Bible with some system of thinking concerning God and God's revealed truths. He sees everything in Scripture through those mental glasses. In fact, he is only able to receive with understanding ideas that fit somewhere into the systematic arrangement of ideas already in his mind. Therefore, not only are all Christians theologians, all people are theologians. The only difference is that some are better theologians than others.

Ernest Best describes this theological bent, which is common to every person:

> All interpretation of Scripture is controlled by the theology of the person who interprets. It may not be true that a particular interpreter has a consistent theological position; but his theology and world view always control his interpretation.[1]

If it is true that the Bible is God's Word, and that the human mind constantly seeks a coherent relationship among the ideas accepted for belief, what approach should be used to avoid error in discovering the true meaning of Scripture? How can a person work through the maze of his own preconceptions and those of other Bible interpreters to get at the message God reveals in Scripture? Answering those questions will be a major part of this study in chapters 15 and 16.

The process of synthesizing biblical teaching is not unlike the scientist's use of induction and deduction. The interpreter begins with a particular passage, establishing the meaning intended by the author. He does this for all passages dealing with the the same and related themes, seeking to correlate them into a unified whole. The interpreter then forms a plausible model, or hypothesis, confident of the Scripture's ultimate unity. The model in turn becomes the basis for study of other passages. A thoroughly tested model, held with conviction, becomes a theological system by which the interpreter understands the Scripture.

Arriving at a system is not the final step in interpretation, however, because interpreting the Bible is a lifelong process. Scripture must always control the system; the system must never be allowed to control the Scripture. The interpreter, furthermore, is responsible to incorporate *all* biblical teaching into his or her system, or abandon the system. In addition, aspects of any system that cannot be substantiated by direct biblical evidence should be held with humility and tentativeness.

1. See Ernest Best, *From Text to Sermon: Responsible Use of the New Testament in Preaching* (Atlanta: John Knox, 1978), pp. 97-99.

There is, therefore, a legitimate use of a system of doctrine in studying Scripture. The problem arises when the system itself becomes the authority, sitting in judgment on the independent authority of any given passage of Scripture. The Bible is misinterpreted when the interpreter uses the dogmatic assumptions of the system to force the passage to conform to the dogma, rather than to modify the dogma to conform to Scripture.

Because of a God-given zeal to understand all of God's truth, scholars and lay people alike, through the ages, have first constructed what to them are coherent systems and then have interpreted all passages of Scripture on the basis of their systems. That is called the dogmatic approach. The presupposition of a dogmatic hermeneutic is this: all the teaching of Scripture is from God and must be seen as a coherent whole; after that systematized whole has been discovered, specific interpretation must conform to it.

A dogmatic framework is built of materials provided in Scripture, and of logical deduction from the biblical data. Then every passage is made to conform to that system. For that reason, in recent years, many scholars have ceased to speak of *hermeneutics,* or a set of guidelines by which a person may interpret Scripture. Rather, they speak of a *hermeneutic,* in the singular. That means that a person frankly acknowledges not only his presuppositions but his entire system. Then on the basis of that system he seeks to understand Scripture. Today we have the New Hermeneutic, the Calvinistic hermeneutic, the dispensational hermeneutic, and many others.

Although I said *recently,* that was the basis of interpretation in the Middle Ages as well:

> During the Middle Ages, many, even of the clergy, lived in profound ignorance of the Bible. . . . It became an established principle that the interpretation of the Bible had to adapt itself to tradition and to the doctrine of the Church. It was considered to be the acme of wisdom to reproduce the teachings of the Fathers, and to find the teachings of the Church in the Bible. . . . Hugo of St. Victor even said: "Learn first what you should believe and then go to the Bible to find it there."[2]

2. Louis Berkhof, *Principles of Biblical Interpretation* (Grand Rapids: Baker, 1950), p. 23.

In the middle of the sixteenth century the Council of Trent established the dogmatic approach as the official hermeneutical presupposition of the Roman Catholic church. The Council stated that both the Scripture *and* the church were infallible, effectively making the church's dogma the controlling factor in interpretation.

What of the Reformers? There is only one explanation for Luther's low view of the book of James. Luther's basic system was found in Romans 1:17. Since the book of James departed from that norm, as Luther understood it, it was to him a "right strawy epistle."

By any recognized principle of biblical interpretation, could John 3:16 mean: "For God so loved the *elect*"? There would seem to be no way it could, except on the basis of dogmatic presuppositions, that is, by a system that has been constructed by which that passage is held to mean something other than its plain, normal meaning. Likewise, a system can be used to eliminate repentance as a prerequisite for God's acceptance, or the Lord's Prayer as suitable for Christian lips.

The system determines the meaning. Milton Terry speaks to the issue of interpreting on the basis of dogmatic presuppositions:

> When a theologian assumes the standpoint of an ecclesiastical creed, and thence proceeds, with a polemic air, to search for a single text of Scripture favorable to himself or unfavorable to his opponent, he is more than likely to overdo the matter. His creed may be as true as the Bible itself; but his method is reprehensible. Witness the disputes of Luther and Zwingli over the matter of consubstantiation. Read the polemic literature of the antinomian, the Calvinistic, and the sacramentarian controversies. The whole Bible is ransacked and treated as if it were an atomical collection of dogmatic prooftexts. . . . It should be remembered that no apology is sound, and no doctrine sure, which rests upon uncritical methods, or proceeds upon dogmatic assumptions. Such procedures are not exposition, but imposition.[3]

3. Milton S. Terry, *Bible Hermeneutics* (1909 repr.; Grand Rapids: Zondervan, 1974), p. 172.

When taken to an extreme, the dogmatic approach to Scripture clearly has undesirable results. The Bible is no longer its own authority. Although it provided the raw material that was built into the system, a great deal of logical deduction is also built into the system. That structure is then superimposed on any given passage of Scripture, thus becoming the authority by which the normal meaning of the passage is set aside.

The dogmatic approach as defined here, though accepting both the supernatural and natural characteristics of the Bible, nevertheless hinders objective study to determine the author's intended meaning. Ultimately, it can do more than inhibit good interpretation. It can replace the independent authority of Scripture with the authority of a man-made system.

There are three typical sources of dogma that control interpretation. Coherence—either among the teachings of Scripture or with one's own situation—is achieved by an uncritical submission to dogma from one of three sources: tradition, another Christian, or personal experience.

Tradition

Tradition can be viewed positively or negatively. As a doctrine or doctrinal system adopted by a body of Christians and passed to succeeding generations, tradition is helpful by showing what truths have stood the test of time. It offers today's church the insight of the historic church. How difficult it would be for Christians if each new generation had to think through such matters as a definition of the Trinity, the relationship between the human and divine in Christ, or justification by grace through faith. Historically, the Holy Spirit has directed the church in establishing interpretations that stood the test of Scripture then and have now stood the test of time. Tradition, however, can also hamper faithful interpretation of the Bible if traditional interpretations are adopted without adequate scriptural justification. Unexamined inherited propositions often function as a set of blinders that prevent Christians from seeing in Scripture what falls outside their field of vision. Furthermore, restricted vision distorts what *is* seen.

A system of doctrine that has been inherited needs to be maintained or modified under the rigorous authority of Scripture

—allowing the Scripture to control one's faith and behavior even when a particular passage doesn't seem to fit the system. Though there is reassurance when one's system is held in common by many other believers, that does not mean that every Christian must fit exactly into a traditional system, such as covenant or dispensational, Calvinist or Arminian, Lutheran or Anabaptist. Everyone has a system, whether operating explicitly or only implicitly. But whatever the system, inherited tradition or personal construction, interpretation should be done rigorously under the independent authority of Scripture.

Another Christian

A less defensible dogmatic approach to interpretation occurs when one accepts uncritically the teaching of another individual, such as a revered teacher or pastor. Allowing someone else to establish dogma or biblical interpretation without assuming personal responsibility to understand, trust, and obey the teaching of Scripture may come from one of several motivations. Love or admiration for the leader entrusted to interpret Scripture may lead to an uncritical abandonment of personal responsibility. That is easy when the trusted leader knows much more than the follower and especially when such a leader encourages or expects this kind of relationship as a requirement for "discipleship" or "loyalty." There is security in acceptance by the leader or by the group of followers.

Of course, one may abdicate responsibility out of laziness—unwillingness to expend the effort to personally understand and apply Scripture. The fine line between humble learning from the learned and allowing the learned to establish dogma may not always be easy to discern, but each believer is responsible to do his best to bring his thought and life under the direct authority of Scripture.

The problem might not be *what* is believed, but *how* it was arrived at. If any Christian holds dogmatically to an interpretation of the Bible merely because it was offered by another person—no matter how respected that person may be—then the Bible no longer functions as its own authority in that life. The authority of all

Christian leaders is derived; only the authority of Christ through His Word is absolute.

Personal Experience

A third wrong variety of dogmatic approach to Bible interpretation is allowing personal experience to establish dogma. Positively viewed, a Christian's experience with God propels him or her to want to know more about God. The more God is trusted and obeyed, the more He shows Himself faithful. A Christian's experience, however, can become a hindrance to proper biblical interpretation. The Bible is ultimately authoritative, not the subjective evaluation of one's experience with God. For example, a conversion experience is always accompanied by certain ideas about sin, the Person of Jesus Christ, the ministry of the Holy Spirit, and the purposes of the church, to mention a few. If at a later time a Christian refuses to alter his or her views in the light of biblical testimony, saying, "But I know that what I have always believed is true because I experienced it," or, "God was at work in my life then so I know it must be true," then personal experience has become the authority. We must interpret our experience by the Bible and not interpret the Bible by our experience.

In developing a private interpretation of a passage or a personal system of doctrine, we must to do so with great humility. To depart from the common wisdom of the church is hazardous to say the least. Contemporary concepts of individual autonomy notwithstanding, the Holy Spirit guides His church in a way that no independent individual can confidently claim. Having noted that, each of us must give an account of how he handled Scripture: "Do your best to present yourself to God as one approved, a workman who has no need to be ashamed, rightly handling the Word of Truth" (2 Tim. 2:15).

We have considered four approaches to Scripture that can lead the Bible student far astray: supernaturalistic, with its allegorical or mystical interpretations; naturalistic, with its rationalistic interpretations; existentialistic, with its unworkable combination of naturalism and subjectivisim; and the dogmatic approach, which interprets each passage in terms of a dogmatic presupposition. Note that each of these approaches is based on a true assumption about Scripture: that it is supernatural, that it is natural, that it must be applied, or that it is coherent—all its teachings fit together in unity. The problem is that each of these approaches has emphasized one true presupposition about Scripture but has neglected other presuppositions just as true. The solution is to approach Scripture with all the presuppositions it holds about itself.

These Bible presuppositions imply certain principles, which we will now identify. After that, we will discuss guidelines that derive from those principles.

Selected Bibliography for Further Study

Berkhof, Louis. *Principles of Biblical Interpretation. Grand Rapids:* Baker, 1950.

Braga, James. *How to Study the Bible.* Portland, Oreg.: Multnomah, 1982.

Carson, Donald A. *Exegetical Fallacies.* Grand Rapids: Baker, 1984.

Efird, James M. *How to Interpret the Bible.* Atlanta: John Knox, 1984.

Fee, Gordon D., and Douglas Stuart. *How to Read the Bible for All Its Worth.* Grand Rapids: Zondervan, 1981.

Ferguson, Duncan S. *Biblical Hermeneutics: An Introduction.* Atlanta: John Knox, 1986.

Inch, Morris A., and C. Hassell Bullock, eds. *The Literature and Meaning of Scripture.* Grand Rapids: Baker, 1981.

Longenecker, Richard. *Biblical Exegesis in the Apostolic Period.* Grand Rapids: Eerdmans, 1975.

Kearley, F. Furman, Edward P. Myers, and Timothy D. Hadley, eds. *Biblical Interpretation: Principle and Practice.* Grand Rapids: Baker, 1986.

Mickelsen, A. Berkeley. *Interpreting the Bible.* Grand Rapids: Eerdmans, 1963.

Ramm, Bernard. *Protestant Biblical Interpretation.* Grand Rapids: Baker, 1970.

Shultz, Samuel, and Morris A. Inch, *Interpreting the Word of God Today.* Chicago: Moody, 1976.

Sproul, R. C. *Knowing Scripture.* Downers Grove, Ill: InterVarsity, 1977.

Terry, Milton. *Bible Hermeneutics.* Reprint. Grand Rapids: Zondervan, 1974.

Stott, John R. *Understanding the Bible.* 2d ed. Grand Rapids: Zondervan, 1985.

Virkler, Henry A. *Hermeneutics: Principles and Processes of Biblical Interpretation.* Grand Rapids: Baker, 1981.

6
Basic Principles for Understanding the Bible

Context of the Author

Since the Bible is of human authorship, it must be treated in the same way as any other communication. The goal is to determine the author's intended meaning. But certain barriers—differences in language and culture—divide the author and the reader. To understand the author's meaning, the reader must understand the context from which the author writes. Only that way can the effect of the differences between author and recipient be overcome and true understanding become possible.

In subsequent chapters we will study the methods and develop the skills necessary to penetrate the context of biblical writings, use that understanding to interpret Scripture, and, finally, apply it to our lives. At this point we will simply establish the principle itself. God chose to reveal Himself and His will, not in a catalog of propositional truths recorded in a celestial language, but to people in history by using human language. Therefore, it is our responsibility to study the Bible as we would any other human communication to determine as accurately as possible what the authors intended us to understand, believe, and obey.

To do that, we will consider two contexts: the historical and the literary. The historical context includes the physical, geographical, cultural, and ideological context of the authors and the people to whom they wrote, as well as historical events. The literary context includes the language itself, the type of literary form, and the immediate context of the passage under consideration.

The Truth of Scripture

Since God is the Author behind the authors—the ultimate source of revelation—Scripture must be interpreted as true in all its parts, and the unity of all its parts must be sought.

TRUE IN ALL ITS PARTS

Since Scripture is true in all its parts, it will not do to distort one's interpretation of Scripture or to disallow a portion of Scripture because it might seem to be in conflict with a scientific theory, a historical source, or some contemporary psychological, sociological, or anthropological theory. For example, God created the world; it did not spontaneously arise. So, any understanding of the first chapters of Genesis must treat those chapters as true, or the interpreter will have used naturalistic presuppositions. Did God command Israel to destroy certain people, or was that Moses' idea? Who wrote the book called "Isaiah"? There are many passages whose interpretation depends on answers to questions like those, but the interpreter who accepts the evaluation of Jesus Christ concerning the Bible must make every interpretation on the assumption that the Bible is true.

THE UNITY OF ITS PARTS

If, indeed, the Bible is true in all its parts, a true unity must be sought by the one who would understand Scripture. Scripture must be compared with Scripture, and the context of the writer and the first receiver of the writing must be examined. Questions might arise such as: How does the Old Testament relate to the New? What does one do with historical records that do not seem to agree, such as certain genealogies in the Old Testament or accounts of Christ's life in the New Testament? The task of harmonizing Scripture requires certain skills that we shall study in some detail in chapter 15. But we must begin with the basic principle that because all parts of Scripture are true, the harmony is already there, and our task is to search it out.

The searcher for truth is responsible for compiling all that the Bible says on a particular subject. Furthermore, it is a worthy task to seek to relate all biblical teaching in a comprehensive understanding of the whole body of biblical truth. Guidelines and methods for interpreting Scripture by Scripture, for building an exhaustive consideration of any biblical theme, and for constructing a comprehensive arrangement of all Bible doctrine (systematic theology) will be part of our study in chapter 16. At present, however, we may conclude that all Scripture is trustworthy, simply because God is the Author. Therefore, it is not only legitimate but necessary to work toward finding the unity among all the teachings of Scripture to understand more fully the will of God.

The Authority of the Bible

The Bible, and only the Bible, is the absolute authority for faith and life. Therefore, all principles and techniques for deriving the meaning of a biblical passage must conform to the principle that the Bible itself is the final authority. Consider four major implications of that principle.

THE PURPOSE OF DIVINE REVELATION

God revealed Himself in the Bible for the purpose of human salvation. That "salvation" is complete—from initial reconciliation with God through the transforming of the believer into the moral likeness of God to the final loving unity with God in eternity. God's purpose is man's salvation.

> You have known the sacred writings which are able to give you the wisdom that leads to salvation through faith which is in Christ Jesus. All Scripture is inspired by God and profitable for teaching, for reproof, for correction, for training in righteousness; that the man of God may be adequate, equipped for every good work. (2 Tim. 3:15-17)

To say that salvation is the purpose of Scripture means that revelation is limited. The Bible is not given to teach all there is to know about an infinite God or all about His universe. God did not inspire the biblical writers to provide a definitive record of ancient history or even to teach all there is to know about the nature of man. To use the Bible as a textbook on biology, psychology, or sociology is to misappropriate Scripture and to undermine its authority. To be sure, when the Bible touches on those areas, it is wholly trustworthy. It does not teach error. However, that is not the purpose of revelation. Rather, it is to reconcile people to God and, through that reconciliation, restore them to all that God designed them to be.

THE GOAL OF BIBLICAL STUDY

Since the Bible is the authoritative revelation of spiritual truth, the initial goal of biblical study must be to understand the author's meaning. If the Bible is to have any independent authority, we must determine the author's meaning.

If the purpose of Scripture is our salvation, that purpose can never be fulfilled unless God's message is understood. That is the task of the interpreter. However, to understand the Bible will not bring salvation. The message must be *believed* and *obeyed.* That is the task of application.

> Exegesis, to be true to the intention of the writer, must include application.[1]

> A learning of the Word of God can be validated only by a transformed life. . . . The only teaching that can rightly be called "Bible teaching" focuses, not on processing information, but on hearing and responding to God's own loving voice.[2]

In summary, the purpose of divine revelation is the salvation of individuals. For the Bible to be effective in man's salvation, the first step is understanding the author's intended meaning. The next step is to apply that meaning to the contemporary setting for faith and obedience. Only then will the purpose of divine revelation be fulfilled and Scripture be fully authoritative in the lives of people.

1. William Larkin, Jr., *Faculty Handbook* (Columbia, S.C.: Columbia Bible College and Seminary, 1990). p. F-3.
2. Larry Richards, "Church Teaching: Content Without Context," *Christianity Today,* 15 April 1977, p. 16.

EXTENT OF AUTHORITY

We have already seen that God's authority does not rest upon our fallible interpretation of Scripture but only upon Scripture itself. But does that authority reside only in the teaching of Scripture, or does it also extend to the words of Scripture? If so, does it extend to every part of Scripture equally? First, our presupposition is that *all* Scripture is God-breathed and infallible. This is not the place to defend the position of verbal inspiration or scriptural inerrancy. However, it is appropriate to remember that our models for interpretation are Jesus Christ and the New Testament writers. They treated the Old Testament Scriptures as not only authoritative but also as wholly trustworthy—even to the individual words. Following that example, we affirm that the authority of Scripture covers the words as well as the concepts. Some interpreters affirm the truth of the concepts of Scripture while holding that some of the words are in error. But there is no meaning without words true to that meaning. Furthermore, the "inspired concept" theory violates the independent authority of Scripture. The criteria for distinguishing between true meanings or concepts, and untrue words through which the meaning is given, shifts the authority to those criteria or to the one using them.

John Warwick Montgomery uses a parallel with a legal document to make this point clear:

> Concerning the interpretation of legal documents in general, Lord Bacon offered these telling aphorisms:
>
> > "Interpretation that departs from the letter of the text is not interpretation but divination."
> >
> > "When the judge departs from the letter, he turns into a legislator."
>
> Sir Roland Burrows makes the point with admirable clarity: "The Court has to take care that evidence is not used to complete a document which the party has left incomplete or to contradict what he has said, or to substitute some other wording for that actually used, or to raise doubts, which otherwise would not exist; as to the interpretation, it is always restricted to such as will assist the Court to arrive at the meaning of the words used, and thus to give effect to the intention as expressed."

> As with wills, deeds, and statutes, the faithful interpreter of the Bible will construe the text in a manner to give it validity rather than invalidity"; will operate with a "presumption against absurdity"; and, once the clear meaning of the text has been determined, will accept its application and enforcement in his life "though the results may seem harsh or unfair or inconvenient" (C. E. Odgers, *The Construction of Deeds and Statutes,* fourth edition, 1956, pp. 186, 188). The believing Christian interpreter of the testamentary Scripture will assume that in reference to it also "every part of a will means something and must be given effect and harmonized, if possible, by construing it in connection with all other parts" (F. H. Childs); and he will interpret the Old Testament always in light of the New on the ground that "the last testamentary expression prevails."[3]

Though all Scripture is from God, and thus trustworthy, not all Scripture is of equal authority for the obedience of Christians in the church age. That principle will be discussed in some detail when the principles for applying Scripture are studied in chapter 19. Scripture itself, as the final authority, must designate which part of it has enduring and universal application, and which part is limited. If the distinction between universal and limited applicability is made by any other principle or person, that principle or person becomes the authority, displacing Scripture's final word concerning itself.

LIMITATIONS IMPLIED BY THE PRICIPLE OF AUTHORITY

The authority of Scripture does put specific limitations on the principles of context of the author and the unity of Scripture. If that were not true, the Bible would not itself be the final authority. Let us look at those limitations.

Limitations of human context. As we have noted earlier, because the Bible came through human authors, the interpreter inevitably deals with two contexts: (1) he seeks to understand as fully as possible the context of the biblical writer, and (2) he seeks to interpret and apply biblical truth in the light of the contemporary context. Often those two endeavors are combined and usually

3. John Warwick Montgomery, "Testamentary Help in Interpreting the Old and New Testaments," *Christianity Today*, 5 May 1978, p. 55.

overlap. The key question is this: How can those helpful and legitimate tools for understanding Scripture be used without violating the authority of Scripture? On what basis does one distinguish between the authoritative and enduring message of the author, and the temporary, historical context?

Several approaches have been suggested. Some hold that a teaching is to be believed and obeyed if it is in the order of creation or of the nature of God (e.g., love). If a teaching of Scripture is not in the order of creation or of the nature of God, it may be assumed that the teaching is a temporary captive of the transient cultural form or specific historical context. The present-day interpreter must free the enduring truth for present-day application or rejection. Others hold that any command that deals with a universal principle, an ethical requirement made in all cultures of all times (e.g., not stealing), may be applied universally with the authority of God's certain will, but a culturally limited particular teaching may not be so applied. Commands concerning the role relationships in marriage are culturally limited particulars, and may not be applied with authority as God's certain will in all cultures at all times.[4]

Still others say teaching that is inherently moral and theological is authoritative, but nonmoral, nontheological teaching does not have the same authority.[5]

The problem with each of those approaches is, how does one decide? Since the Bible does not give us such a basis for interpreting Scripture, the interpreter, perhaps unwittingly, usurps the authority of Scripture by imposing his own external criteria on what teaching of Scripture may be accepted as authoritative and what teaching may be disregarded. The problem is a real one. The solution is not easy. But the abiding principle that puts strict limitations on cultural understanding is the authority of the Bible itself.

At this point let's distinguish between interpretation and application. The first task is to interpret; that is, to determine with certainty the intended meaning of the author. For that, cultural

4. Charles H. Kraft, "Interpreting in Cultural Context," *Journal of the Evangelical Theological Society,* December 1978, p. 257.

5. Gordon Fee, "The Genre of New Testament Literature and Biblical Hermeneutics," in *Interpreting the Word of God*, ed. Samuel J. Schultz and Morris A. Inch (Chicago: Moody, 1976), p. 133.

understanding is useful in illuminating the text. In making application from the text to a contemporary setting, it is necessary to examine the general principle that lies behind any specific instruction. In this way the seeker can determine and obey the will of God as revealed in the authoritative Word of God.

Consider an example alluded to earlier. "Wives, be subject to your own husbands" (Eph. 5:22) is clear enough. It will not do to say that is a culturally conditioned statement, and therefore no longer applicable. To do so would mean that the next command, "Children, obey your parents" (Eph. 6:1), should also be relativized, and the prior command to obey God could suffer the same fate. Paul's meaning to any objective observer is very clear. That meaning cannot be changed through interpretation if the interpreter recognizes the independent authority of God's Word. However, when it comes to application, the way in which the biblical teaching concerning the husband's role as head of the house should be applied will certainly differ from culture to culture. For example, a much more democratic atmosphere will prevail in the American home than in the Japanese home, whereas both may be obedient to the clear teaching of Scripture.[6]

To discern the principle behind a culturally conditioned teaching of Scripture is quite legitimate and necessary in applying the Scripture for present-day faith and obedience. That does not violate scriptural authority, but implements it. On the other hand, to use that approach in interpretation so that the plain meaning of Scripture is set aside replaces the authoritative text with contemporary cultural understanding. That not only violates Scripture, it becomes a tool that can manipulate Bible teaching into virtually any form desired by the interpreter.

Limitations of seeking the unity of all Scripture. The principle of the authority of Scripture puts certain limitations on implementing the principle of treating the Bible as an understandable human communication. It also puts limitations on the principle that the interpreter should work to harmonize the teaching of Scripture. Later we will study the guidelines and methods for harmonizing Scripture (chaps. 15-16).

6. See J. Robertson McQuilkin, "The Limits of Cultural Interpretation," *Journal of the Evangelical Theological Society*, June 1980, p. 113.

To summarize, the authority of Scripture is violated in two primary ways by those who work toward harmonizing apparently incompatible passages of teaching:

1. Obscure passages, uncertain interpretations, or minor biblical emphases are made to prevail over clearer passages or more pervasive teaching. On the surface, it would seem that the method is simply allowing Scripture to fight it out with Scripture. However, when an uncertain teaching is made to prevail over far clearer revelation, it is the interpreter or his interpretation that has become authoritative.
2. The interpreter violates the authority of Scripture through logical deduction from clear Bible teaching. That kind of deduction violates the authority of Scripture when (1) it is treated as infallible truth, or worse, (2) it is turned against other clear teaching of Scripture. It then becomes an extrabiblical philosophical position that has been used to subvert the plain intent of the biblical author.

The authority of the Bible must reign supreme if God's Word is to be understood, believed, and obeyed.

Prerequisites for Interpreting Scripture

Although God desires to communicate to every person, not just anyone can understand Scripture. The Bible is clear on that point. *Faith* is the prerequisite for truly understanding God's Word. A person who reads without faith may understand some revealed truth, but he cannot expect to *fully* understand any truth revealed in Scripture. There are several aspects of faith, all of which are essential for the student who would interpret the meaning of Scripture.

REGENERATION

Initial faith is necessary, for the unbeliever cannot understand the things of the Spirit. Regeneration is essential. This is explicitly taught in 1 Corinthians 2:6-16 and 2 Corinthians 2:15-18.

> The thoughts of God no one knows except the Spirit of God. Now we have received . . . the Spirit who is from God, that we might know the things freely given to us by God. . . . But a natural man does not accept the things of the Spirit; for they are foolishness to him, and he *cannot understand them,* because they are spiritually appraised. . . . For who has known the mind of the Lord, that he should instruct Him? But we have the mind of Christ. (1 Cor. 2:11-12, 14-16; italics added)

The Holy Spirit is the great Interpreter (John 16:13). Without Him all our efforts at fully understanding His Word are doomed to failure.

COMMITMENT

Regeneration is essential, but it alone will not qualify the believer to understand the truth of God. The believer must have confidence in Scripture, for faith is not mere intellectual assent. Rather, faith means *commitment,* yielding to the Book; to its message, its meaning, and its divine Author. Faith predisposes one to discover the meaning the biblical writer intended, not to read into the text his own desired meaning. Only the one with full confidence in the Scripture will make the commitment necessary to fully understand its meaning.

> If any man is willing to do His will, he shall know of the teaching, whether it is of God, or whether I speak from Myself. (John 7:17)

A person must be determined to obey the Word if he expects to understand it. Commitment to obedience has another characteristic: hard work. The person truly committed to obey God will study to show himself approved to God, a hard worker who has no need to be ashamed of his workmanship. "Faith" does not mean the Bible student lays aside his intellect and relies on feelings or subjective impulses to understand Scripture. No, the kind of faith that believes the Bible is God's own Word will drive the student to use all the resources God has given him to understand Scripture so that he may obey it.

PRAYER

Faith in the Author of the Word, the indwelling Holy Spirit, must be actively expressed. Prayer is the evidence of true faith, and the only atmosphere in which full understanding of God's intent can occur. It is simply not enough that He indwells us by faith and that we are open to His will with an obedient heart. We must actively ask, seek, and knock. There must be active dependence on the Holy Spirit, our Interpreter.

> I am Thy servant; give me understanding, that I may know Thy testimonies. (Ps. 119:125)

> But if any of you lacks wisdom, let him ask of God, who gives to all men generously and without reproach, and it will be given to him. (James 1:5)

The prerequisite for understanding the Bible is faith. Only one who is indwelt by the Holy Spirit, rightly related to God with an obedient heart, and actively seeking the wisdom that is from above can know the truth. Nevertheless, only the Bible is infallible, not we or our interpretations. We are illuminated by the Holy Spirit through the Word, not inspired. For that reason, there is a fourth element in faith necessary to an understanding of the Word of God.

HUMILITY

Humility is appropriate since we are dealing with the Word of God. It is also appropriate because of our nature. We are finite and subject to error. Furthermore, we are fallen and see reality only indirectly, veiled by sin. Therefore, an attitude of humility before the Word of God is essential if we would come to a knowledge of the truth. In this way we may be able to discern between that which is certain and that which may be our own fallible or sin-distorted interpretation of that Word.

Summary

In this chapter we have considered the biblical principles for interpreting Scripture. They come directly from the presuppositions that Scripture has concerning itself.

1. Since the Bible was written by human beings, it must be treated as any other human communication in determining the meaning intended by the author.
2. Since Scripture is God-breathed and true in all its parts, the unity of its teaching must be sought and its supernatural elements recognized and understood.
3. Since Scripture is God-breathed, it is absolute in its authority for doctrine and life. Therefore, all guidelines and techniques for understanding and applying it must treat the Bible itself as the final authority.

We turn now to the implementation of these principles. Our course of study will concern the methods by which we will be able to determine, with some degree of certainty, the author's intended meaning and how that meaning relates to us today.

PART TWO

GUIDELINES AND SKILLS

HUMAN AUTHORSHIP

PRINCIPLE:

Since the Bible was written by human beings, it must be treated as any other human communication in determining the meaning intended by the writer.

7

Understanding Human Language

Introduction

When God created individuals in His own likeness, He created them with the ability to communicate. The gift of human language, the ability to communicate, is indeed wonderful. In fact, it is so wonderful that meaning in life depends on it. A relationship of love gives the ultimate significance in human life, and such a relationship depends on understanding what the other person is thinking. That is what communication is all about: enabling the other person to understand what one is thinking.

Successful communication depends on both the sender and the receiver of the communication. The sender of information must accurately put into words his own thoughts, and the receiver must accurately understand those words. In the case of Scripture, God is the sender through human transmitters. We are the receivers, and our task is to make sure of the human author's intended meaning. That is what interpretation is all about.

To correctly understand the meaning intended by an author might be difficult, as no two people have the same set of experiences and ideas. Words are not altogether precise, particularly when important abstract concepts are to be communicated. So the person who would understand another must work at it.

A person may not work too hard at understanding the communication of the salesman with a product he does not want. But he will work very hard to understand the one whose love he hopes to win. That accounts for the different level of interest in understanding the Bible on the part of one who views it as a product he does not want, and on the part of another who loves God. But in the case of Scripture, the problem of communication is greatly intensified because we do not live in the same age or cultures from which the Scriptures came.

Walter Kaiser gives a clear statement of this basic truth concerning human communication and Scripture:

> The general rules for interpreting oral or written speech are not learned, invented, or discovered by men; rather, they are part and parcel of our nature as individuals made in the image of God. This art has been in use since God gave the gift of communication and speech itself. Thus the person spoken to is always the interpreter; the speaker is always the author.
>
> This is not to argue that everyone is automatically and completely successful in the practice of the art and science of hermeneutics just because each possesses this gift of communication as part of the image of God. Precisely at this point the distinctiveness of the cultural context of the reader/interpreter becomes most embarrassingly obvious. Certainly even when the speaker and listener/reader share the same culture and age there may still be some general subjects and vocabularies that may not be a part of the interpreter's experience and therefore his ability to interpret is frustrated. In this case, it will be necessary for the interpreter to engage first in some serious study before he can be a successful interpreter.
>
> But when the interpreter is removed from the original author by many years, governments, societies, and even religious conditions, how can the general rules for interpreting be part and parcel of our natures as made in the image of God? Again, the answer is the same. This question merely confuses one type of learning—which is only preparatory and an antecedent study—with the task of interpretation which still must follow. Had birth and Providence favored us so that we would have been present and would have participated in that culture from which the writing emanated, we would have dispensed with the search into background, culture and even at times languages. But we would still have been obligated to engage in the task of interpreting the text. Thus we will contend that the principles of interpretation are as natural and universal as speech itself.[1]

1. Walter Kaiser, "Meaning from God's Message: Matters for Interpretation," *Christianity Today,* 5 October 1979, pp. 31-32.

Because the language of Scripture is normal human language, we will first study some commonsense guidelines for understanding meaning through ordinary language. Sometimes those guidelines are called "principles." I do not call them principles because I have reserved the word *principle* to identify biblically based, unalterable standards. The laws of human language are nowhere stated in Scripture. As Kaiser has reminded us, they are part of our creation in the image of God. Therefore, we will seek to develop skills in the art of understanding human communication. I suggest three basic guidelines:

1. To understand the meaning of a speaker or author, one begins with the ordinary meaning of the language.
2. One must identify the type of language being used (e.g., poetry or prose, figurative or literal).
3. Ordinarily, the interpreter is seeking a single meaning from what the speaker or writer has said.

Those guidelines should form the basis for subsequent study and skill development. Let us consider the three in more detail.

Seek the Ordinary Meaning of the Language

The most natural, clear, and evident meaning must be identified. As we approach Scripture, we are approaching a set of books written in languages that are not familiar to us, and written in a far distant setting. It might be said that we are learning communication at the receiving end almost as an infant learns communication or as a tribal translator learns an unwritten language without the help of an interpreter. How does the infant or translator go about it?

First, he begins to identify meaning through the setting in which he finds himself. The infant is aware of his mother's body and voice, and gradually becomes aware of the room and his crib. He begins to understand language on the basis of what his senses tell him. The same process must be followed in learning a new language without an interpreter. In that way our first series of guidelines for determining the ordinary meaning will have to do with understanding the historical, physical, and cultural setting in which a given passage was written.

Next, the person learning a new language begins to learn the meaning of individual words. *Mama, Daddy,* and *no* are some of the first words an infant understands. Our second set of guidelines will concern methods for making sure of the meaning of words. Particularly, we must analyze words that are not simple or clear in meaning. In the next phase of learning word meaning, the infant or translator begins to hear the words connected with larger units of thought: sentences, and then paragraphs. It is essential to understand the relationship of individual words if the meaning the author had in mind is to be communicated. So the next set of guidelines will deal with ways of making sure of the flow of thought through clarifying sentence structure.

As the child matures in understanding human communication, and as the translator learns enough to reduce the language to writing, earlier understandings may be modified and clarified through relating each communication to its larger context. Therefore, our final set of guidelines will have to do with understanding meaning in a passage through relating it both to its immediate context and to the larger context of the entire book.

In summary, since our quest is for the most natural, clear, and evident meaning, we must study guidelines that will help us identify that meaning.

Identify the Literary Style of the Language

Should we treat every passage of Scripture as literal? The print and electronic media speak condescendingly, at times derisively, of "biblical literalists." It seems a foregone conclusion that the Bible cannot be taken literally. However, for one who takes the Bible seriously, a literal approach follows the basic principle that Scripture is a human communication.

Actually, the battleground is ill-chosen. The real battle is the question of trustworthiness, not literalness. Are those portions of Scripture that purport to be literal actually true? And more basic, is the teaching of Scripture, whether literal or figurative, true? The trustworthiness of the Bible must be identified as the key issue, not its literalness.

We have been pushed into the position of defending a "literal" position by allegorical interpreters and certain rationalistic interpreters who find secondary meanings, myths, and other mysterious things in the Bible. However, if the Bible is to be authoritative, it must be understandable.

As in all human communication, one begins with the assumption that the speaker or writer is saying something to be taken in its literal meaning. But the receiver should always be alert to the possibility that the language may be figurative or poetic. In fact, a great deal of humor in English is based on the initial perception that the speaker is using ordinary literal language that, in the end, turns out to be figurative. To us, that can be very funny precisely because the normal expectancy is for language to be used in a literal way.

So we must study guidelines for determining the type, or genre, of language being used, and then determine the meaning of that specific type of language. How does one determine the author's intent when a parable is used? What was intended by a specific figure of speech? Those questions are not as easily answered as questions concerning literal meanings, but they are certainly legitimate forms of human communication that are intended to be understood, and can be understood.

Therefore, literal language must be interpreted literally; figurative language, figuratively; and poetic language, poetically. Did Jerusalem and all Judea literally go out to hear John the Baptist (Matt. 3:5)? That is, did the physical city move out into the wilderness? No, we say that is a figurative expression—it means the people of Jerusalem went out. But does it mean that every single person living in Judea went out into the wilderness to hear John the Baptist? No, for figurative language must be interpreted figuratively. Simple guidelines exist that enable us to identify the many kinds of figures in human language and to understand their meaning.

One problem is that many interpreters take literal language and turn it into a figure or a myth. Creation and the resurrection are often treated in that way. When human language is so distorted, it can carry almost any meaning the interpreter wishes to put on it. It is not just the rationalistic interpreter who misuses Scripture in that way; Bible-believing people can do the same thing —and often do, as we have seen in the case of "spiritual" or allegorical interpretation. It is also quite possible to take figurative language and understand it as a literal statement. For example, Jesus said concerning the bread, "This is My body" (Matt.26:26). That expression is taken as literal by more than half of those who call themselves Christians, and a major doctrine is built on it. We must learn guidelines that enable us to identify the type of language being used, and then to understand the meaning of that particular type of language. With those tools we can interpret each specific passage.

Seek the Single Meaning Intended by the Author

The author of any written or spoken communication normally seeks to convey a single meaning. Since the Bible is written in human language, any passage has only one meaning, unless the author says there is another meaning. A second meaning may be intended, as that is a legitimate literary device. But for the interpreter to be dogmatic about a second meaning, the author must first have affirmed it.

Note that figurative or poetic language might *appear* to have more than one meaning, but the author might be really intending to communicate one particular meaning through that type of language. The question of a double meaning has to do with the author's having in mind two meanings at the same time. For example, he may intend to communicate something concerning a historic event, and at the same time he may be using that to prophesy some other event yet to take place. Interpreters are not agreed as to whether that is ever true in Scripture. This guideline is of use only to those who hold that a second or hidden meaning occasionally may be present, particularly in prophetic Scripture. For them, such a restriction must be carefully observed lest Scripture become putty in the hands of the interpreter to mold into any form he desires. Once again, the author himself must identify any hidden meaning. In the case of the Bible, if the Lord Jesus or the Holy Spirit, through a subsequent biblical writer, designated such a meaning, that meaning may be accepted with equal authority as the initial, plain meaning of the passage.

To determine the single meaning is the objective of biblical interpretation. Otherwise, the fancy of the interpreter, or the preconceptions he imposes on the text, becomes the authority. Guidelines for handling any possible exceptions will be discussed under the interpretation of prophecy (chap. 18).

To say that there is only one meaning does not mean that all interpreters will agree on that meaning, or that the meaning is easily understood in every passage. In a passage where the one true meaning is not clear, there may be more than one plausible interpretation. For example, concerning the creation account of Genesis 1 and 2, there are several interpretations, each of which seeks to treat the passage as the authoritative revelation of historic truth. The interpreter may not need to decide with finality which of those is *the* true interpretation. He may accept the fact that there are several possible interpretations and leave the final decision for further light.

To concede several possible interpretations does not mean that all the possibilities are equally valid. The author had one meaning in mind. When that meaning is not clear, the position of humility in interpretation will prevent the Bible student from dogmatically affirming a specific uncertain interpretation and from building a theological superstructure on the foundation of such a passage. We will study guidelines on that in chapters 15-16 when we consider comparing Scripture with Scripture and building a systematic theology.

To say that there is a single meaning does not, however, imply that there is a single application. For any Bible teaching there may be many legitimate applications. For example, "You shall love your neighbor as yourself" (Lev. 19: 18) must be applied in many ways to many circumstances if we are to be obedient to that authoritative word from God. "Whatever a man sows, this he will also reap" (Gal. 6:7) was used in the context of giving and has to do with the use of money. That identifies the single meaning. However, that principle could legitimately apply to other areas of life such as good or evil behavior. Later we will study a number of guidelines that will enable us to make valid application of Scripture. But at this point, we must reemphasize that our search is for the single meaning intended by the author.

Those, then, are the implications of the principle that the Bible is considered a thoroughly human, understandable communication. We will now examine in greater detail the guidelines implied by the principle, guidelines that will enable the careful student to determine with confidence the meaning of any typical passage of Scripture.

8
Historical, Physical, and Cultural Setting

Guideline: Base the study on the historical, physical, and cultural setting.

The "setting," as used here, is the context that formed the original message. Whether it be an infant learning his mother's language or a translator learning an unwritten language, examining the setting is a good way to begin learning the language. Without understanding that context, communication of meaning is difficult, if not impossible.

Historical Setting

The Bible is revelation in history, unlike the teachings of many religions. Some religions are rooted in mythology, such as Shintoism or Hinduism. Others were founded by a historic individual, but large elements of their religious teachings today are mythological, such as in Buddhism. In contrast to those, Scripture is rooted in history and claims to be a historical document, the record of God's self-revelation to man. As such, we must understand it in the context of its history.

PERSONAL SITUATION OF THE AUTHOR

The author's situation often throws light on the meaning of a passage. Many of the psalms take on fresh meaning when studied in the light of the personal situation from which David wrote. David said, "Against Thee, Thee only, I have sinned" (Ps. 51:4). The meaning of that statement influences one's interpretation of the entire psalm. Is David speaking of some inward, spiritual offense that does not involve other people? Understanding that that great confession was written in response to David's conviction over the sin with Bathsheba and Uriah enables one to comprehend David's profound meaning. All sin against another person, no matter how violent, is ultimately and primarily a sin against God. Only with the personal situation of the author in mind does that come into focus.

Paul tells us, "Rejoice in the Lord always; again I will say, rejoice! Let your forbearing spirit be known to all men. . . . Be anxious for nothing . . . the peace of God, which surpasses all comprehension, shall guard your hearts and your minds in Christ Jesus" (Phil. 4:4-7). Those are beautiful sentiments, almost idyllic. But what was Paul's condition as he dictated those glorious words? Paul was in prison (Phil. 1:13-14)! His very life was in danger when he wrote, "But even if I am being poured out as a drink offering upon the sacrifice and service of your faith, I rejoice and share my joy with you all. And you too, I urge you, rejoice in the same way and share your joy with me" (Phil. 2:17-18). In fact, the Christians in Philippi had the model of Paul as a prisoner on an earlier occasion; one who, bleeding from the lacerations inflicted by a Roman whip, could sing at midnight (Acts 16:12, 22-25). Knowing that heightens and deepens our understanding of his simple exhortation to rejoice. No reader with the knowledge of Paul's situation could respond, "He can talk about rejoicing, but he never knew *my* circumstances."

HISTORICAL REFERENCES WITHIN SCRIPTURE

Often the historical setting can be found in Scripture itself. An understanding of Old Testament history is necessary for grasping the New Testament. Books like the letter to the Hebrews would be beyond our understanding without the historical background of the Old Testament.

Jesus once made a passing reference to an Old Testament historic event, a reference that holds the key to understanding an entire passage. He told Nicodemus, "As Moses lifted up the serpent in the wilderness, even so must the Son of Man be lifted up; that whoever believes may in Him have eternal life" (John 3:14-15). If we do not understand the Old Testament accounts of sin, judgment, faith, and God's healing, Christ's reference will be an enigma that could obscure the meaning rather than throw light on the purpose of His death on the cross.

Some said that Jesus was Elijah reincarnated; others said He was Jeremiah (Matt. 16:14). What characteristics in Jesus evoked memories of Elijah and Jeremiah? There is no way of knowing without studying those two Old Testament prophets.

Not only is Old Testament history essential to the understanding of much of the New Testament, but it is also needed to understand many passages in the Old Testament itself. For example, the prophets must be read in the context of the historical books. Many have found it helpful to chart Old Testament history chronologically from the historical books, and place the prophets on the chart to be sure of the historical background for each prophecy.

For example, Ezekiel tells us of a valley filled with dry bones (Ezek. 37:1-6). And earnest preachers have subjected God's people to marvelous interpretations of that passage! Usually the passage is spiritualized, often referring to a description of the new birth, when a person is brought from death to life by the power of the Holy Spirit. Yet, for an understanding of that passage, knowledge of its historical setting is of vital importance: "Now it came about in the twelfth year of our exile, on the fifth of the tenth month, that the refugees from Jerusalem came to me, saying, 'The city has been taken' " (Ezek. 33:21). Immediately following the vision the Lord tells the prophet, "Son of man, these bones are the house of Israel; behold, they say 'Our bones are dried up, and our hope has perished. We are completely cut off.' Therefore prophesy, and say to them, 'Thus says the Lord God, "Behold, I will open your graves and cause you to come up out of your graves, My people; and I will bring you into the land of Israel" ' " (Ezek. 37:11-12). The historical setting helps us understand that the vision refers to Israel and its restoration to the land of promise.

Furthermore, New Testament history often helps in understanding New Testament passages. Consider the closing words of Acts:

> And he stayed two full years in his own rented quarters, and was welcoming all who came to him, preaching the kingdom of God, and teaching concerning the Lord Jesus Christ with all openness, unhindered. (Acts 28:30-31)

Paul's circumstances provide the setting for the prison epistles and illuminate passages like these:

> And pray on my behalf, that utterance may be given to me in the opening of my mouth, to make known with boldness the mystery of the gospel, for which I am an ambassador in chains; that in proclaiming it I may speak boldly, as I ought to speak. (Eph.6:19-20)

> According to my earnest expectation and hope, that I shall not be put to shame in anything, but that with all boldness, Christ shall even now, as always, be exalted in my body, whether by life or by death. For to me, to live is Christ, and to die is gain. . . . Yet to remain on in the flesh is more necessary for your sake. And convinced of this, I know that I shall remain and continue with you all for your progress and joy in the faith. (Phil. 1:20-21, 24-25)

> All the saints greet you, especially those of Caesar's household. (Phil. 4:22)

Be sure that the passages you use are truly parallel. For example, do not use Acts 28 (above) as the background for 2 Timothy and Paul's imprisonment recorded there. And do not use his situation recorded in 2 Timothy (in the Mamertine dungeon, according to tradition) as the background for the prison epistles. Second Timothy and Philippians are parallel only in the sense that Paul was in prison on both occasions. But Ephesians and Philippians no doubt refer to the same experience, that described in Acts. Those comparisons throw light on one another, filling out the picture of Paul's situation and providing the background for his teaching.

Historical background provided by Scripture can be found in many sources:

1. Marginal references found in a good cross-reference Bible

2. A Bible concordance where a name is traced in other passages (Excellent concordances are *Strong's Exhaustive Concordance of the Bible*, by James Strong, and *Young's Analytical Concordance to the Bible*, by Robert Young.)
3. A Bible dictionary or encyclopedia (See the bibliography at the end of this chapter.)

EXTRABIBLICAL SOURCES

Although a great deal of historical background can be found in Scripture itself, often extrabiblical historical sources are helpful in understanding a passage.

The vision of the great image recorded in Daniel 2:31-45 traces in advance the rise and fall of Babylon, Medo-Persia, Greece, and Rome. The various sections of the image were obviously not chosen at random. They were intended to identify characteristics of each of those empires. But one must study the historical background from other sources to understand the characteristics of those subsequent empires. And to discover from historical records the precision of Daniel's predictions is surely a profound reinforcement of faith in the Bible as God's miracle Book, and in Daniel as God's authentic spokesman. No matter how late the liberal higher critic may date the origin of the book of Daniel, it is still a precise prophecy that must be supernatural. Without extrabiblical historical records, much of the force of those facts would be lost.

Another example is found in the book of Revelation. Its constant reference to Babylon can be understood only in the light of the history of Rome at the time of its writing. Furthermore, the seven churches in Asia Minor were historical places we can learn about through historical and archaeological studies. Those characteristics shed light on the Word of our Lord to the church in each location (Rev. 1-3). Who were the Nicolaitans? What was the "synagogue of Satan" in Smyrna? What was Satan's throne in Pergamum? Who was Jezebel in Thyatira? Answers to those and many other questions must be sought in sources outside the Bible.

In seeking to find the meaning of any passage, the interpreter needs first to discover all he can concerning the author: who he was, where and when he wrote, and under what circumstances he wrote. Furthermore, the interpreter should seek to know the audience: to or for whom the passage was written, and the historical setting in which they read that passage. If there is a reference to some event, that event must be traced out to be certain of the meaning intended. Historical background not found in the Bible may be found in several outside sources:

1. Bible dictionaries, encyclopedias, and handbooks
2. Books on the history of biblical times
3. Books on Bible introduction and introductory materials in commentaries (See the bibliography at the end of this chapter.)

The historical setting is of great importance for understanding many passages of Scripture and, indeed, of crucial importance in interpreting many of those. But there are other elements in the setting.

Physical Setting

GEOGRAPHICAL REFERENCES

The *geography* of the setting is often helpful in understanding a passage. Geography can be as simple a matter as the direction a river flows. In Ezekiel 47 we read of a river that flows from the Temple and "heals" a sea. When particular care is given to identify each of the physical elements in that passage, it is immediately apparent that in this passage the river flows east, not west, and that it is the Dead Sea that is brought to life in the prophetic dream.

In another example, Hosea is typical of the prophets by being rooted both in the history and in the geography of the land:

> For you have been a snare at Mizpah, and a net spread out on Tabor. . . . I know Ephraim, and Israel is not hidden from Me; for now, O Ephraim, you have played the harlot, Israel has defiled itself. . . . Blow the horn in Gibeah, the trumpet in Ramah. Sound an alarm at Beth-aven: "Behind you, Benjamin!" . . . When Ephraim saw his sickness, and Judah his wound, then Ephraim went to Assyria and sent to King Jareb. But he is unable to heal you, or to cure you of your wound. (Hos. 5:1, 3, 8, 13)

As are so many, that particular passage is unintelligible without a thorough investigation of the places named.

The story of Deborah's delivering Israel is powerful without an understanding of the historical setting. But to locate each of the tribes on a map and study the lineup of those who fought and those who did not brings the entire passage into clear focus (Judg. 4-5). The drama is between those who helped the Lord and those who did not. It is easy to see how the impact of a passage and the spiritual truth found there is greatly diminished without a thorough study of the geographical setting.

Refer to the map of the twelve tribes (next page) and locate Zebulun, Issachar, and Naphtali. Note that they are all clustered around the scene of the battle at Mount Tabor and the Brook Kishon. A historical atlas or encyclopedia will tell you more about those tribes. They were poor, living among and oppressed by wealthy Canaanites. They are the people who fought and won God's approval, along with Benjamin and Ephraim, where Deborah held court.

Now locate on the map Dan, Asher, and Reuben. "Gilead" was probably Gad and the part of Manasseh that was across the Jordan River. Note that all of those tribes lived on the fringes of the battle. Historical background reveals that they were also much better off economically. Dan was affluent through trade. Asher, though closer to the conflict, was secure and had made peace with the enemy. Across the river, Gad and eastern Manasseh were safe, along with Reuben. But the Reubenites also had a great deal to lose as wealthy sheepherders. In the end they did not go, and came under God's curse.

How does western Manasseh fit in? Note that it is not even mentioned in the text, but is close to the scene of battle. Does "Machir" refer to that tribe? And how could nine hundred iron chariots be swept away by a brook? Even more unlikely, how could an experienced military leader let his armored vehicles get into a torrent capable of sweeping them away? An atlas will provide answers to those questions, which are crucial to understanding the passage.

The physical circumstances of Paul the apostle when he wrote the second letter to Timothy illuminate the meaning of the

THE GREAT SEA
ASHER
ZEBULUN
NAPHTALI
MANASSEH
Brook Kishon
Mt. Tabor
ISSACHAR
MANASSEH
GAD
EPHRAIM
DAN
BENJAMIN
REUBEN
JUDAH
SIMEON

entire book, especially the fourth chapter. Tradition tells us that Paul was in the Mamartine Dungeon, a dank hole with irregular slabs of stone as a partial floor above the Tiber River that flowed beneath the dungeon. He told Timothy to be sure to come before winter (2 Tim. 4:21) and to bring his coat with him (4:13). Here, Paul the aged, in a smelly, cold dungeon, faced death in loneliness: "At my first defense no one supported me, but all deserted me" (4:16). The physical setting helps put Paul's words into perspective:

> Endure hardship, . . . for I am already being poured out as a drink offering, and the time of my departure has come. I have fought the good fight, I have finished the course, I have kept the faith; in the future there is laid up for me the crown of righteousness, which the Lord, the righteous Judge, will award to me on that day. (2 Tim. 4:5-8)

Several sources are available for understanding the geographical setting. In addition to maps and charts in historical atlases and atlases in Bibles, the student can find geographic descriptions in Bible dictionaries. Bible encyclopedias also discuss geographical settings. (See the bibliography at the end of this chapter.)

REFERENCES TO ANIMAL LIFE

The physical setting might also require an understanding of biblical animals. For example, the Bible is full of references to sheep—lost sheep, found sheep, sacrificial sheep, and the Lamb of God. For those who have not had contact with sheep, it would be helpful to study the characteristics of that particular animal. Sheep are helpless, unable to care for themselves, nonresistant, unprotected, and dull. Those and other characteristics of sheep help us to understand Psalm 23, Isaiah 53, Ezekiel 34, John 10, and many other passages. The way a shepherd related to his sheep in ancient Palestine is also an important study for understanding sheep/shepherd passages in Scripture. However, that is a cultural matter more than a physical question of the nature of the animal itself.

REFERENCES TO PLANT LIFE

It is often helpful in understanding a passage to study the characteristics of plant life in ancient Israel. For example:

> And on the next day, when they had departed from Bethany, He became hungry And seeing at a distance a fig tree in leaf, He went to see if perhaps He would find anything on it; and when He came to it, He found nothing but leaves, for it was not the season for figs. And He answered and said to it, "May no one ever eat fruit from you again!" (Mark 11:12-14)

That is a strange passage. It seems that Christ cursed an innocent tree for not doing what it was not even supposed to be doing: bearing fruit out of season. Perhaps He was doing that as a demonstration to encourage the faith of His disciples, which, in fact, He did. And certainly, as the Lord of all creation, He had the right to dispense with a single tree. Men, in general, have had no conscience about destroying whole forests for lesser purposes.

Nevertheless, the story is a curious one and difficult to understand until we learn some facts concerning fig trees. An investigation would indicate that fig trees have small nodules before leafing (a physical matter), which the people of the region were accustomed to eating (a cultural matter). Therefore, if a tree at that season of the year had leaves, it certainly could be expected to have the early growth that would satisfy a hungry person. But here was a tree with nothing but leaves. Later that same day Christ was to clean out the Temple profiteers and, after that, curse the hypocritical Pharisees (Matt. 23). Was He enacting in advance a parable of God's view of hypocrisy—those who have "leaves of profession," but lack the "fruit of possession"? At any rate, a study of the physical characteristics of the fig tree is helpful for understanding the passage.

Cultural Setting

The way the people lived—their social and religious customs and legal requirements—is the context from which a writing comes. To understand the relevant culture is to understand the meaning of a writing more clearly.

CULTURAL BACKGROUND LEARNED FROM THE BIBLE

Some customs and cultural background can be learned from the Bible itself. In Matthew 15:2, the Pharisees and scribes wanted to know why the disciples of Christ did not wash their hands before they ate. That would seem to be a reasonable question. Is it not strange that the disciples did not wash before eating? Why does it appear that Christ is against such a sanitary practice? Mark gives us a parenthetical explanation of the custom involved (7:3-4). He explained that it was a religious ceremony and that the baptisms are not only for one's hands, but for everything else involved in the meal. It becomes clear that the confrontation was not over a question of sanitation but over a matter of religious ceremony in which Christ was true to His personal tradition of opposing the bondage of man-made religious requirements.

In another example, it seems incredible to us that a man would vow to make a burnt offering of whatever came out of the doors of his house to meet him (Judg. 11:30-40). Vow or no vow, it seems so incomprehensible that a man would then sacrifice his only child that some interpreters have held he did not sacrifice his daughter, but simply sent her away. Since it is said that "she had no relations with a man," some conclude that the "offering" was a commitment to celibacy. However, the entire passage seems to indicate that the common practice of sacrificing one's own child is precisely what took place. There is continual reference in Scripture to the custom of surrounding nations of sacrificing their own children. That was one of the great sins of Israel as well (Lev.: 18:21; 20:2-5; Deut. 12:30-31; Ps. 106:37).

Though much of the cultural background needed to understand the New Testament can be found in the Old Testament, sometimes we must consult archeological sources and other records from that day for help in understanding a passage.

CULTURAL BACKGROUND FROM EXTRABIBLICAL SOURCES

Cultural backgrounds from sources outside the Bible are helpful in understanding the meaning of many passages. In the above-mentioned Scripture references, the abomination of the people in surrounding nations was to cause their "seed" to "pass through the fire." Actually, a giant metal idol was made as a furnace that could be heated red-hot. Into the fiery outstretched hands of the god a parent would place his own infant, a sacrifice to appease the gods or to gain some great favor. That background helps in understanding the frequent reference to "passing through the fire."

In John 9, it seems strange that the parents of the blind man were so afraid of "being put out of the synagogue" that they would not stand with their own son (v. 22). Even stranger, the context reveals that they were not in a synagogue at all, but that the healing took place in the Temple. Knowing the Jewish culture, however, solves the puzzle. From extrabiblical sources we learn that membership was not in the Temple, but in the local synagogue. To be "put out" was an excommunication that involved virtual disenfranchisement. As far as the Jewish community was concerned, excommunication was the loss of citizenship rights. Against that background, the courage of the blind man in speaking the way he does to the religious leaders is astounding.

Christ told the parable of the wedding guest who could not get in because he did not have a wedding garment (Matt. 22:11). That really seems unfair, particularly since the guests did not ask to come but were "drafted" from the highways and hedges. It seems even more unreasonable when the one without a wedding garment was tied hand and foot and thrown out! A study of the cultural background helps to unravel the mystery. The wedding garment was provided by the host. One who would refuse that provision by the host would thereby prove himself to be a usurper and be deliberately disqualified.

In the same passage Christ responded to a trick question from the Herodians. He told them that they should "render to Caesar the things that are Caesar's" (Matt. 22:21). Whole theologies of cultural integration have been built on that enigmatic statement. However, it is plain from the context that Jesus was giving an answer in kind to those who would trap Him with an insincere question. Research into the cultural background indicates that "secular" money was not legitimate as an offering in the Temple. That is why there were money changers in the Temple. Temple offerings had to be made in Temple currency, so there were money exchange banks on the premises. The Herodians were trying to trap Jesus into making an unpatriotic statement. Either He would have to oppose the law of the land, the hated Roman taxation, and thus be unlawful; or He would have to favor the taxation and be a traitor to His own people. In the face of that, He sidestepped the question by indicating that if a coin had a man's name and face on it, it must belong to him! Similarly, Temple coins should be put in the Temple offering, not used to pay Roman taxes.

By His answer Jesus remained both a law-abiding subject of Rome and a loyal son of Israel. Profound teaching concerning a cultural mandate to be involved in the affairs of this world will have to be sought elsewhere in Scripture. Hence, the cultural background can help considerably in the understanding of a passage.

But one must be very careful in seeking for understanding from extrabiblical sources. For example, a contemporary preacher has reinforced his "doctrine of prosperity" by saying that Christ riding on a donkey was the cultural equivalent of driving a luxurious automobile today. A comfortable doctrine, but hardly what the prophet predicted concerning the lowly Messiah who did not arrive on a prancing war-horse:

> Behold, your king is coming to you; He is just and endowed with salvation, humble, and mounted on a donkey. (Zech. 9:9)

How does one find answers to questions about the historical, physical, and cultural setting? What are the tools that must be used? As we have seen, a careful reading of the context often will shed light on the question of setting, and that is where a person begins his study.

Perhaps the most useful tools of all are cross-references given in the margins of any good study Bible. Topical Bibles serve the same purpose. In other words, the Bible itself usually provides the information needed concerning the historical and cultural setting of a given passage. When a Bible student has advanced enough to know where parallel passages and historical background are given, such a tool may not be needed as often. However, for most Bible students it is necessary to locate parallel passages for further light on historical events and cultural background that would help interpret the passage under study.

Those are the basic tools. However, much more can be gleaned from the works of those who have done special studies on cultural matters. For that reason, books on Bible background, Bible dictionaries, and Bible encyclopedias are a great help in researching the cultural setting of the Bible.

The specialist who has used those guidelines for interpreting Scripture will write his findings in a "critical" commentary. Critical commentaries are different from devotional commentaries in that they deal with questions of meaning. Devotional commentaries do not normally deal with questions of textual criticism and careful exegesis of a passage. Rather, they concentrate on applying a passage to life. By using all the guidelines of hermeneutics, the critical commentator endeavors to draw out the meaning of a text. Such a commentator has already done what we are now learning to do.

Even for the experienced Bible student it is best to consult the commentary *after* one has made his own independent study. There are several reasons for that. First, no commentator is infallible, nor is any commentator an expert on every passage of Scripture. Often a commentator will rely on the work of earlier commentators. Therefore, to preserve one's independent judgment and the integrity of one's own work, it is best to do personal study first by exegeting or drawing out the meaning of the passage with the basic tools. On the other hand, it is never wise to conclude one's study without referring to several of the best commentators on a given passage. In that final stage of study, the commentator provides a check for one's own conclusions and also provides additional insight before one's work is complete. Furthermore, the commentator provides appropriate background sources that can be checked.

Summary

The student must examine carefully the setting of any Bible passage. He must ask himself how the passage fits into the flow of historical events, and how geography or other physical features condition the meaning. He must determine what cultural factors need attention to make sure of the author's intended meaning.

Selected Bibliography for Background Study

CONCORDANCES

Goodrick, Edward W., and John R. Kohlenberger III, eds. *NIV Complete Concordance.* Grand Rapids: Zondervan, 1981.

Strong, James. *Strong's Exhaustive Concordance of the Bible.* Rev. ed. Nashville: Abingdon, 1980.

Thomas, Robert L., gen. ed. *New American Standard Exhaustive Concordance of the Bible.* Nashville: Holman, 1981.

Young, Robert. *Young's Analytical Concordance of the Bible.* Grand Rapids: Eerdmans, 1955.

ATLASES

Aharoni, Yohanan, and Michael Avi-Yonah. *The Macmillan Bible Atlas*. Rev. ed. New York: Macmillan, 1977.

Beitzel, Barry J. *The Moody Atlas of Bible Lands.* Chicago: Moody, 1985.

May, Herbert G., ed. *The Oxford Bible Atlas,* 2d ed. London: U. Press, 1974.

Pfeiffer, Charles F. *Baker's Bible Atlas*. Rev. ed. Grand Rapids: Baker, 1987.

Prichard, James B. *The Harper Atlas of the Bible.* New York: Harper & Row, 1987.

Rasmussen, Carl G. *The Zondervan NIV Atlas of the Bible.* Grand Rapids: Zondervan, 1989.

ENCYCLOPEDIAS, DICTIONARIES, AND HANDBOOKS

Achtemeier, Paul J., gen. ed. *Harper's Bible Dictionary.* San Francisco: Harper & Row, 1985.

Alexander, David, and Pat Alexander, eds. *Eerdmans' Handbook to the Bible*. Rev. ed. Grand Rapids.: Eerdmans, 1983.

Bromiley, Geoffrey W., gen. ed. *International Standard Bible Encyclopedia*. 4 vols. Grand Rapids: Eerdmans, 1979-88.

Douglas, James Dixon, ed. *The New Bible Dictionary*. Rev. ed. Wheaton, Ill.: Tyndale, 1982.

Douglas, J. D., and Merrill C. Tenney, eds. *The New International Dictionary of the Bible*. Rev. ed. Grand Rapids: Zondervan, 1987.

Elwell, Walter A., gen. ed., *Baker Encyclopedia of the Bible*. 2 vols. Grand Rapids: Baker, 1988.

Harrison, R. K., ed. *The New Unger's Bible Dictionary.* Chicago: Moody, 1988.

Larson, Gary. *The New Unger's Bible Handbook.* Chicago: Moody, 1984.

Myers, Allen C., ed. *The Eerdmans' Bible Dictionary.* Grand Rapids: Eerdmans, 1987.

Packer, James I., Merrill C. Tenney, and William White. *The Bible Almanac.* Nashville: Nelson, 1980.

Pfeiffer, Charles F., Howard F. Vos, and John Rea, eds. *Wycliffe Bible Encyclopedia.* Chicago: Moody, 1975.

Tenney, Merrill C. *The Zondervan Pictorial Bible Encyclopedia*. 5 vols. Grand Rapids: Zondervan, 1975.

INTRODUCTIONS AND SURVEYS

Archer, Gleason. *Survey of Old Testament Introduction*. Rev. ed. Chicago: Moody, 1974.

Gromacki, Robert G. *New Testament Survey.* Grand Rapids.: Baker, 1974.

Guthrie, Donald. *New Testament Introduction.* Downers Grove, Ill.: InterVarsity, 1975.

Harrison, R. K. *Introduction to the Old Testament.* Grand Rapids: Eerdmans, 1969.

Jensen, Irving Lester. *Jensen's Survey of the New Testament*. Chicago: Moody, 1981.

———. *Jensen's Survey of the Old Testament*. Chicago: Moody, 1979.

LaSor, William S., David A. Hubbard, and Frederic W. Bush. *Old Testament Survey: The Message, Form, and Background of the Old Testament.* Grand Rapids: Eerdmans, 1982.

Tenney, Merrill C. *New Testament Survey.* Rev. ed. Grand Rapids: Eerdmans, 1985.

CULTURAL FEATURES

Gower, Ralph. *The New Manners and Customs of Bible Times.* Chicago: Moody: 1987.

Matthews, Victor H. *Manners and Customs in the Bible.* Peabody, Mass.: Hendrickson, 1988.

Miller, Madeleine S., and J. Lane Miller, eds. *Harper's Encyclopedia of Bible Life.* San Francisco: Harper & Row, 1971.

Thompson, John A. *Handbook of Life in Bible Times.* Downers Grove, Ill.: InterVarsity, 1986.

Tidball, Derek. *The Social Context of the New Testament: A Sociological Analysis.* Grand Rapids: Zondervan, 1984.

Van der Woude, A. S., gen. ed. *The World of the Bible.* Translated by Sierd Woudstra. Grand Rapids.: Eerdmans, 1986.

ARCHAEOLOGY

Avi-Yonah, Michael, and E. Stern, eds. *Encyclopedia of Archaeological Excavations in the Holy Land.* 4 vols. London: Oxford U., 1976-78.

Blaiklock, E. M., and R. K. Harrison, eds. *New International Dictionary of Biblical Archaeology.* Grand Rapids: Zondervan, 1986.

McRay, John. *Archaeology and the New Testament.* Grand Rapids: Baker, 1990.

Pfeiffer, Charles F., ed. *The Biblical World: A Dictionary of Biblical Archaeology.* Grand Rapids: Baker, 1966.

9
A Method for Word Study

Guideline: Research each unclear and important word.

Words are the basic building blocks for understanding the meaning of any passage. In seeking the author's intended meaning, we must consider the meanings of individual words. Their meanings, in many cases, are not always self-evident.

An example of the misunderstanding of words comes from a student who spoke at a Bible college chapel on the verse "I being in the way, the Lord led me" (Gen. 24:27, KJV). She took the expression "being in the way" as referring to her own resistance to the will of God. Although she felt she often stubbornly obstructed God's purposes ("being in the way") she also felt that God led her despite her obstruction because she was His child! Through the misunderstanding of words, the interpreter came to an opposite meaning of that intended by the author. She concluded that God will lead even when a person resists His will, whereas the verse says He will lead when we follow His precepts.

Why are words so troublesome? Because they seldom have a precise meaning that is identical in all contexts. Rather, they have a range of meaning, so that in one context an emphasis, or even a meaning, differs from that intended by the use of that same word in a different context. Even in one's native tongue, understanding another person is a constant exercise in interpretation.

In translation, the problem is compounded since a word in one language rarely means precisely what a word means in another language. For example, when Paul exhorts us to pray always, he literally said "all the time" (Eph. 6:18), and when Christ said He would be with us always, the literal words are "all the days" (Matt. 28:20). For our understanding of the intent, we would probably have reversed the choice of words. We would like to think that Christ is with us without interruption (all the time), and that we should pray on a daily basis, not without interruption (twenty-four hours a day). But the range of meaning in Paul's "all the time" can be from literal "without interruption" to "consistently"—a general habit of life. The interpreter must discern which of the possible meanings Paul had in mind when he gave that exhortation.

Thus, the task of the translator is to define as precisely as possible the meaning of a word in the way the author used it in its specific context, and then search for a word or expression in his language that gives as nearly as possible that same meaning. The translator has done that as carefully as possible, but since the task is basically one of interpretation, the serious Bible student will make a direct study of every word that is crucial to the meaning of the passage he is studying. Sometimes a single word in translation will not do; an explanation might be necessary.

To say that there is a range of meaning does not mean that one can identify the whole range and then pick the meaning or nuance that best suits what he would like the author to have said. No, the author had a very specific meaning in mind. A word study will assist the interpreter in locating the range of meanings of a word; through a careful examination of the context, the student can identify the meaning in a particular text. If God the Holy Spirit took the care to inspire the very words, we must be careful to search out the intent of the author in his choice of words.

Biblical Words Used in a Special Sense

Because they are used in a special sense, technical words like *justification,* figurative words like *death,* and profound words like *sin* must be carefully studied. For example, the non-Christian society does not have a word for the biblical concept of love. Neither was there such a word in the days of the New Testament. *Agapē* was used occasionally in the classics and emphasized the great value of the object loved, though it tended to be cold and intellectual. But the Holy Spirit chose that word rather than *philia, eros,* or *storgē* and poured the divine meaning into it. By command, description, and example, a new meaning was given to an old word.

There are many elements in the biblical concept of love that the unregenerate world never discovers. For example, loving behavior depends on the quality or character of the one doing the loving, not on the worth or lovability of the object of love. Again, the emphasis shifts from *love* as a noun describing how one feels to the verb describing how one behaves toward another. That basic shift in meaning lays the groundwork for another basic truth concerning love. A person can behave lovingly, even though his feelings may not direct him to do so. There are many other elements in the biblical concept of love, but those cannot be known to the interpreter without a thorough study of the word.

The serious student of the Bible should make it a goal to study in depth all of the great words of Scripture. That kind of study would be the task of a lifetime, but it is one of the most exciting and profitable areas of biblical study.

Words Having More Than One Meaning

A word might not be instantly or fully understood because its wide range of meaning may span very different concepts. For example, *death* is a word that can be very confusing because it is used in many different ways. In a brief passage between Colossians 2:12 and 3:5, the word is used in four different ways. It refers (1) to the physical death of Christ; (2) to the fact that people are "dead" before they become Christians; (3) to people "dying" as they become Christians; and (4) to the idea that those who have died are now to "put to death" the deeds of the body. And that is just a beginning.

There are many other uses of the word *death* in Scripture. For example, Paul "died daily," and there is the "second death." It is of utmost importance to know the meaning. Great confusion has come to the church concerning how the Christian life is to be lived because Bible students have not taken care to study the various meanings to determine which meaning the author intended in a given passage. One must know all the potential meanings to understand the specific meaning within a passage.

Unclear Words Because of Translation Problems

Some basic problems are inherent because we are not studying Scripture in its original language. Even if we were, the problems inherent in translation are still present in the gospels because they render in Greek the original Aramaic that Christ and His disciples normally spoke.

DIFFERENT WORDS IN THE ORIGINAL MAY BE TRANSLATED BY THE SAME ENGLISH WORD

Perhaps the word translated "love" in John 21:15-19 is the most famous illustration of that problem. When Christ asked Peter if he loved Him, Peter answered with a different word. That difference is indeed difficult to translate into English and, as a result, is not normally translated. Yet it is important to study the two words that are used. Milton Terry explains that there are four sets of synonyms in these verses, not merely the one on love, which is commonly known.[1]

New is another important word in this category. In the Greek text, *neos* refers to a new existence (i.e., brand-new), whereas *kainos* refers to a new aspect, new depth, new fullness, or new scope. When Christ says, "A new commandment I give to you, that you love one another" (John 13:34), it is important for the understanding of that passage to know that John used *kainos*, a new aspect of an old command.

Another example of difficulty in translation comes from the use of the word *perfect*. One senses immediately the great theological importance of knowing that *perfect* does not always mean "absolute lack of any flaw." But to determine that, it is necessary to study all the words that have been translated "perfect" in our English Bible. Consider the following texts.

> Therefore, you are to be perfect, as your heavenly Father is perfect. (Matt. 5:48)

> Power is perfected in weakness. (2 Cor. 12:9)

1. Milton S. Terry, *Bible Hermeneutics* (1909 repr.; Grand Rapids: Zondervan, 1974), p. 200.

> Are you now being perfected by the flesh? (Gal. 3:3)
>
> [I] might perfect what is lacking in your faith. (1 Thess. 3:10, KJV)
>
> That the man of God may be perfect. (2 Tim. 3:17, KJV)
>
> I have not found thy works perfect before my God. (Rev. 3:2, KJV)

"Perfect" in each of the passages is translated from an entirely different Greek word. Obviously, the nuance of meaning will differ with each word, though there may be an overlap in meaning in some cases.

A WORD IN THE ORIGINAL MAY BE TRANSLATED BY DIFFERENT ENGLISH WORDS

Just as more than one word may be translated "perfect" in English, the same word in the original may be translated "perfect" in one passage, and something else in other passages. Here are some examples (italics added):

> *Mending* their nets. (Matt. 4:21)
>
> Everyone, after he *has been fully trained*, will be like his teacher. (Luke 6:40)
>
> Vessels of wrath *prepared* for destruction. (Rom. 9:22)
>
> *Restore* such a one in a spirit of gentleness. (Gal. 6:1)
>
> Will Himself *perfect,* confirm, strengthen and establish you. (1 Pet. 5:10)

By reading only an English text, it would be difficult to imagine that the one word in Greek could be translated by so many English words. And yet, it is that difference that needs recognition to fully understand the meaning of individual words.

A crucial example concerning theology and apologetics is the Hebrew word *yom,* translated "day" in the first few verses of Genesis. Those who say the days of creation are not twenty-four-hour days point out that *yom* is also translated "time," "age," "space," and "season" in the book of Genesis alone. Furthermore, even when it is translated "day," it can refer to daytime, a twenty-four-hour day, a period of time ("in the day that the Lord God made earth and heaven," Gen. 2:4), or a specific point in time ("in the day that you eat from it," Gen. 2:17). Whatever the conclusion of the lively debate in evangelical circles as to whether God created in six twenty-four-hour days or in six periods of time, it is important to recognize that day may have a variety of meanings.

In summary, the Bible may use words in a special sense, or a single word may have several meanings. Again, some words are unclear because of translational problems where different words in the original may be translated by the same English word, or a word in the original may be translated by different words in English. Because of those factors, it is essential to become skillful in identifying the meaning of individual words.

A Method for Word Study

It is possible to do a competent word study without a working knowledge of the original languages. However, if the serious student can quickly learn both the Hebrew and Greek alphabets and their standard transliterations into English, he is then equipped to use more efficiently concordances, dictionaries, and commentaries. The following is a suggested procedure for determining the meaning of important or unclear words of the Bible for those with no working knowledge of the original languages.

USE OF THE WORD IN THE BIBLE

First, to find all the occurrences of a word, refer to an exhaustive Bible concordance, such as Strong's (for the KJV; see fig. 1) or the *New American Standard Exhaustive Concordance*, to identify the word in the original language.[2] Since more than one word in Hebrew, Aramaic, or Greek may be translated by the same English word, as we have seen, be careful to check only those occurrences

2. James Strong, *Exhaustive Concordance of the Bible*, rev. ed. (Nashville: Abingdon, 1980); and *The New American Standard Exhaustive Concordance of the Bible* (Nashville: Holman, 1981). In addition, the *NIV Exhaustive Concordance* (Grand Rapids: Zondervan, 1990) serves the same purpose for those using the *New International Version*.

of the word used in the original. That can easily be done by noting the number in the right-hand margin. In the case of "perfect" in Matthew 5:48, the number is 5048. All the words with the same number translate the same word from the original language. If the number differs, the word in the original may be quite different. Those numbers refer to the lexicon (dictionary) in the back of the concordance, where you can find the word used in the text you are studying. Note all the occurrences (identified by the proper number) of that word listed in the concordance.

For *perfect,* you will find the same word in John 17:23; 2 Corinthians 12:9; Philippians 3: 12; and throughout Hebrews, James, and 1 John. (Note also that words with a different number in *Strong's Concordance of the Bible* may actually be the same root. That can be easily discovered as it is indicated in the case of each word in the lexicon.) It is possible to quickly scan the occurrences of a given word, reading the portion of the text quoted in the concordance. In most cases, it is possible to identify through the brief context of the quotation given in the concordance whether or not the use of the word in other passages corresponds to the use in the passage you are studying. When there are only a few occurrences in Scripture, as in the case of the word *perfect,* it is wise to examine all of the passages that use the word. When there are many occurrences, and you do not need to do an exhaustive word study, you need only choose those passages that seem to have the possibility of different nuances or meanings. Make a note of those passages and examine the context of each usage. That very simple comparative study will enable you to learn a great deal about the meaning of the word under consideration.

However, you might now face a problem. As we have seen, the word in the original of the text may have been translated into different English words in other passages. For a thorough word study, you need to examine the word as it is used in those other passages.

Studying a Hebrew word. In order to study such occurrences in the Old Testament, the first step is to refer to the *Englishman's Hebrew and Chaldee Concordance* or to the *Word Study Concordance.* Toward the back of the *Englishman's Hebrew Concordance* is an English dictionary that gives the page number where the Hebrew original of your English word may be found (see fig. 2)[3]. Though you may not be able to read the Hebrew, you can quickly find the biblical reference where your word is found. In the case of *day*, your second try, page 508, turns out to be the one you are interested in (see fig. 3).[4] That identifies the specific Hebrew word, and you can immediately compare that occurrence with all other occurrences of the word in the Old Testament.

Studying a Greek word. With New Testament words, the process is much simpler. You may go directly from the number listed in *Strong's Concordance* to the same number in the *Word Study Concordance,* and there find listed all occurrences of that word in the New Testament (see fig. 4).[5] In fact, in the case of the New Testament, it is possible to use the *Word Study New Testament,* in which the number of the Greek word is listed directly beneath the English word in this King James Version of the New Testament (see fig. 5).[6] That number takes you directly to the listing of the Greek word in the *Word Study Concordance* (see fig. 4).

When a word is used a limited number of times, every passage using the word should be studied. As a result, the student will be able to formulate a tentative definition derived from the most important source of word definition, the context in which the word is used. This is called the *usus loquendi*, or the way the word was used at the time it was written. The use made by the author of the passage is the most important, so his usage in all of his writings merits special attention.

Sometimes a word is used so often that it seems impractical to study every passage in which it occurs. When that is the case, it is helpful to make a list of at least one representative passage for each different meaning of the word discovered through a brief examination of the passages listed in the concordance. Those passages should then be studied.

Not only is it important to study the usage of the word throughout the New Testament and to concentrate on the usage

3. *Englishman's Hebrew and Chaldee Concordance* (Grand Rapids: Zondervan, 1976).
4. Ibid.
5. George V. Wigram and Ralph D. Winter, *Word Study Concordance* (Pasadena, Calif.: William Carey Library, 1978).
6. Ralph D. Winter and Roberta H. Winter, *Word Study New Testament* (Pasadena, Calif.: William Carey Library, 1978).

MAIN CONCORDANCE.

Ac 8:23 For I p' that thou art in the gall of *3708
10:34 I p' that God is no respecter of 2638
17:22 I p' that in all things ye are too 2334
27:10 I p'...this voyage will be with hurt "
28:26 and seeing ye shall see, and not p': 1492
2Co 7: 8 p' that the same epistle hath made *991
1Jo 3:16 Hereby p' we the love of God. *1097

perceived

Ge 19:33, 35 he p' not when she lay down. *3045
J'g 6:22 Gideon p' that he was an angel *7200
1Sa 3: 8 And Eli p' that the Lord had called 995
28:14 And Saul p' that it was Samuel. 3045
2Sa 5:12 David p'...the Lord had established "
12:19 David p' that the child was dead: 995
14: 1 p' that the king's heart was toward 3045
1Ki 22:33 p' that it was not the king of Israel *7200
1Ch 14: 2 David p'...the Lord had confirmed 3045
2Ch 18:32 p'...it was not the king of Israel. *7200
Ne 6:12 I p' that God had not sent him; *5234
16 p' that this work was wrought of 3045
13:10 p' that the portions of the Levites "
Es 4: 1 Mordecai p' all that was done, * "
Job 38:18 thou p' the breadth of the earth? * 995
Ec 1:17 I p' that this also is vexation of 3045
2:14 and I myself p' also that one event "
Isa 64: 4 have not heard, nor p' by the ear, 238
Jer 23:18 and hath p' and heard his word? *7200
38:27 him; for the matter was not p'. 8085
M't 16: 8 Which when Jesus p', he said unto *1097
21:45 they p' that he spake of them. "
22:18 Jesus p' their wickedness, and said "
M'r 2: 8 when Jesus p' in his spirit that *1921
Lu 1:22 they p' that he had seen a vision "
5:22 when Jesus p' their thoughts, he * "
9:45 hid from them, that they p' it not: * 143
20:19 p' that he had spoken this parable 1097
23 But he p' their craftiness, and said 2657
Joh 6:15 p'...they would come and take him *1097
Ac 4:13 p' that they were unlearned and 2638
23: 6 p'...the one part were Sadducees, 1097
29 I p' to be accused of questions of *2147
Ga 2: 9 p' the grace that was given unto 1097

perceivest

Pr 14: 7 p' not in him the lips of knowledge *3045
Lu 6:41 p' not the beam that is in thine *2657

perceiveth

Job 14:21 low, but he p' it not of them. 995
33:14 once, yea twice, yet man p' it not. *7789
Pr 31:18 p' that her merchandise is good: 2938

perceiving

M'r 12:28 p' that he had answered them well. *1492
Lu 9:47 Jesus, p' the thought of their heart, * "
Ac 14: 9 p' that he had faith to be healed, * "

perdition

Joh 17:12 of them is lost, but the son of p'; 684
Ph'p 1:28 is to them an evident token of p', "
2Th 2: 3 of sin be revealed, the son of p'; "
1Ti 6: 9 drown men in destruction and p'. "
Heb 10:39 not of them who draw back unto p'; "
2Pe 3: 7 of judgment and p' of ungodly men. * "
Re 17: 8 of the bottomless pit, and go into p': "
11 is of the seven, and goeth into p'. "

Peres (*pe'-res*) See also UPHARSIN.
Da 5:28 P'; Thy kingdom is divided, and 6537

Peresh (*pe'-resh*)
1Ch 7:16 a son, and she called his name P'; 6570

Perez (*pe'-rez*) See also PEREZ-UZZAH; PHARES.
1Ch 27: 3 Of the children of P' was the chief 6557
Ne 11: 4 of Mahalaleel, of the children of P'; "
6 sons of P' that dwelt at Jerusalem "

Perez-uzza (*pe''-rez-uz'-zah*) See also PEREZ-UZZAH.
1Ch 13:11 that place is called P' to this day. 6560

Perez-uzzah (*pe''-rez-uz'-zah*) See also PEREZ-UZZA.
2Sa 6: 8 name of the place P' to this day. 6560

perfect See also PERFECTED; PERFECTING; UNPERFECT.
Ge 6: 9 Noah was a just man and p' in his 8549
17: 1 walk before me, and be thou p'. "
Le 22:21 sheep, it shall be p' to be accepted; "
De 18:13 shalt be p' with the Lord thy God. "
25:15 shalt have a p' and just weight, 8003
15 a p' and just measure shalt thou "
32: 4 He is the Rock, his work is p': 8549
1Sa 14:41 Lord God of Israel, Give a p' lot. * "
2Sa 22:31 As for God, his way is p'; the word "
33 power: and he maketh my way p'. "
1Ki 8:61 Let your heart therefore be p' 8003
11: 4 his heart was not p' with the Lord "
15: 3 his heart was not p' with the Lord "
14 nevertheless Asa's heart was p' "
2Ki 20: 3 thee in truth and with a p' heart. "
1Ch 12:38 came with a p' heart to Hebron. 8003
28: 9 serve him with a p' heart and with "
29: 9 with p' heart they offered willingly "
19 unto Solomon my son a p' heart, "
2Ch 4:21 made he of gold, and that p' gold; 4357
15:17 heart of Asa was p' all his days. 8003
16: 9 them whose heart is p' toward him. "
19: 9 faithfully, and with a p' heart. "
25: 2 of the Lord, but not with a p' heart. "
Ezr 7:12 unto Ezra the priest,...p' peace, 1585
Job 1: 1 and that man was p' and upright, 8535
8 a p' and an upright man, one that "
2: 3 a p' and an upright man, one that "
8:20 God will not cast away a p' man, "
9:20 if I say, I am p', it shall also prove "
21 Though I were p', yet would I not "
22 destroyeth the p' and the wicked "
22: 3 that thou makest thy ways p'? 8552
36: 4 he that is p' in knowledge is with 8549
37:16 of him which is p' in knowledge? "
Ps 18:30 As for God, his way is p': the "
32 strength, and maketh my way p'. "
19: 7 law of the Lord is p', converting "
37:37 Mark the p' man, and behold the 8535
64: 4 they may shoot in secret at the p': "
101: 2 behave myself wisely in a p' way. 8549
2 within my house with a p' heart. 8537
6 he that walketh in a p' way, he 8549
138: 8 will p' that which concerneth me: 1584
139:22 I hate them with p' hatred: I 8503
Pr 2:21 land, and the p' shall remain in it. 8549
4:18 more and more unto the p' day. 3559
11: 5 righteousness of the p' shall direct 8549
Isa 18: 5 when the bud is p', and the sour *8552
26: 3 Thou wilt keep him in p' peace, whose
38: 3 thee in truth and with a p' heart, 8003
42:19 who is blind as he that is p', and *7999
Eze 16:14 it was p' through my comeliness, 3632
27: 3 thou hast said, I am of p' beauty, "
11 they have made thy beauty p'. *3634
28:12 full of wisdom, and p' in beauty. 3632
15 Thou wast p' in thy ways from the 8549
M't 5:48 Be ye therefore p', even as your 5046
48 your Father which is in heaven is p'. "
19:21 If thou wilt be p', go and sell that "
Lu 1: 3 having had p' understanding of all *199
6:40 that is p' shall be as his master. *2675
Joh 17:23 that they may be made p' in one; *5048
Ac 3:16 hath given him this p' soundness 3647
22: 3 p' manner of the law of the fathers, *195
24:22 more p' knowledge of that way, * 197
Ro 12: 2 and acceptable, and p', will of God. 5046
1Co 2: 6 wisdom among them that are p': ‡ "
13:10 But when that which is p' is come, "
2Co 12: 9 strength is made p' in weakness. 5048
13:11 Be p', be of good comfort, be of *2675
Ga 3: 3 are ye now made p' by the flesh? *2005
Eph 4:13 unto a p' man, unto the measure *5046
Ph'p 3:12 attained, either were already p': 5048
15 Let us therefore, as many as be p', 5046
Col 1:28 every man p' in Christ Jesus: "
4:12 that ye may stand p' and complete "
1Th 3:10 might p' that which is lacking 2675
2Ti 3:17 That the man of God may be p', * 739
Heb 2:10 the captain of their salvation p' 5048
5: 9 And being made p', he became the "
7:19 For the law made nothing p', but "
9: 9 make him that did the service p', "
11 a greater and more p' tabernacle, 5046
10: 1 make the comers thereunto p'. 5048
11:40 without us should not be made p'. "
12:23 to the spirits of just men made p'. "
13:21 Make you p' in every good work 2675
Jas 1: 4 But let patience have her p' work, 5046
4 be p' and entire, wanting nothing. "
17 and every p' gift is from above, "
25 looketh into the p' law of liberty, "
2:22 and by works was faith made p'? 5048
3: 2 not in word, the same is a p' man, 5046
1Pe 5:10 suffered a while, make you p', 2675
1Jo 4:17 Herein is our love made p', that 5048
18 but p' love casteth out fear: 5046
18 that feareth is not made p' in love. 5048
Re 3: 2 have not found thy works p' †‡4137

perfected

2Ch 8:16 So the house of the Lord was p'. 8003
24:13 and the work was p' by them, 5927,724
Eze 27: 4 thy builders have p' thy beauty. 3634
M't 21:16 and sucklings thou hast p' praise? 2675
Lu 13:32 and the third day I shall be p'. 5048
Heb 10:14 by one offering he hath p' for ever "
1Jo 2: 5 in him verily is the love of God p': "
4:12 in us, and his love is p' in us. "

perfecting

2Co 7: 1 p' holiness in the fear of God. 2005
Eph 4:12 For the p' of the saints, for the 2677

Figure 1
Strong's Concordance of the Bible

DAS (1506) DEC

dasheth in pieces, that
פּוּץ Hiphil 1014
daub, to
חָמַר Kal............. 441
טוּחַ Kal............. 479
daubing
טִיחַ 480
daughter
בַּיִת (כ׳)............ 214
בֵּן (כ׳)............ 232
בַּת 280
daughter in law
כַּלָּה 600
dawning
עָלָה Kal............. 934
עַפְעַפַּיִם 968
פָּנָה Kal.............1021
dawning of the day
נֶשֶׁף 849
dawning of the morning
נֶשֶׁף 849
day
בֹּקֶר 266
יוֹם 508
יוֹם Ch.............. 521
יוֹמָם 521
שַׁחַר 1252
day †
אוֹר 32
עֶרֶב 976
*** day †**
בֹּקֶר 266
day, *see* break, dawning, feast, holy, midday, next, noonday
day, by
יוֹמָם 521
day by day
יוֹם Ch...............521
day, each
יוֹם 508
day, in the
יוֹמָם 521
days, *see* three
days agone
יוֹם 508
days, now a
יוֹם 508
days,† these *three*
תְּמוֹל 1349
days, two
יוֹם 508
daysman
יָכַח Hiphil 525
dayspring
שַׁחַר 1252
daytime, by
יוֹמָם 521
daytime, in the
יוֹמָם 521

dead
מוּת Kal............. 675
מָוֶת 680
נֶפֶשׁ 829
רְפָאִים 1188
שָׁדַד Kal.............1237
dead, *see* body, carcase
dead, be
מָוֶת 680
dead, to be
גָּוַע Kal............. 302
מוּת Kal............. 675
dead body
גְּוִיָּה 302
מוּת Kal............. 675
פֶּגֶר 1010
dead man
מוּת Kal 675
dead of itself
נְבֵלָה 787
dead, one
מוּת Kal............. 675
deadly
נֶפֶשׁ 829
dead*ly*
מָוֶת 680
deadly, *see* wounded
deaf
חֵרֵשׁ 467
deaf, to be
חָרַשׁ Kal............. 466
deal, to
חָלַק Piel............. 435
עָשָׂה Kal............. 981
פָּרַם Kal.............1046
deal, *see* bitterly, corruptly, deceitfully, falsely, foolishly, ill, perversely, proudly, subtilly, tenth, treacherously, unfaithfully, unjustly, well, wickedly, wisely, worse
deal bountifully, to
גָּמַל Kal............. 311
deal hardly with, to
עָנָה[3] Piel............. 964
deal subtilly, to
נָכַל Hithpael 818
deal with, to
עָשָׂה Kal............. 981
dealer, *see* treacherous
dealing, *see* violent
dear
יַקִּיר 558
dearly, *see* beloved
dearth
בַּצֹּרֶת 264
רָעָב 1183
dearth †
דָּבָר 325
death
מוּת Kal............. 675
מָוֶת 680
מוֹת Ch.............. 681
מוּת 681
תְּמוּתָה 1349
death, *see* shadow
death, to put to
מוּת Hiphil 675
רָצַח Kal.............1190
death, to be put to
מוּת (כ׳) Kal 675
מוּת Hophal.......... 675
death seize, let
יְשִׁימוֹת (כ׳)............. 576
death, worthy of
מוּת Kal............. 675
deaths
מָמוֹת 730
debase, to
שָׁפֵל Hiphil 1321
debate
מַצָּה 752
debate, to
רִיב Kal.............1171
debt
יָד 489
מַשָּׁאָה 767
נְשִׁי 847
*** debt**
נָשָׁא[2] Kal 846
debtor
חוֹב 405
decay, to
חָרֵב / חָרַב } Kal 458
מָכַךְ Niphal 699
decay, to be fallen in
מוֹט Kal.............. 670
decayed, to be
כָּשַׁל Kal............. 621
decayed place
חָרְבָּה 461
deceased
רְפָאִים 1188
deceit
מִרְמָה 765
מַשָּׁאוֹן 767
רְמִיָּה 1176
שֶׁקֶר 1325
תֹּךְ 1346
תַּרְמוּת 1358
תַּרְמִית 1358
deceitful
כָּזָב 594
מִרְמָה 765
עָקֹב 974
עָתַר[2] Niphal 1008
רְמִיָּה 1176
שֶׁקֶר 1325

Figure 2
Englishman's Hebrew and Chaldee Concordance of the Old Testament

יום (508) יום

יוֹם *yōhm*, m.

Gen 1: 5. God called the light Day,
— evening and the morning were *the* first *day*.
8. the evening and the morning were *the* second *day*.
13. the evening and the morning were *the* third *day*.
14. divide *the day* from the night;
— for seasons, *and for days*,
16. the greater light to rule *the day*,
18. to rule *over the day*
19. the evening and the morning were *the* fourth *day*.
23. evening and the morning were *the* fifth *day*.
31. evening and the morning were *the* sixth *day*.
2: 2. *on the* seventh *day* God ended his work
— he rested *on the* seventh *day*
3. God blessed *the* seventh *day*,
4. *in the day that* the Lord God made
17. *in the day that* thou eatest thereof
3: 5. *in the day* ye eat thereof,
8. the cool of *the day*:
14. dust shalt thou eat all *the days of* thy life:
17. (of) it all *the days of* thy life;
4: 3. in process of *time* it came to pass,
14. thou hast driven me out *this day*
5: 1. *In the day that* God created man,
2. *in the day when* they were created.
4. *the days of* Adam
5. all *the days* that Adam lived
8. all *the days of* Seth
11. all *the days of* Enos
14. all *the days of* Cainan
17. all *the days of* Mahalaleel
20. all *the days of* Jared
23. all *the days of* Enoch
27. all *the days of* Methuselah
31. all *the days of* Lamech
6: 3. *his days* shall be an hundred and
4. giants in the earth *in those days*;
5. evil continually. (marg. every *day*)
7: 4. For yet seven *days*,
— to rain upon the earth forty *days*
10. it came to pass after seven *days*,
11. *the* seventeenth *day* of the month, *the* same *day* were all the fountains
12. the rain was upon the earth forty *days*
13. In *the* selfsame *day* entered Noah,
17. the flood was forty *days* upon the earth;
24. an hundred and fifty *days*.
8: 3. the end of *the* hundred and fifty *days*
4. *the* seventeenth *day* of the month,
6. at the end of forty *days*,
10, 12. he stayed yet other seven *days*;
14. *the* seven and twentieth *day* of the month, was the earth dried.
22. While the earth remaineth, (marg. as yet all *the days of* the earth)
— *and day* and night shall not cease.
9: 29. all *the days of* Noah were 950 years:
10: 25. *in his days* was the earth divided;
11: 32. *the days of* Terah were 205 years:
14: 1. to pass *in the days of* Amraphel
15: 18. *In* the same *day* the Lord made a covenant
17: 12. he that is eight *days* old
23. in *the* selfsame *day*, as God had said
26. *the* selfsame *day* was Abraham
18: 1. the heat of *the day*;
11. well stricken *in age*;
19: 37. the father of the Moabites unto *this day*.
38. children of Ammon unto *this day*.
21: 4. being eight *days* old,
8. made a great feast *the* (same) *day*
26. neither yet heard I (of it), but *to day*.
34. in the Philistines' land many *days*.
22: 4. *on the* third *day* Abraham lifted up his eyes,
14. as it is said (to) *this day*,
24: 1. well stricken *in age*:
12. send me good speed *this day*,
42. I came *this day* unto the well,
55. Let the damsel abide with us (a few) *days*,
25: 7. these (are) *the days of* the years
24. when *her days* to be delivered
31. Sell me *this day* thy birthright.
33. Swear to me *this day*;
26: 1. *in the days of* Abraham.

Gen 26: 8. when he had been there *a* long *time*, (lit. when *days* were prolonged to him there)
15, 18. *in the days of* Abraham his father,
32. it came to pass *the* same *day*,
33. of the city (is) Beer-sheba unto this *day*.
27: 2. I know not *the day of* my death:
41. *The days of* mourning for my father
44. tarry with him a few *days*,
45. deprived also of you both in one *day*?
29: 7. (it is) yet high *day*,
14. he abode with him the *space* of a month. (marg. a month of *days*)
20. they seemed unto him (but) a few *days*,
21. *my days* are fulfilled,
30: 14. *in the days of* wheat harvest,
32. I will pass through all thy flock *to day*,
33. answer for me *in time* to come, (lit. *in the day of* to-morrow)
35. he removed that *day* the he goats
36. he set three *days*' journey betwixt
31: 22. it was told Laban *on the* third *day*
23. pursued after him seven *days*' journey;
39. (whether) stolen by *day*,
40. *in the day* the drought consumed me,
43. what can I do *this day* unto these
48. witness between me and thee *this day*.
32: 32(33). unto this *day*:
33: 13. if men should overdrive them one *day*,
16. Esau returned that *day*
34: 25. it came to pass *on the* third *day*,
35: 3. answered me *in the day of* my distress,
20. the pillar of Rachel's grave unto *this day*.
28. *the days of* Isaac were 180 years.
29. (being) old and full of *days*:
37: 34. mourned for his son many *days*.
38: 12. And in process of *time* (lit. *the days* were multiplied)
39: 10. spake to Joseph *day by day*, (lit. day, day,)
11. it came to pass about *this time*,
40: 4. they continued *a season* in ward.
7. Wherefore look ye (so) sadly *to day*?
12. three branches (are) three *days*:
13, 19. Yet within three *days*
18. The three baskets (are) three *days*:
20. it came to pass *the* third *day*, (which was) Pharaoh's birth*day*,
41: 1. at the end of two *full* years,
9. I do remember my faults *this day*:
42: 13. the youngest (is) *this day* with our father,
17. all together into ward three *days*.
18. Joseph said unto them *the* third *day*,
32. the youngest (is) *this day* with our father
43: 9. bear the blame for ever: (lit. all *the days*)
44: 32. I shall bear the blame to my father for ever. (lit. all *the days*)
47: 8. How old (art) thou? (marg. How many (are) *the days of* the years of thy life)
9. *The days of* the years of my pilgrimage
— few and evil have *the days of* the years of my life been, and have not attained unto *the days of*
— *in the days of* their pilgrimage.
23. I have bought you *this day*
26. a law over the land of Egypt unto this *day*,
28. the whole age (marg. *the days of* the years of his life) of Jacob
29. *the time* drew nigh that Israel must die:
48: 15. all my life long unto this *day*,
20. he blessed them that *day*,
49: 1. which shall befall you in *the* last *days*.
50: 3. forty *days* were fulfilled for him;
— so are fulfilled *the days of*
— threescore and ten *days*.
4. when *the days of* his mourning were past,
10. made a mourning for his father seven *days*.
20. *as* (it is) this *day*,
Ex. 2: 11. it came to pass *in* those *days*,
13. he went out *the* second *day*,
18. How (is it that) ye are come so soon *to day*?
23. *in* process of *time*, (lit. *in* those many *days*)
3: 18 & 5: 3. three *days*' journey into the
5: 6. Pharaoh commanded *the* same *day*
13. (your) *daily* tasks, (marg. a matter of *a day in his day*)
14. both yesterday and *to day*,
19. your *daily* task. (lit. the affair of *the day in its day*)

Figure 3
Englishman's Hebrew and Chaldee Concordance of the Old Testament

5055

1Joh. 3: 1. that we should be called the *sons* of God: (lit. *children*)
2. now are we the *sons* of God, (lit. *children*)
10. In this the *children* of God are manifest, and the *children* of the devil;
5: 2. we know that we love the *children* of God,
2Joh. 1. unto the elect lady and her *children*,
4. that I found of thy *children* walking in truth,
13. The *children* of thy elect sister greet
3Joh. 4. to hear that my *children* walk in truth.
Rev. 2:23. And I will kill her *children*
12: 4. to devour her *child* as soon as
5. her *child* was caught up unto God, and (to) his throne.

5044 1 816/936 5043,5142
τεκνοτροφέω, *teknotropheo.*

1Ti. 5:10. if she *have brought up children*,

5045 2 816/936 rt 5098
τέκτων, *tektōn.*

Mat.13:55. Is not this the *carpenter's* son?
Mar 6: 3. Is not this the *carpenter*,

5046 19 816/936 8:49 5056
τέλειος, *telīos.*

Mat. 5:48. Be ye therefore *perfect*, even as your Father which is in heaven is *perfect*.
19:21. If thou wilt be *perfect*, go (and)
Ro. 12: 2. and acceptable, and *perfect*, will of God.
1Co. 2: 6. wisdom among them that are *perfect*:
13:10. when that which is *perfect* is come,
14:20. but in understanding be *men*.
Eph 4.13. unto a *perfect* man, unto the measure of
Phi. 3:15. Let us therefore, as many as be *perfect*,
Col. 1:28. that we may present every man *perfect* in Christ Jesus:
4:12. that ye may stand *perfect* and complete
Heb 5:14. belongeth to them that are *of full age*,
9:11. greater and more *perfect* tabernacle,
Jas. 1: 4. let patience have (her) *perfect* work, that ye may be *perfect* and entire,
17. and every *perfect* gift is from above,
25. looketh into the *perfect* law of liberty,
3: 2. the same (is) a *perfect* man, (and)
1Joh.4:18. but *perfect* love casteth out fear:

5047 2 817/936 8:49 5046
τελειότης, *telīotees.*

Col. 3:14. which is the bond of *perfectness*.
Heb 6: 1. let us go on unto *perfection*;

5048 24 817/936 8:49 5046
τελειόω, *telīoō.*

Lu. 2:43. And *when* they *had fulfilled* the days,
13:32. the third (day) I shall be *perfected*.
Joh. 4:34. and to *finish* his work.
5:36. the Father hath given me to *finish*,
17: 4. I *have finished* the work which
23. that they may be *made perfect* in one;
19:28. that the scripture *might be fulfilled*,
Acts20:24. that I might *finish* my course with joy,
2Co.12: 9. my strength *is made perfect* in weakness.
Phi. 3:12. either *were* already *perfect*:
Heb. 2:10. *to make* the captain of their salvation *perfect*.
5: 9. And *being made perfect*, he became
7:19. For the law *made* nothing *perfect*,
28. the Son, *who is consecrated* for evermore.
9: 9. that could not *make* him that did the service *perfect*,
10: 1. *make* the comers thereunto *perfect*.
14. For by one offering he *hath perfected* for ever
11:40. that they without us *should* not *be made perfect*.
12:23. to the spirits of just men *made perfect*,
Jas. 2:22. by works *was* faith *made perfect*?
1Joh.2: 5. in him verily *is* the love of God *perfected*:
4:12. and his love is *perfected* in us.
17. Herein *is* our love *made perfect*, that
18. He that feareth *is* not *made perfect* in love

5049 1 818/937 5046
τελείως, *telīōs.*

1Pet. 1:13. and hope *to the end* (lit. trust *perfectly*) for the grace

---

5050 2 818/937 8:49 5448
τελείωσις, *telīōsis.*

Lu. 1:45. there shall be a *performance* of those
Heb 7:11. If therefore *perfection* were by the Levitical priesthood,

---

5051 1 818/937 8:49 5048
τελειωτής, *telīotees.*

Heb 12: 2. Jesus the author and *finisher* of (our)

5052 1 818/937 5056,5342
τελεσφορέω, *telesphoreo.*

Lu. 8:14. and *bring* no *fruit to perfection*.

5053 12 818/937 5055
τελευτάω, *telūtao.*

Mat. 2:19. But *when* Herod *was dead*,
9:18. My daughter *is* even now *dead*:
15: 4. *let* him *die* the death.
22:25. the first, when he had married a wife, *deceased*,
Mar 7:10. *let* him *die* the death:
9:44. Where their worm *dieth* not,
46. Where their worm *dieth* not,
48. Where their worm *dieth* not,
Lu. 7: 2. was sick, and ready *to die*.
Acts 2:29. David, that he *is* both *dead* and buried,
7:15. So Jacob went down into Egypt, and *died*,
Heb 11:22. By faith Joseph, *when* he *died*, (lit. *dying*)

5054 1 818/937 5053
τελευτή, *telūtee.*

Mat. 2:15. And was there until the *death* of Herod:

5055 26 818/937 8:49 5056
τελέω, *teleo.*

Mat.10:23. Ye *shall* not *have gone over* the cities
11: 1. when Jesus *had made an end* of commanding his
13:53. when Jesus *had finished* these parables,
17:24. *Doth* not your master *pay* tribute?
19: 1. when Jesus *had finished* these sayings,

727

Figure 4
Word Study Concordance

ST. MATTHEW 5, 6 15

and take away thy coat, let him have thy
cloak also.
41 And whosoever shall compel thee to go
a mile, go with him twain.
42 Give to him that asketh thee, and from
him that would borrow of thee turn not thou
away.
43 Ye have heard that it hath been said,
Thou shalt love thy neighbor, and hate thine
enemy.
44 But I say unto you, Love your enemies,
bless them that curse you, do good to them
that hate you, and pray for them which
despitefully use you, and persecute you;
45 That ye may be the children of your
Father which is in heaven: for he maketh his
sun to rise on the evil and on the good, and
sendeth rain on the just and on the unjust.
46 For if ye love them which love you,
what reward have ye? do not even the publicans the same?
47 And if ye salute your brethren only,
what do ye more than others? do not even
the publicans so?
48 Be ye therefore perfect, even as your
Father which is in heaven is perfect.

Jesus' Teaching on Almsgiving

6 Take heed that ye do not your alms before men, to be seen of them: otherwise
ye have no reward of your Father which is in
heaven.
2 Therefore when thou doest thine alms, do
not sound a trumpet before thee, as the

Figure 5
Word Study New Testament

by the author, but any Old Testament usage of the word also deserves study. The Hebrew word can be very important for understanding the Greek word, because the thought pattern of most of the New Testament authors is more Hebrew than Greek. Consequently, the word usage is often formed by Hebrew thinking. That can be discerned only through a study of Old Testament usage. So, for the theological words and other words with special importance, it is necessary to trace the concepts back to their Old Testament roots.

Without a knowledge of the original languages it is impossible to make a comparative study of words that have limited usage. But for biblical words like *love*, used throughout the Old and New Testaments, it is possible to do a thorough word study using only an English translation and *Strong's Concordance*. By studying both Old and New Testament usage, the New Testament will be illuminated by the Old Testament, and the Old Testament may be deepened or heightened by the New Testament usage.

For example, to understand the New Testament concept of faith, one is spared from grave error and a very one-sided perception if he studies the Old Testament concept along with the New. In the Old Testament, faith is consistently used objectively, and could be translated "faithful." "My righteous one shall live by his *faithfulness*" (Hab. 2:4, author's translation) emphasizes the true meaning. Since Paul quoted that passage twice, and the author of Hebrews once, it is of crucial importance to know that they did not set aside the Old Testament usage, but expanded it with the additional Greek nuance of the subjective—reliance on God. If, however, the understanding of faith in the New Testament is limited to a subjective attitude, the interpreter has gone astray on one of the key theological concepts, and he has done so by ignoring the Old Testament, from which the concept came.

RESEARCHING A WORD

After the student completes his or her own study of a specific word, he should turn to Bible dictionaries and encyclopedias, theological dictionaries, commentaries, and translations. However, the initial personal study is important to maintaining one's independent judgment should he encounter different interpretations. Translations, in a sense, are commentaries on the meaning of the text inasmuch as it is impossible to translate without doing some interpreting. So it is also helpful to check as many English translations as possible.

TRACING THE HISTORY OF A WORD

Tracing the history of a word can help one in understanding its meaning. Root meanings may be helpful in shedding light on the meaning of the word at the time it was used in Scripture, but the etymology of a word can be very misleading in itself. For example, the word *church* means, literally, "called out," but that is of little help in understanding the way the term is used in the New Testament. One should never imply that the word means "a group called out by God." That may be true theologically, but the word itself did not have that connotation.[7] The current usage (*usus loquendi*) controls the meaning of the word, not its root meaning or etymology. *Agapē* is another example of a word in which a study of the classical use will lead one far astray from understanding the New Testament use of the term *love*. *Repentance* in its root meaning may refer to a simple change of mind. But is that the way the New Testament uses the word? Some contemporary preachers and superficial interpreters have misunderstood great biblical words like *confess* and *Lord* by a simplistic use of the historical root without allowing the biblical context itself to identify the meaning.

However, we may shed some light on the meaning of a word by researching its etymology and root meaning, provided that approach is used with great caution. For example, studying the root meaning of various words translated "glory," "glorious," and "glorify" in the Old Testament can illuminate all the facets of God's character. In the Hebrew Old Testament, ten different words coming from entirely different roots are translated in the King James Version as "glory." One word has the root idea of "grandeur," "imposing appearance," and "majesty." The idea eventually came to mean "magnificent beauty" or "splendor." Another word derived from its root meant "heavy." In fact, several of the ten have the original idea of "being weighty." God's dignity is the predominant idea in those words. Another word came from the root idea of "clear," whether of sound or color, and came to mean "gleaming," "shining," or

7. James Barr, *Semantics of Biblical Language* (New York: Oxford U., 1961), p. 107.

"highly visible." Similarly, another word originally had the idea of "clean," and came to mean "unadulterated," "pure," "innocent," or "bright." Another word meant "loud" or "conspicuous," and gradually incorporated the idea of "triumph and praise."

By putting them all together one may discover that to glorify God is to make brilliantly visible His magnificent excellence. Tracing out the roots of those words gives greater dimension and emotional impact to that key biblical word used of God.

COMPARING NUANCES OF MEANING

Often it is helpful in comprehending the nuance of a word to compare it with other words, both synonyms and antonyms. A simple study of that kind can be accomplished with *Strong's Concordance.* One can check all the different words in the original that have been translated by the same English word. For example, more than twenty different Hebrew and Greek words are translated "perfect" in *Strong's Concordance* (see fig. 1). That kind of study has an additional advantage in that the student will not fall into error through uncritically using one passage to explain another in which the same English word, but different Greek word, is used.

The comparison of words with overlapping meaning is useful for highlighting the precise meaning of the particular word under study. For example, authority and power are closely related in both Greek and English. Christ bases His great commission on the fact that He has been given all authority in heaven and on earth (Matt. 28:18). It is true that He also has all strength and might. We might think that is the basis for accomplishing our difficult task of discipling all nations. But comparing the two words, both of which could be translated "power," gives the deep underlying reason for our confidence when we obey His command. The release of the dynamism of His strength through us is based squarely on His total authority over all. The study of synonyms thus helps define more carefully the area of meaning intended.

SUMMARY OF STEPS

Let us summarize the steps one must consider in determining the meaning intended by the author for a particular word. To determine a word's specific meaning, determine the following:

1. Immediate context
2. Other occurrences within the book
3. Occurrences in other writings by the same author
4. Usage of the word by other authors
5. Old Testament root concept of New Testament words
6. Nonbiblical usage

All of those steps are directed at finding the uses of a word through the study of the various contexts in which that word is found. Other sources outside the context include:

1. Historical root meaning found in lexicons and commentaries
2. Synonyms and antonyms that may throw light on the range of meaning

After studying a word, it may be helpful to put the results of your study into the following format:

1. Define the word as concisely as possible. Do not fall into the error, however, of trying to define a word in a mechanically uniform way. Words in the Bible, like words in the newspaper today, vary in shades of meaning from context to context, and change in meaning from generation to generation. The definition should not be confined to the meaning found in a single passage, but should set the meaning of that passage in the context of the whole range of meaning you have discovered.
2. List problems yet to be solved.
3. List the bibliography of book and periodical material that you have consulted on the word so that you will be able to check your sources and conduct further studies as necessary.
4. Note all devotional thoughts, applications, and sermonic material you may have derived from your study.

Word Study Example: Covetous

To put the above guidelines into practice, let us go through the steps with the word *covetous*. We will not do a complete word study but will demonstrate the use of each guideline. If you use the resources previously mentioned, this procedure will prove to be very helpful.

IMMEDIATE CONTEXT

First Corinthians 6:9-10 will be the springboard for our study of the word *covetous:*

> Or do you not know that the unrighteous shall not inherit the kingdom of God? Do not be deceived; neither fornicators, nor idolators, nor adulterers, nor effeminate, nor homosexuals, nor thieves, nor the *covetous,* nor drunkards, nor revilers, nor swindlers, shall inherit the kingdom of God. (Italics added)

We recognize that the passage itself does not throw much light on the specific meaning of the word because it is listed with a number of different words that describe an unrighteous person. There is no hint as to what *covetous* means. But there is one thing we can learn from the context: *covetous* is in pretty bad company! A sin that most of us would consider fairly common and not-so-bad is listed along with idolatry, adultery, homosexuality, and theft.

Furthermore, the context lets us know that God views it as very serious: a covetous person will never get into God's kingdom. One other thought from the more distant context: the whole passage is dealing with those who have brought lawsuits against fellow Christians. "Why not rather be defrauded?" Paul asks. In other words, "covetous" is not an incidental item in that terrible list—it seems to have been the key sin Paul had in mind.

But the context does not help us define the word, so we must look for its use elsewhere.

USAGE WITHIN THE BOOK

Now we go to *Strong's Concordance* and find that our word, *pleonektēs,* is #4123. Immediately we see that the same word is found twice in 1 Corinthians 5:10-11. In that context we find:

> I did not at all mean with the immoral people of this world, or with the *covetous* and swindlers, or with idolators; for then you would have to go out of the world. But actually, I wrote to you not to asso-

ciate with any so-called brother if he should be an immoral person, or *covetous,* or an idolator, or a reviler, or a drunkard, or a swindler —not even to eat with such a one. (Italics added)

Paul's use here in an adjoining passage reinforces our sense that the sin of covetousness—whatever it is—is very serious. It is included here in a similar list of sins, and we are warned not to have anything to do with someone who calls himself a Christian, but is covetous. And we have the idea that one sign of having that sinful characteristic is that a person would take a brother to court to recoup his financial or material losses.

Before we go to the next step, note from *Strong's Concordance* that another word (a different number) appears as "covet" in 1 Corinthians: "Covet earnestly the best gifts" (12:13), and "Covet to prophesy" (14:39).

We naturally wonder if *covetous* and *covet* come from the same root. *Covet* in this passage is #2206, and on checking it out, we find that it has a different root—there is no connection. Although that does not help us define our word, we will hold it for possible use when we look at synonyms.

OTHER USES BY THE SAME AUTHOR

Paul uses *pleonektēs* (#4123) in Ephesians 5:5, and the context helps define the term. He says a covetous person is an idolator. One who covets is worshiping someone or something other than God. No wonder Paul treated this sin so seriously! In the same passage we find *covetousness* and note that it is #4124 in *Strong's Concordance.* Checking it out, we see it is another form of the same word, so that gives us other passages to check. Several of those, like 1 Corinthians 5-6 (above), are lists of sins. One interesting fact to note is that covetous usually appears in a list of sexual sins. Perhaps sexual covetousness is intimated. In Colossians 3:5 we find the "covetousness is idolatry" theme again. Furthermore that passage indicates that the wrath of God comes upon non-Christians for that kind of behavior (or attitude?), and that Christians must put off that sort of thing.

Paul uses the word in 2 Corinthians 9:5 in a peculiar way. In the passage where he is exhorting believers to give generously he tells them to prepare their offering in advance. Why? So that the gift might be as a matter of bounty, and not of covetousness. The King James Version seems to contrast *bounty* with *covetousness.* It does not make much sense, since it seems to imply that a person could give a lot because he is covetous—the opposite of what is reasonable! A quick check of the Greek lexicon (dictionary) in *Strong's Concordance* gives another possible meaning: "extortion." A look at other translations shows that the word does fit Paul's meaning here: give generously because you want to, not because it is forced out of you (extortion). So the word often translated "covetousness" really should be translated some other way here. Do not err by trying to use this passage in defining covetousness.

Paul helps us to understand that covetousness is a terrible thing and that it is a form of idolatry. It can be seen in the person who defrauds another or who fights in the wrong way to keep or get back his possessions. Often the sin is associated with sexual sins. But we still have no definition.

USAGE BY OTHER AUTHORS

When we further check New Testament usage we find the same sort of thing: lists of sins without definitions. We seem to be at a dead end in finding a definition. But are there any occurrences of this word that are translated by other English words? If so, they would escape us in our English translation, not appearing under *covetous* in *Strong's Concordance.* A quick check of the *Word Study Concordance* shows that there are no other occurrences in the King James Version. That means that for *covetous,* if you are using the King James Version, you have been able to check every occurrence with your *Strong's Concordance.* But if you are using some other translation, the probability is that you would have needed to check the *Word Study Concordance* to find all occurrences.

When we study synonyms, we will find abundant resources for defining *covetous* through New Testament passages that contain great detail concerning its meaning, evidence, and consequences. In 2 Peter 2:14, we find a valuable hint on its meaning. Here we find another list, but the list is in the context of an example: Balaam. Peter points us back to the Old Testament for a definition. Many New Testament ideas come from the Old Testament.

Balaam was a prime example of covetousness. His struggles, defeat, and destruction through covetousness is a graphic picture of the meaning of the term and the results of that sin. Let us turn to the Old Testament.

OLD TESTAMENT USAGE

We find definitions of the term as soon as we turn to the Old Testament. Among the Ten Commandments we read: "You shall not covet your neighbor's house, you shall not covet your neighbor's wife or his male servant, or his female servant, or his ox, or his donkey, nor anything that belongs to your neighbor" (Ex. 20:17). In Caanan, Achan said he saw the loot, he coveted it, and took it (Josh.7:26). We see a definition emerging from the use of the word in the Old Testament—to desire something that is not rightfully yours.

That is reinforced in other Old Testament usage. For example, "All day long he is craving, while the righteous gives and does not hold back" (Prov. 21:26). Desiring to get is contrasted with freely giving, so covet is defined by its opposite. Micah the prophet tells about the kind of coveting that even materialistic Americans can abhor:

> Woe to those who scheme iniquity, who work out evil on their beds! When morning comes, they do it, for it is in the power of their hands. They *covet* fields and then seize them, and houses, and take them away. They rob a man and his house, a man and his inheritance. (Mic. 2:1-2)

A new dimension is added in Psalm 10:3. Not only must we ourselves refrain from coveting, we must join God in abhorring those who are covetous! The prophets thunder against covetousness and link it constantly with other sins. Paul was doing nothing but following the precedent of the Old Testament. And yet, when we check all the references in *Strong's Concordance* for *covet,* there really are not very many. Could there be other passages in which the same Hebrew words are translated by English words other than *covet*? To find out we must turn to the *Englishman's Hebrew and Chaldee Concordance.* In the English word list under covet we find the page numbers: 29, 263-64, and 437. Now we have struck a gold mine! The word translated *covet* in the tenth commandment is used throughout the Old Testament, and almost always with a good sense: the lovers in Song of Solomon *delighted* in one another (Song of Sol. 2:3), God's Word is to be *desired* more than gold (Ps. 19:10), God Himself *desires* (Ps. 68:16), and His creation is *pleasant* (Gen.2:9). There is also the negative: sexual *lust* (Prov. 6:25). Another word translated "covet" only twice is used twenty-seven times with the ideas of "lust, " desire," or "longing." The third major word that seems closer to our New Testament usage is *bâtsa'* (p. 263), found in Psalm 10:3. It almost always has the negative idea and describes God's feeling about the greedy, those who go after gain. Sometimes (but not always) it is translated "dishonest gain."

An adequate study of Old Testament usage, examining the context of key passages, is beyond the scope of this brief word study model. But by checking only the concordance we have discovered the root source of meaning for *covet.* God seems to abhor covetousness almost as much as idolatry and immorality, those two great Old Testament sins.

NONBIBLICAL USAGE

A Greek-English Lexicon of the New Testament and Other Early Christian Literature[8] quotes many sources other than the Bible for the word used in 1 Corinthians 6:9-10, *pleonektēs.* The idea seems to be stronger than our common use of *covetous*: greedy, avaricious, and insatiable.

HISTORY OF THE WORD

Strong's Concordance indicates the combination of two root words, the idea of "more'" and "hold." There is not much additional insight, except that the root idea is stronger than merely wishing for something one does not have.

8. William F. Arndt and Wilbur F. Gingrich, *A Greek-English Lexicon of the New Testament and Other Early Christian Literature* (Chicago: U. of Chicago, 1952).

SYNONYMS AND ANTONYMS

In considering both Greek and Hebrew synonyms, we have already cast considerable light on the meaning. Now returning to Strong's references to *covet, coveted, coveteth, covetous*, and *covetousness,* we discover additional, very important synonyms. Probably the key passage in all Scripture on the subject of covetousness is Luke 16. Here the Pharisees are described as covetous (#5366; earlier editions have #5566, a typographical error). The word itself, as well as the passage, is instructive. The root of *philarguros* is a combination of "love" and "bright things," and came to refer to silver coinage or money. So the Pharisees were, literally, lovers of money. Luke 16 tells us much about the end result of that kind of life—rather the opposite of what Jewish theology of that day taught. Another use of this synonym is to have an *alpha* prefixed to it (*a* in the Greek), which makes it negative: *un*avaricious. That is one of the qualifications for an elder (1 Tim. 3:3). Another synonym not often used is *hēdone* (#2237). The word is important because a key passage examining the nature and results of covetousness uses that word, James 4:1-4. The word is translated "lust" in the King James Version, but "covet" in the *New International Version* (NIV).[9] As we have seen earlier, the opposite of coveting is giving generously. Another antonym is *contentment.* "Godliness with contentment is great gain" (1 Tim. 6:6).

HELP FROM DICTIONARIES AND COMMENTARIES

The most renowned of all dictionaries, the *Theological Dictionary of the New Testament,*[10] devotes eight pages to the word *covetous.* In the scope of our study here we can note only representative insights.

In the non-Jewish and non-Christian Greek world, the word originally meant "having more," then came to mean "receiving more," and finally "wanting more." It meant a strong desire not only for more possessions but also for more power; more fame; more pleasure, specifically, sexual desire. The word was often used

9. *The Holy Bible: New International Version* (Grand Rapids: Zondervan, 1984).

10. Gerhard Kittel and Gerhard Gingrich, *Theological Dictionary of the New Testament.* 9 vols. (Grand Rapids: Eerdmans, 1964).

of going beyond desire to actually taking what belongs to another. It was considered the greatest evil because the inner harmonics of a person and of human society fall victim to covetousness. The ideal is contentment and moderation.

In Jewish literature written in Greek, such as the Septuagint, the idea is "unlawful gain."

New Testament use of that particular Greek word is usually by Paul (fifteen out of nineteen instances), and the sense "striving for material possessions" is possible in every case (apart from 2 Cor. 2:11). Taking advantage of one's neighbor is obviously the main thought. The idea of "immoderate eating and drinking" is also included in New Testament use.

Two important points we missed in our earlier study are brought to light by the *Theological Dictionary of the New Testament.* In Romans 1:29, covetousness is "one of the basic facts in which the total abandonment of the human race by God works itself out."[11] In fact, God gave up mankind because people were not grateful. We also learn about the special emphasis on covetousness as a sin of Christian leaders. We saw earlier that the absence of that sin was a prerequisite for holding office. But in addition to that, Paul went to great pains to show that his own motivation was not covetousness (2 Cor. 7:2, 8-9; 1 Thess. 2:5).

SUMMARY OF FINDINGS

From this study of the word *covet* we can draw several conclusions about the word and the word-study process itself:

1. *Definition.* To covet is to seek for something, someone, some position, some recognition, or some pleasure not in the will of God for you.

Notice that I used the word *seek* rather than *desire.* To be sure, such a sin begins with desire, but it grows into action. It lies at the root of every variety of sin (1 Tim. 6:10). It is not simply wishing for more, but going after it, lusting for it, or working to hold onto it.

2. *Problems remaining.* The chief problem is to define precisely the degree of covetousness intended when it is listed with those grave sins that keep a person out of the kingdom of God. Is it

11. Ibid., 6:272.

simple desire for something one does not have? Is it a greedy and avaricious way of life? Is it both, or something in between?

3. *Bibliography*. The sources I consulted are listed throughout the word study model given above.

4. *Application*. As can be seen in the course of this study, the applications are many. To note a few examples: covetousness is so terrible a sin that it separates a person from God, destroys community, breaks fellowship in the church, is the just object of church discipline, and brings the wrath of God on mankind in this age and the wrath of God on the covetous person in eternity. It is a special temptation for the Christian minister and rightly debars him from service. It is a form of idolatry, substituting things for the living God.

A desire to have things, enjoy pleasure, and be successful is not evil in itself. However, the distortion of those God-given desires, aiming at what is not in the will of God for a person, is a terrible and destructive sin. A covetous spirit becomes visible in those who steal, defame others, lust sexually, fight with a Christian brother to recover material losses. A covetous spirit also pervades those who scheme to make unjust gain, who pursue recognition, or give sparingly and grudgingly. No wonder the Bible treats covetousness so ruthlessly!

We have covered in this chapter a running report of an actual word study, recorded step-by-step. It is not a finished product with final conclusions, but rather a model of the kind of study you can do *now* with the tools you have. If you follow the guidelines, you will find the study of Bible words one of the most fulfilling and exciting forms of Bible study.

Selected Bibliography for Further Study

Balz, Horst, and Schneider, Gerhard, eds. *Exegetical Dictionary of the New Testament.* Vol. 1. Translated by Virgil P. Howard and James W. Thompson. Grand Rapids: Eerdmans, 1990.

Botterweck, G. Johannes, and Helmer Ringgren, eds. *Theological Dictionary of the Old Testament.* 6 vols. Translated by John T. Willis. Grand Rapids: Eerdmans, 1978.

Brown, Colin, ed. *Word Meanings in the New Testament.* Grand Rapids: Baker, 1986.

Goodrick, Edward W., and John R. Kohlenberger, *NIV Exhaustive Concordance.* Grand Rapids: Zondervan, 1990.

Harris, R. L., Gleason Archer, and Bruce K. Waltke, eds. *Theological Wordbook of the Old Testament.* 2 vols. Chicago: Moody, 1980.

Kittel, Gerhard, and Friedrich Gerhard, eds. *Theological Dictionary of the New Testament.* 10 vols. Translated by Geoffery W. Bromiley. Grand Rapids: Eerdmans, 1964.

Kohlenberger, John, ed. *The Expanded Vine's Expository Dictionary of New Testament Words.* Minneapolis: Bethany House, 1984.

The New American Standard Exhaustive Concordance of the Bible. Nashville: Holman, 1981.

Robertson, A. T. *Word Pictures in the New Testament.* 6 vols. Grand Rapids: Baker, 1982.

Terry, Milton S. *Bible Hermeneutics.* 1909 reprint. Grand Rapids: Zondervan, 1974.

Wigram, George V., and Ralph D. Winter. *Word Study Concordance.* Pasadena, Calif.: William Carey Library, 1978.

Winter, Ralph D., and Roberta H. Winter. *Word Study New Testament.* Pasadena, Calif.: William Carey Library, 1978.

Wuest, Kenneth, *Wuest's Word Studies of the New Testament.* 4 vols. Grand Rapids: Eerdmans, 1966.

10
Analyzing Thought Structure

Guideline: Analyze the structure of the basic unit of thought, the sentence.

Individual words are not suspended in isolation, but linked together with other words to form a thought structure. Since the initial goal of Bible study is to determine the single meaning intended by the author, we have considered guidelines for discovering the historical, physical, and cultural setting of the passage and for defining individual words that have special importance or are not easily understood. We now turn to guidelines for understanding meaning through the analysis of thought structure.

Two elements constitute thought structure: the sentence and the context. The basic unit of thought in the grammatical structure is the sentence, which we will consider in this chapter. But sentences, in turn, are linked together. So, to trace the flow of thought, the context of each sentence must be also considered. That larger context will be the subject of our study in chapter 11.

Basic Unit of Thought: The Sentence

We study sentence structure to analyze the flow of thought and gain insight into the meaning. More than any other part of biblical study, grammatical analysis depends on a knowledge of the original language. The flow of thought is not determined by the structure in English but by the structure in the original language. Ordinarily, that structure is apparent to the translator and can be fully translated into the English language. But sometimes the flow of thought is not clear in the original language either. At other times it is clear in the Hebrew or Greek text, but because English is not structured like those languages, it is difficult to translate with clarity.

For those reasons, the interpreter who does not have a working knowledge of the original languages depends on the translator and the commentator for analysis of the flow of thought in the sentence structure. That is true of grammatical study more than of any of the other guidelines used to determine the meaning of a passage. Although a working knowledge of the original languages is helpful with other guidelines and is important in word studies, it is essential for grammatical analysis.

In most instances, the flow of thought is clear enough in the original language, but sometimes problems can arise. Often such problems are not immediately apparent in a translation, as a good translator is charged with the task of making the flow of thought understandable. How can the English reader be aware of such problems? Two ways, basically: (1) by comparing different translations, and (2) by checking critical commentaries. If several translations do not agree on a given flow of thought, you may be fairly sure that the original text has some ambiguity that needs to be searched out.

There is good news for the English-language student who feels handicapped at this point. First, because he is limited in his ability to analyze the grammatical structure, he is likely to give greater attention to the other guidelines for determining the meaning of a passage. Of course, those other guidelines are equally open to the student of the original languages. However, those with a knowledge of the original languages have a tendency to concentrate far more on grammatical analysis. As a result, they may be tempted not to give adequate weight to other skills and guidelines that may be even more crucial in determining the meaning of a given passage. In other words, the English-language student may find it easier to have a balanced, full-range kit of tools as he builds an understanding of the passage.

Second, the other major guidelines are fully available to the English-language student, and therefore, he is wholly dependent only in the area of grammatical analysis. It is important to emphasize that the English reader must consult others for any final conclusions or important interpretations based on grammatical structure.

Although an authoritative analysis of the grammatical structure may not be made without a knowledge of the original language, in the vast majority of passages in Scripture the student can analyze with confidence the flow of thought in a good English translation.

What is a "good" translation? All translators must "interpret" or discern the meaning of the author in order to put that meaning into another language. But what does the translator do when the meaning is not clear? Some translators emphasize form and seek to reproduce as nearly as possible the language of the original. If there is uncertainty or ambiguity in the original, the translators seek to reflect that in translation. For the serious student, that is a "good" translation since it alerts him to questions of interpretation and gives him the opportunity to use his guidelines and skills to determine the meaning. The *American Standard Version* (ASV), the *New American Standard Bible*, and the *Revised Standard Version* (RSV) are examples of this kind of translation.

Other translators emphasize meaning more than "formal" or "literal" correspondence between the original text and the translation. For them the task of the translator is to decide on the meaning and put that into the other language. The task of interpretation is done as much as possible for the English reader. For the casual Bible reader that is a "good" translation since it interprets difficult or ambiguous passages for him. Paraphrases are of this kind. *Good News for Modern Man* (Today's English Version [TEV]), the *New English Bible* (NEB), and *The Living Bible* (TLB) are examples of this approach.

Other versions fall in between. The *New International Version* is an example of a mediating version, good for more accurate correspondence with the original than a paraphrase, but not the best for serious study.

In following the thought flow, it is helpful to ask the following questions about each unit of thought:

1. *What or who is the main subject of the thought*? The subject will be a noun, or a pronoun, or a phrase standing in place of the noun.

2. *What action does the subject do?* The verb indicates the action, state, or condition and is called the predicate.
3. *What or who is the object of the action?* This can be either a direct object or an indirect object.
4. *How have the parts of the thought been modified by a word or a phrase?* Modifiers include adjectives and adverbs.
5. *What are the relationships among the various parts of the thought?* Prepositions and conjunctions are words indicating relationship.
6. *How does the key idea or thought relate to those before and after it?*

Let us look at some examples in which the flow of thought and sentence structure affect the meaning of the text. I will not attempt to solve each problem in each text but will simply demonstrate how it is essential to analyze the grammatical structure if one is to be certain of the meaning.

The subject of the sentence and the verb identifying the action or condition of the subject form the nucleus of every sentence. Every sentence has both. They need to be the first elements identified in a sentence's structure.

THE SUBJECT

Sometimes the subject is understood rather than expressed, as in commands. For example, "[you] Beseech the Lord of the harvest to send out laborers into his harvest" (Luke 10:2). Who, exactly, is the "you"? Not all interpreters agree. A subject can also be a compound where more than one person or thing is doing the action of the verb.

Additional work might be necessary for the interpreter when the subject is a pronoun. When *he, she, it, this, that, you, we*, and other substitutes are used it is important to know who or what is referred to, and whether the subject is singular or plural, male, female, or neuter. Such matters are not always clear in English translations. For example, John tells us that Jesus "came to His own, and those who were His own did not receive Him" (1:11). Note the following ways that verse has been translated:

> He came unto his own, and his own received him not [KJV*]
>
> He came to that which was his own, but his own did not receive him [NIV]
>
> He came to his own home, and his own people received him not [RSV]
>
> He entered his own realm, and his own would not receive him [NEB]
>
> Even in his own land and among his own people, the Jews, he was not accepted [TLB]

These five translations indicate that the subject of the thought is not altogether clear. Who or what are "His own"? By consulting a commentary one might discover that "His own" has a different gender in the two occurrences in that verse. The first "His own" is neuter and could be translated "His own things," whereas the second "His own" is masculine and refers to people. In some translations that is not clear. But the interpretation hinges on this awareness: His own people, the Jewish people who should have received Him, were the very ones who rejected Him.

THE VERB

Verbs possess many features that make an analysis of them probably the most important aspect of examining thought structure. Interpreters need to ask the following questions: Is the action past, present, or future (tense)? Does the verb express a fact of reality, a command, or a conjecture (mood)? Does the subject perform the action of the verb or does it receive the action of the verb (voice)? Is the action complete or incomplete (aspect)?

For instance, in the famous Romans 12:1-2 passage, the change of tense of the Greek verbs is important to notice:

> I urge you therefore, brethren, by the mercies of God, to present your bodies a living and holy sacrifice, acceptable to God, which is your spiritual service of worship. And do not be conformed to this world, but be transformed by the renewing of your mind, that you may prove what the will of God is, that which is good and acceptable and perfect.

*King James Version.

It is essential to know that the first verse speaks of a simple action that can be completed: "I plead with you to make a great presentation." On the other hand, the verbs in verse 2 are in the form of a continuing action. "Conformed" has the idea of "stop being molded by the influences of this world, and keep on resisting the pressure to conform." Again, being "transformed" is not something that is done at a church altar, once for all, or in an instant decision. The force of the verb is a continuous action: "keep on being transformed by the renewing of your mind." Furthermore, the two verbs in verse 2 are commands. Obedience is not optional.

The kind of action described by a verb might not always be clear in the English translation because the English language does not have the same kinds of verb forms. The English-language student, therefore, must develop a sensitivity to hidden nuances in any action word. If the meaning of a given sentence would be greatly affected, depending on a possible different thrust in the original, he should be certain to check that out in a commentary.

THE OBJECT

In most cases, the subject performs action on some object either directly or indirectly. When Jesus said, "I will give you the keys of the kingdom" (Matt. 16:19), the keys were directly acted upon, being given, with "you" as the indirect object receiving the result of the action. But who is "you"? Is "you" singular or plural? Is Christ addressing Peter and his successors, as the Roman Catholic church would hold? Is He addressing the leaders of the church, or is He addressing all Christians?

Consulting a commentary or the Greek text would reveal that "you" is singular in the original. Then the question is whether it refers to Peter alone, or to persons like Peter. In seeking the solution, it is helpful to look at a parallel passage two chapters later where the same promise is repeated. "Whatever you shall bind on earth shall be bound in heaven; and whatever you loose on earth shall be loosed in heaven" (Matt. 18:18). On that occasion *you* is plural. He follows with what seems to be an explanation, indicating that if two agree on earth concerning anything, it shall be done for them by the Father who is in heaven. Immediately following that is the promise "Where two or three are gathered together in

My name, there I am in their midst" (Matt. 18:20). Is not the promise, then, to those who pray unitedly in the name of Christ, in the presence of their Lord? Peter and those like him are able, through prayer, to identify with God in His purposes. Other principles or guidelines can be used to determine what the object is, once it is settled from the grammatical structure what the options or limitations are.

Different interpretations are given to the promise "He will give you the desires of your heart" (Ps. 37:4). Does the psalmist mean to indicate that God will answer prayer by giving what the person desires? Or does he mean that the desire or "want" a person ought to have will be given to him?

The answer to that question can be settled by a simple word study that indicates that the Hebrew word translated "desires" actually means "petitions." Another way to determine the meaning is to check parallel passages. For example, Psalm 78:29-31 reads: "So they ate and were well filled; and their desire He gave to them. Before they had satisfied their desire, while their food was in their mouths, the anger of God rose against them."

Obviously in that passage they were not given the right kind of desires, but rather were provided with what they had pled for. The psalmist is promising that those who delight themselves in the Lord are the ones who will have their prayers answered.

MODIFIERS

Modifiers such as adjectives and adverbs modify or qualify the meaning of other words. Adjectives may tell us the answer to questions such as Which one? How many? and What kind? Adverbs will answer questions such as When? Where? How? and To what degree? Even the most simple modifiers can have great significance. For example, our sonship is distinguished from Jesus' sonship because, according to John 3:16, Jesus was God's only begotten Son. The meaning and significance of that modifier is the difference between heresy and truth. Entire clauses can also serve as adjectives.

Adverbs are often one-word modifiers of verbs, typically ending in "ly." It is significant that Jude tells readers to "contend *earnestly* for the faith" (v. 3) and that Jesus promises to come *quickly*

(Rev. 22:20). Adverbs can be a whole clause as well. For example, we know that perfection in Christlikeness awaits a definite future event because John says, "When He appears, we shall be like Him" (1 John 3:2).

Conditions imposed by adverbs and adjectives must be carefully noted.

WORDS SHOWING RELATIONSHIPS

A word that shows relationships among other words that come before and after it must be given special attention.

Prepositions. Prepositions have the pre-position: they stand before nouns or pronouns for the purpose of showing the relationship of that noun or pronoun to some action or state, or to some other word in the sentence. For example, "the God *of* hope" could mean that God is a hopeful God, that "hope" is one of His attributes; or that God is the source of our hope and the reason we are hopeful. Grammatically, both interpretations are allowable. Therefore, the interpreter must examine the context and make a choice in the interpretion.

Conjunctions. Conjunctions are often the key to understanding, for they join thoughts. Those thoughts may be words, short parts of the sentence, or larger units of thought. Conjunctions often indicate the relationship of the thoughts they join. The connective words used in identifying those relationships are as follows:

1. *Time:* after, as, before, now, then, until, when, while
2. *Place:* where, wherever, in
3. *Reason or cause:* because, for, since, as, whereas
4. *Result:* so, then, therefore, thus
5. *Explanation:* now, for
6. *Purpose*: in order that, so that, that
7. *Contrast:* but, nevertheless, however, yet, otherwise, whereas
8. *Comparison:* also, as, as. . . so, likewise, so also, moreover, than
9. *Continuation:* and, or, either . . . or, neither . . . nor
10. *Concession:* although, even though
11. *Condition:* if
12. *Emphatic:* indeed, only

An example of how a conjunction is used is found in Paul's first letter to the Corinthians: "*That* there should be no division in the body, but that the members should have the same care for one another" (1 Cor. 12:25, italics added). Does the word *that* (in order that) refer only to verse 24 or to the entire preceding thought? Did God plan to give greater honor to those parts of the body that were inferior that there should be no schism in the body? If so, "that" must refer only to the thought immediately preceding. The interpreter is then pressed to figure out why giving honor to the inferior part will keep the body from being divided. Grammatically *that* could also refer to the entire preceding thought, so the meaning is that each part was designed to function as a corporate whole, which prevents schisms in the body. It is important to become sensitive to connecting words so that all options can be examined.

CONTEXT

In considering the grammatical structure, one must keep in mind the immediate context. We must determine how the key thought relates to other thoughts within that context.

Sentences are often long and complicated. Colossians 1:9-20 is an example of one long sentence in Greek. After it is translated into English as one long sentence (even if broken into smaller parts by colons, semicolons, and commas) it is very difficult to follow. The *New American Standard Bible* uses seven sentences, whereas the King James Version uses only three. Often a comparison of different versions will help enable the English-Bible student to sort out the train of thought.

Second Peter 1 is another example of a long, complicated, and interdependent series of ideas. The interpreter must trace the relationship from verse to verse, discerning the flow of thought from verse 1 to 11. For example, verse 4 says, "That by them you might become partakers of the divine nature." What could be of greater importance than to know what it is that enables us to become partakers of the divine nature? Is it the knowledge of God and Jesus our Lord (v. 2)? Is it His divine power (v. 3)? Is it all the things that the divine power has given us (v. 3)? Or is it His own glory and virtue (v. 3)? The only answer to this vital question is to trace the flow of thought from beginning to end, noting the connecting words.

Examine the flow of thought in Paul's beautiful prayer in Ephesians 3:14-19:

> For this reason, I bow my knees before the Father, from whom every family in heaven and on earth derives its name, that He would grant you, according to the riches of His glory, to be strengthened with power through His Spirit in the inner man; so *that* Christ may dwell in your hearts through faith; and *that* you, being rooted and grounded in love, may be able to comprehend with all the saints what is the breadth and length and height and depth, and to know the love of Christ which surpasses knowledge, *that* you may be filled up to all the fulness of God. (Italics added)

Notice the single connecting word *that* (in order that), and see how it builds a crescendo of purpose in Paul's prayer, with each request leading to the possibility of a higher and greater purpose. Grammatically *that* could introduce three separate prayer requests, but the ideas themselves seem to indicate a connection in which each builds on the preceding thought. Practically speaking, with such a crescendo of requests, each leading to a grander result, we are given a plan of action.

Analysis by Diagram

In the above, I have sought to outline a simple approach to help the English-language student of Scripture ask the right kind of questions about the flow of thought as seen in the grammatical structure. There are other approaches. Some with a solid knowledge of English grammar would prefer to begin with an analysis of the various parts of speech. But one way or another, to get the meaning that the author had in mind, the student must see how each phrase fits into the overall message of the entire passage. Each thought must be understood as part of the connected thread of the whole paragraph. Two helpful approaches for analyzing the structure or flow of thought are to (1) diagram the passage and (2) develop it in a "mechanical layout."

GRAMMATICAL DIAGRAM

A *grammatical diagram* helps the student to rearrange the words of a passage in such a way that he can see at a glance the central theme and the actual grammatical and thought structure of the passage. The diagram should show the relationships of words, clauses, and sentences. A diagram uses only the words of the passage itself in a textual recreation without the intrusion of comment from outside. That kind of diagramming necessitates changing the order of the words. Those who are skilled in this approach may prefer to analyze the thought structure in that way.

MECHANICAL LAYOUT

A simplified kind of diagram is a *mechanical layout* of the text. Unlike the grammatical diagram, the words in a mechanical layout are left in the same order in which they occur in the text; such a layout emphasizes relationships between clauses and phrases more than the grammatical function of individual words.

Developing a mechanical layout has two purposes. First, the finished product allows the student to see at a glance the primary elements of a passage and their relationship to each other. He can immediately see the main clause or clauses, and the modifying phrases or clauses, and their relationships as well.

Second, the process of developing the layout forces the interpreter to ask questions and make observations about the structure of the passage. If there is ambiguity in thought flow, he must face it to decide where a thought fits in the layout. He will have to make judgments concerning each part of the sentence. That will keep him from assuming he understands the flow of thought before he has actually studied each part of the sentence and paragraph. Thus, details become prominent—a vital element of Bible study, since each word is God-breathed.

A mechanical layout has two practical advantages: (1) it becomes an ideal worksheet for recording notes and observations from the application of all the hermeneutical guidelines to the text; and (2) it is a good intermediate step between studying the text and composing a teaching outline from the passage. Each main clause and its modifiers, linked by all of the connectives, helps one think about the major and minor points of the author.

There is no one right way to lay out each passage of the Bible, although careful and practiced students will agree as to the relationships between most clauses and phrases. Nevertheless, one

must be consistent in the way the work is done to preserve the fruit of the study for future use.

The thoroughness with which a layout is made will depend on the passage and the purpose of the study. Some passages, such as most historical narratives, require little or no layout. Other passages may become clear with a simple layout. But many passages, in the epistles, for example, are very complex. The argumentation is closely reasoned, involved, and extensive. Such passages become clear, and the flow of thought more certain, through a careful and detailed mechanical layout.

Although the mechanics of the layout are fairly simple, they demand a degree of grammatical awareness. Consider the following three grammatical structures.

Independent clauses. Place the independent clauses (complete thoughts) at the left-hand margin and on the same line write the subject, verb (action word), and word or phrase indicating the direct object (object acted on). That line will represent what the sentence is primarily talking about.

Dependent clauses. Dependent clauses (incomplete thoughts) or modifying phrases are placed on the next line under the word they describe. Modifiers include prepositional phrases, adverbial phrases and clauses, and relative clauses. And those phrases or clauses may also contain other modifiers that would be placed below them, so that the final product might appear terraced.

Connectives. Connecting words (coordinating conjunctions) may be placed above the line or joined to the phrases or clauses they join with bracketing lines.

In addition, the student should leave enough space between lines so that he or she can write in observations and comments. It is well to write comments in a different color so that when the study is used at a later time, the Bible text can be clearly distinguished from the comments of the interpreter.

THE TEXT OF MATTHEW 6:1-4

A careful study of the following example of a layout will be the best means of learning what is involved in making a layout.

Matthew 6:1-4:

(v. 1) Beware of practicing your righteousness
before men
to be noticed by them;
otherwise
you have no reward
with your Father
who is in heaven.
(v. 2) When therefore you give alms,
do not sound a trumpet
before you,
as the hypocrites do
in the synagogues
and
in the streets,
that they may be honored by men.
Truly I say to you, they have their reward
in full.
(v. 3) *But*
when you give alms,
do not let your left hand know what your right hand is doing
(v. 4) that your alms may be in secret;
and
your Father
who sees in secret
will repay you.

Now that you have examined the process, it would probably be helpful to try it on a simple passage in which you have a particular interest before considering the next, more complex example.

THE TEXT OF PHILIPPIANS 1:9-11

Consider now the important, difficult, and beautiful text of Philippians 1:9-11. There are basic problems in this passage. The flow of thought is not altogether clear, though it may appear so on first glance.

Philippians 1:9-11:

```
(v. 9)  And
        this I pray,
          that your love may abound
                        still more and more
                      / in real knowledge
              and <
                      \ discernment,
        (v. 10) so that you may approve the things
                                       that are excellent,
                 in order to be sincere and blameless
                        until the day
                            of Christ;
        (v. 11) having been filled with the fruit
                                  of righteousness
                                  which comes
                                    through Jesus Christ,
                                    to the glory and praise
                                              of God.
```

COMMENTARY ON PHILIPPIANS 1:9-11

The above layout pictures the flow of thought as decided by one interpreter. But there are other possibilities. Consider the five major questions of structure in this passage.

1. *"That"* (v. 9). When Paul said he was praying "that," he could have meant:
   a. "I am praying the following things."
   b. "I am praying in order that the following may take place."

   The indention in the diagram does not indicate which option is correct, nor does the sentence structure. The decision will probably be made on other grounds, such as one's theology of prayer. For example, a person believing strongly in God's sovereign decrees would likely choose option a.
2. *"So that"* (v. 10). Does this mean the ability to approve what is excellent is the result of love that abounds in knowledge and discernment?

The layout indicates such a meaning. If, on the other hand, Paul meant that to be a second request, it would be diagrammed with both requests beginning at the same margin, as follows:

that your love may abound
(so) that you may approve.

3. *"In order to be"* (v. 10). The layout indicates that being sincere and blameless until the day of Christ is the result of approving the things that are excellent. If, on the other hand, Paul meant that that good condition until the day of Christ was the result of abounding love, the phrase should be written parallel with the earlier phrase, "so that you may approve," as follows:

   that your love may abound . . .
           so that you may approve the things . . .
           in order to be sincere and blameless.

4. *"Having been filled"* (v. 11). The subject is understood as "you," the Christians in the church at Philippi: "*you* having been filled." Note that they do not fill themselves. Note also that the condition is complete—"having been filled." But that condition will be completed at the day of Christ after Paul's prayer for them has been answered.

   The original layout, by making "having been filled" parallel with "in order to be sincere" and indented from "so that you may approve," indicates the meaning that being filled with the fruit of righteousness is the condition or prerequisite for being able to approve the things that are excellent. It could read, "You may approve the things that are excellent, having been filled with the fruit of righteousness." But it could mean that they will be sincere and blameless because they have been filled with the fruit of righteousness. If that is the meaning, it would be diagrammed as follows:

   in order to be sincere and blameless
           until the day
                   of Christ;
           having been filled with the fruit
                           of righteousness.

5. *"Which comes through Jesus Christ"* (v. 11). Is it the fruit that comes through Christ, or the righteousness? The original lay-

out indicates that it is the fruit that comes through Christ. This option was chosen because of the agreement of cases in the Greek text. The other, *incorrect* option, that Paul is speaking in this passage of righteousness through Christ, would be diagrammed as follows:

having been filled with the fruit
    of righteousness
        which comes
        through Jesus Christ.

The flow of thought as diagrammed might be expressed in this way:

> I pray that your love may grow abundantly still more and more, both in real knowledge and in discernment. The result of this will be your ablity to approve (or distinguish) what is excellent. This, in turn, will result in a life that is sincere and without blame, extending right up to the "day of Christ." How can one live that kind of life? Only because you already have been filled with the fruit of righteousness. How did that happen? It comes through Jesus Christ. And the purpose of His filling you in this way is to bring glory and praise to God.

Summary

In this chapter we have mentioned four different approaches for tracing the flow of thought in a passage and have given a detailed explanation of two of those: (1) basic questions to ask concerning a passage, and (2) a mechanical layout. Actually, these are more effective when combined as a single approach, although they may be used independently. To combine them in a single approach, the questions are asked concerning a passage, and the answers are pictured in the form of a mechanical layout.

Whatever approach is used, it is essential to trace the flow of thought as accurately as possible. When there is ambiguity or uncertainty as to the flow of thought, the English-language student can become fairly certain of what options are legitimate in interpreting the meaning of the text by comparing several critical commentaries or biblical versions. Sometimes ambiguity will remain because the flow of thought might not be altogether certain in the original. In cases where the grammatical structure permits more than one meaning, the decision on which meaning was intended by the author will usually be based on other guidelines, once the grammatical options are clear. The choice never should be made merely on the basis of what one would like the passage to say but on the basis of careful use of guidelines such as the immediate and distant contexts, parallel passages, word studies, and the historical, physical, and cultural setting. Until we have a complete "kit of tools," we are handicapped, since all the guidelines are interdependent. For example, context is needed to understand word meaning, and word meaning is needed to understand thought flow. But since we cannot study all the guidelines simultaneously, we must be patient, mastering the skills one by one until we can use them all together.

Selected Bibliography for Further Study

Jensen, Irving L. *Independent Bible Study*. Chicago: Moody, 1963.

Kaiser, Walter C., Jr. *Toward an Exegetical Theology: Biblical Exegesis for Preaching and Teaching.* Grand Rapids: Baker, 1981.

Traina, Robert A. *Methodological Bible Study: A New Approach to Hermeneutics.* Wilmore, Ky.: Robert A. Traina, 1952.

Wald, Oletta. *The Joy of Discovery.* Rev. ed. Minneapolis: Augsburg, 1975.

11
Examining the Context

Guideline: Examine the immediate context: the passage as a whole; the book as a whole.

As we have seen, the primary source for understanding the setting of a passage is its context. The most important element in a word study is the word's use in a particular context. Again, ambiguities in grammatical structure are often resolved through reference to the context. In the guidelines we will yet study, the context will be crucial, whether involving figurative language, parables, or Hebrew poetry. In fact, it might even be said that "context is king." It is through the context of any passage, in the final analysis, that we determine meaning.

In chapter 5 we used the term *context* in its broadest sense, referring to the entire historical and literary setting in which the author wrote. In that broad sense, the writer's context derives from the fact that the Bible was written by human beings. We used the term in another sense in chapter 2 when we looked at those who approach the Bible from the point of view of cultural relativism. We discovered various levels of "contextualization." That narrower use of the term was mentioned again in chapter 8, when we discussed the cultural setting, or cultural *context*.

In this chapter we use that same word in an even narrower sense. The term has been used most commonly in the history of Bible interpretation to refer to the text immediately surrounding the verse in question. The broader and quite legitimate meanings used earlier in this textbook have been used more in recent years.

That should not be confusing, however, because we have learned that the meaning of a word must be determined by its use in its context.

Since we shall use *context* in the traditional way in this chapter, it may be divided into three elements: the purpose of the Bible book; the plan of the book; and the immediate context.

The Purpose of the Book

Although we are aware that every book of the Bible shares in the combined purpose of revealing God and His salvation, almost every book in Scripture differs in its purpose from the other books. So it is of particular importance to know why an author wrote his particular book. Some books seem to have more than one purpose—even many purposes. But most have a chief purpose, a central theme, or a main thrust.

DETERMINING THE PURPOSE

How does one go about discovering the purpose of a book of the Bible? A few books explicitly reveal their purpose. For example, the book of John says: "These have been written that you may believe that Jesus is the Christ, the Son of God; and that believing you may have life in His name" (John 20:31). Several key elements in that purpose statement help us in understanding the book of John. "These" refers to the term John uses to describe miracles. He calls them "signs" (v. 30). They are not simply wonderful works; they have a purpose. They are signs pointing to the deity of Christ: "That Jesus is the Christ, the Son of God" (v. 31). That means John was particularly selective in the choice of the miracles he reports. In fact, he records how Jesus used them to teach specific truths.

That seems to be the pattern throughout the book. First, he writes of Christ's giving a "sign" (for example, the feeding of the 5,000); then he follows the account of the miracle with an explanation of the meaning to which the "sign" points. In this case, it is the beautiful discourse on Himself as the Bread of Life. Furthermore, John's purpose statement alerts us to a dual theme—the deity of Christ and the meaning of faith. Without question both the deity of Christ and the meaning of faith are more clearly taught in the book of John than anywhere else in Scripture. Thus, understanding John's purpose in writing his gospel helps us understand his meaning in specific passages.

But how does one determine the purpose of a book if it is not stated clearly? In most books of the Bible, the central or key purpose is not stated in so many words. So it may be necessary to read through an entire book, following the flow of thought, searching for a theme. In that way, it is often possible to discern the purpose.

For example, in Galatians Paul focuses on the problem of Judaistic influences in the church in Galatia. Correcting that error was one obvious purpose for his writing to them. That purpose, in turn, influences the interpretation of specific passages. For example, to what does *law* refer in Galatians? It must be related to the view of the Judaizers. Therefore, *law* in the letter to the Galatian church can hardly refer to just any law or to all law in general. The purpose of the book thus helps us understand specific word meanings.

There are other helpful clues for discerning purpose. In the epistles, we can look in the *opening thanksgiving,* in the *salutation* (Rom. 1:1-7; Col. 1:2; 1 Thess. 1:1-4; James 1:1), and in the closing description (Rom. 15:14-16; James 5:19-20). In the gospels as well, there might be clues at the beginning and end. In books where there is a collection of materials, the book may have a theme, such as practical wisdom (Proverbs) or praise to God (Psalms), but the purpose of each unit (e.g., each psalm) must be the guide for seeking insight.

Sometimes the author indicates the occasion for writing, and that may be a clue for discerning his purpose. But care must be exercised. For example, Paul wrote a thank-you letter to the church in Philippi. That was the occasion. In a sense, it could be called his purpose for writing, but it can hardly be seen as the overriding objective he had in mind while writing the entire book. For that we must look for a theme, or central focus, of the teaching. "Joy in suffering," a theme to which Paul constantly returns, seems to dominate the book of Philippians.

BOOKS WITH MORE THAN ONE PURPOSE

Sometimes a book has several purposes, as in the case of 1 Corinthians, which deals with a series of issues. In such cases, each purpose must be identified, and no overarching purpose may be imposed on a particular passage in a way that would violate the meaning apparent in the immediate context.

It is important to seek an understanding of the purpose through direct reading of the book before consulting the opinions of others. But it would be a mistake to make a final decision without consulting what specialists have concluded. If a Bible introduction book, a Bible handbook, and the introduction of the biblical book in one or two commentaries all concur as to what the purpose is, one can proceed with some confidence on that basis as he studies the book. If there is no general agreement among the specialists, it is probably because no particular purpose is altogether clear. In that case, no purpose should be used as a guideline for interpreting a specific passage, except in a general way.

There are exceptions, however. For example, two widely divergent views exist as to the purpose of the Song of Solomon. In fact, the Song of Solomon is probably the book of the Bible whose purpose is most disputed. Did Solomon write it as a love song, demonstrating the beauty of a biblical and loving relationship between a man and wife? Or did he write it specifically to teach hidden, spiritual truth? The interpretation of every chapter, and of almost every verse, will be determined by one's answer to that initial question of purpose.

In such a case, it is necessary to examine the reason for the divergence. The student should search the book for any hint that it was intended to convey a spiritual meaning. If the book itself appears to speak as a beautiful love song, then there would have to be some compelling external evidence to impose another purpose on it.

The context must decide the purpose. Does Solomon, anywhere in the book, tell us that his meaning is in a spiritual allegory? If not, the interpreter may not impose his spiritual allegory as the purpose of the book and then proceed to interpret it in that light.

First and Second Chronicles do more than relate the history of God's people. Their purpose was to give an interpretation of the spiritual meaning of historic events. Often the writer gave the "inside story," the view of an event from God's perspective. That is helpful not only in interpreting events as recorded in 1 and 2 Chronicles but also in giving a deeper understanding of the same events often reported more "objectively" in the accounts in 1 and 2 Samuel and 1 and 2 Kings. For example, the report of David's final words concerning the Temple and his charge to Solomon (1 Chron. 28-29) give a spiritual dimension not found in Samuel's report. The revival under Hezekiah (2 Chron. 29-31) and God's evaluation of Hezekiah (2 Chron. 32) are filled with insights into God's perspective.

The purpose an author had in mind when writing a book influences every passage in the book. When his purpose can be discerned, it provides the larger context in which every passage should be set before final conclusions are drawn about the author's intended meaning. It is reasonable to assume that the interpretation of each passage should be in conformity with the purpose of the book as a whole.

The Plan of the Book

The human mind, functioning after the pattern of God's way of thinking, seeks for understanding by explaining things coherently, that is, showing relationships. Those relationships may be a simple historic sequence of events, a poetic arrangement for beauty or emotional impact, or a closely reasoned theological discourse. Again, an author may simply make a collection of loosely related maxims or unrelated poetry. The book may be a series of visions. The order of events may be chronological or arranged in some other order to produce a particular effect. Some authors are carefully logical in the presentation of their thoughts, others disjointed. An author may use many possible plans or literary forms, and the interpreter must seek for the meaning of each passage in line with the form the author has chosen.

For example, the book of Proverbs seems to have no overall plan. To impose a flow of thought or a correlation between one verse and the next may lead the interpreter far astray. If it is highly unlikely that there is a connection, verses should be considered independent of one another.

The plan of Matthew seems to be topical rather than chronological. When the interpreter seeks to relate two events as if one caused or led to the other, or interprets the passage as if it were in the historical context of that which precedes or follows, he may well be led astray. Matthew is not written in strict chronological order, but that does not mean Matthew has no plan. He often clusters events or parables to indicate their thematic or theological relationship. Those passages are helpful in seeing the inner meaning of events and the correlation of Christ's various teachings.

INFLUENCE OF THE AUTHOR'S PLAN

The plan of a book influences interpretation. A single thought cannot be interpreted in isolation from its connections to adjoining thoughts. For example, Paul's plan in Romans was to build one concept upon another, systematically arranging basic doctrine in a logical order. No single thought can be extracted and treated in isolation when dealing with Romans, or Paul's meaning will be distorted.

To illustrate this principle, consider the interpretation of 1 Corinthians 12:31: "But earnestly desire the greater gifts." What are the greater gifts?" In verse 28 he describes these: "And God has appointed in the church, first apostles, second prophets, third teachers, then miracles." Some have held that the "first . . . second . . . third" are chronological; that first come the apostolic church starters, then the itinerant prophets, and finally the resident teachers. But in the plan of the book, that interpretation will not hold. The entire passage of 1 Corinthians 12-14 was written to correct an abuse in the church at Corinth. That abuse was in the Corinthians' emphasizing a particular gift (tongues) that Paul said was not so important. The entire passage, then, is dealing with the inherent importance or significance of various gifts. When he speaks of "greater gifts," he means that some are much more important than others. That is very clear when the context is considered. In this case *context* means the entire section of the book. To extract from that section a verse that says "first, second, third," and make it mean something other than the thrust of the entire section of the book, is to miss the key point the author would make.

OUTLINING

In order to discern the plan of the book, we need to outline. That is important not only for the overall plan of the book but also for a specific passage under study. How does one go about outlining a passage or a book of Scripture?

First, a warning: *Do not use the chapter and verse divisions.* Those are not authoritative divisions of thought. They were not in the original text but were added much later. Their great advantage is that they enable all people who are dealing with Scripture to identify the same passage. But in outlining the flow of thought, chapter and verse divisions are not always helpful.

For example, the wonderful passage on love beginning with 1 John 4:7 does not end in chapter 4. In fact, the reader finds a key definition in 5:3: “For this is the love of God, that we keep His commandments.” If one concludes his study at the end of chapter 4, he will miss an integral part of John’s analysis of love, including this definition.

How does one outline the flow of thought? Simply put, one looks for change. If there is a change in events so that one story is concluded and another begun, the outline is fairly simple. In the gospels, however, one must be careful to include the preceding or following commentary on the event as well as the event itself. Change of event may be easy, but change in thought, though more difficult, is of much greater importance.

In the book of Ephesians, the break between chapters 3 and 4 is very clear. Paul had been dealing with doctrinal matters, particularly with the church. In 3:21 his benediction concludes, “To Him be the glory in the church and in Christ Jesus to all generations forever and ever. Amen.” The next verse (4:1) reads, “I, therefore, the prisoner of the Lord, entreat you to walk in a manner worthy of the calling with which you have been called.” Paul has clearly shifted from doctrine to practice, leaving the two major divisions of the book clear.

Less radical changes of thought, in which one idea may gradually flow into another idea, are more difficult to discern. Those would constitute the subdivisions under the main outline. In the case of Ephesians, for example, one might be tempted to make a break between chapters 5 and 6 because chapter 5 is dealing with husbands and wives, whereas chapter 6 begins with the relationship between children and parents. However, looking at the relationship between the two chapters suggests a common theme, subjection to one another.

One can begin at any point in the text and work backward or forward in looking for a change of thought. If one begins at the end of chapter 5 of Ephesians and works backward, he will find the subject centering on the relationship between wives and husbands as an analogy of Christ and the church. There is a clear break between verses 21 and 22, for verse 21 speaks of *subjecting ourselves one to another* in the fear of Christ. And so most versions make a paragraph break at that point. The paragraph break is no doubt legitimate, but the connection between subjecting yourselves one to another in verse 21 and the teaching, beginning with verse 22, that wives should be in subjection to their own husbands obviously has some relationship.

When we return to 6:1 and begin looking in the opposite direction for a change in thought, we immediately find another example of subjection. This time it is the subjection of children to parents. Following the flow of thought further, a break occurs between 6:4 and 6:5, where the subject changes from children and parents to servants and masters. Nevertheless, the thread of thought continues in that servants are to be in subjection to their masters. Not until we reach verse 10 is there a complete break with the original thought of being in subjection one to another in the fear of Christ. To outline the flow of thought in this way obviously sheds a great deal of light on a highly controversial passage.

Here is a possible outline of Ephesians, giving greater detail in division II:

Introduction (1:1-2)
I. Doctrine: The Believer's Standing (1:3–3:21)
II. Practice: The Believer's Walk (4:1–6:20)
  A. Life and service (4:1–6:9)
    1-6. Six topics (4:1–5:20)
    7. Mutual submission (5:21–6:9)
      a. Wife/husband (5:22-33)
      b. Child/parent (6:1-4)
      c. Servant/master (6:5-9)
  B. Warfare (6:10-20)
Conclusion (6:21-24)

Note that the point of division between doctrine and practice represents a major change in thought and is highly visible. We designate those divisions I and II. Within the second section the change from one thought to another is more subtle and less precise. But there are at least two distinct themes (life and service [A]; and warfare [B]). We have put them together under a single major division (II) because they both have in common the idea of the actual living of the Christian life—not the theological standing or relationship the believer has with God (I). Again, within the section on "Life and Service," there are many topics. We divide them into subpoints because they are distinct (1-7). Within the subpoint of "mutual submission" we find three examples or applications of the same principle, so we cluster them under a single heading, but identify them separately (a, b, and c).

With the above, the flow of thought is made clear by showing the major and minor divisions, or changes in thought. As a result, the interpreter can use that structure in analyzing the meaning of any specific passage. Obviously, outlining a book and each passage within the book is far more important than simply providing a framework for easily remembering the content. It is a structured way of tracing the flow of thought. The understanding of the thought flow, in turn, has tremendous importance for the interpretation of each thought within the whole.

The Immediate Context

Discerning the purpose and plan of a book is helpful in putting each passage into its broader context. The immediate context, however, is the most important guideline for determining the meaning of a passage; ironically, it is probably among the most neglected. Studying the immediate context helps the reader understand the intended meaning better, as we can see in studying three different passages in Galatians, Romans, and 1 Thessalonians.

GALATIANS 5:4: FALLING FROM GRACE

When Paul spoke of falling from grace (Gal. 5:4), was he speaking of a person's losing his salvation? A quick check on the context will indicate that is far from the meaning of the expression in that passage. He was speaking of the circumcision party (who sought to bring believers under the bondage of the Old Covenant) and warning the people in Galatia that if a person seeks justification through obedience to the law, he has rejected the way of grace, or is fallen from grace.

ROMANS 14:13–15:1: THE STRONG AND THE WEAK

We might think that a strong person is one who is strong in his opinions, his convictions, his character, or his spirituality. One who is weak is weak in one or more of those areas. That view is legitimate. But is that what Paul was contrasting in Romans 14 when he spoke of the strong and the weak? The context must determine. He was speaking of being strong in faith and weak in faith. The one who is strong in faith has confidence that he may eat anything. The one who is weak in faith lacks that confidence. In Paul's case, he was the strong person and biblical in his convictions. However, it is quite possible to be strong and wrong. Such a person could be weak in character or weak spiritually and still be "strong" in the sense in which Paul used the term here.

It is important for the interpretation of the entire passage to learn from the context what the meaning is. That is, incidentally, another good example of how the context extends beyond chapter divisions. In Romans 15:1 we have additional exhortation and contrast between the strong and the weak: "Now we who are strong ought to bear the weaknesses of those without strength and not just please ourselves." Paul then gives Christ as a model to show how that difficult injunction can be obeyed—all in another chapter but part of the same thought.

1 THESSALONIANS 5:2: THE DAY OF THE LORD

Here Paul tells us that the Day of the Lord will come like a thief in the night. How does a thief come in the night? Many have taken this passage to indicate that the Lord will come stealthily or secretly. Once again, the context must control. The following verse uses another analogy, the way a woman's birth pangs come upon her suddenly, without warning. Then, in verse 4, the contrast between day and night is used in another way, but one that sheds light on the nature of a thief in Pauline usage: "But you, brethren, are not in darkness, that the day should overtake you like a thief." Here again, Paul is speaking of the thief's overtaking or coming suddenly. So it would seem from the context that the characteristic of a thief coming at night does not refer to secrecy or stealth, much less to the immoral behavior of the thief. Rather, it refers to his unexpectedness or suddenness.

For further light, the preceding context would seem to say the very opposite of stealth: "For the Lord Himself will descend from heaven with a shout, with the voice of the archangel, and with the trumpet of God" (1 Thess. 4:1). If 1 Thessalonians 4:16 is taken to mean that thieflike coming refers to secrecy, then those two verses must refer to different events, and the interpretation that "the Day of the Lord" and "the coming of the Lord" are different events would be reinforced. But if the thieflikeness of Christ's coming does not have to do with any other characteristic of a thief except his unexpected coming, the two could fit together very well. I have used several guidelines in analyzing this statement, but chiefly it is the context that yields a more accurate understanding of meanings.

Summary

We have seen examples of the strategic importance of carefully examining the context, for it is the purpose and plan of the book, the flow of thought in a specific passage, and the immediate context that, in the final analysis, determine meaning. The most common failure in interpretation is to violate this most simple and basic principle: *the context must control.*

Since the context is to control, we should begin with the purpose the author had in mind when he wrote the book. We must allow his purpose, rather than our own, to control the interpretation. Then, to see where the passage fits into the thought flow, we should outline the book, giving greater attention to the more subtle changes in thought immediately before and after the passage under study. Finally, we must zero in on the immediate context, allowing it to control the interpretation. We do that by refusing to force a meaning on a word, phrase, or unit of thought that violates any plain implication of context.

Not only is the guideline of context the most obvious and simplest of the guidelines, but, when violated, its consequences are far-reaching. That is because the person who carelessly ignores the context when preparing a sermon or lesson plan has disobeyed the injunction "Be diligent to present yourself approved to God as a workman who does not need to be ashamed, handling accurately the word of truth" (2 Tim.2: 15). It is a shameful thing to carelessly ignore the context. To deliberately violate the context is more than shameful; it is sinful, for it is a deliberate substitution of one's own words for the Word of God.

The student of Scripture, though he may not understand the original languages, nevertheless has at his command the single most important tool—the context. Let him use it diligently!

Selected Bibliography for Further Study

Chisholm, Robert B., Jr. *Interpreting the Minor Prophets.* Grand Rapids: Zondervan, 1990.

Goldingay, John. *Approaches to Old Testament Interpretation.* Downers Grove, Ill.: InterVarsity, 1981.

Longman, Tremper, III. *Literary Approaches to Biblical Interpretation.* Grand Rapids: Zondervan, 1987.

McKnight, Scot, ed. *Introducing New Testament Interpretation.* Grand Rapids: Baker, 1990.

Marshall, I. Howard. *New Testament Interpretation: Essays on Principles and Methods.* Grand Rapids: Eerdmans, 1977.

Schreinder, Thomas R. *Interpreting the Pauline Epistles.* Grand Rapids: Baker, 1990.

Stuart, Douglas. *Old Testament Exegesis: A Primer for Students and Pastors.* Philadelphia: Westminster, 1980.

12
Figurative Language

Guideline: Identify figurative language and determine its literal meaning.

Since the Bible was written by human beings, it must be treated as any other human communication in determining the meaning intended by the author. We have studied guidelines that are derived from that principle; guidelines that enable the serious student to determine the meaning of straightforward, literal language. However, there are many other types of language in the Bible. In addition to history and teaching (didactic) sections, Scripture contains poetry, drama, proverbs, figures of speech, and parables. Those are common to all human language. And the Bible, a human book, is full of such literature.

There are guidelines for understanding the meaning of special language just as there are guidelines for understanding straightforward, literal language. Interpretation goes astray when the type of language is misunderstood and consequently treated in an inappropriate way. Therefore it is very important to identify the type of language in a passage and to interpret it with the guidelines appropriate for understanding that particular type of language.

Although Scripture contains a full range of literary types, we will consider only those that are of major importance for understanding the meaning. First, we will consider various kinds of figurative language. As much of the Old Testament is in poetic form, and much of Christ's teaching is in parabolic form, we will consider Hebrew poetry and the parables as separate literary forms.

Understanding Figurative Language

Figurative language refers to any words that are used with a meaning other than their common, literal sense. When *dog* is used of a human being (e.g., Phil. 3:2), the ordinary, literal designation of an animal is not intended. "The whole world itself would not contain the books" (John 21:25) was never intended as a scientific estimate of available space.

The Bible is filled with that kind of figurative language, and such nonliteral picture-talk is one of the greatest problems of interpretation. To treat figurative language as if it were literal, and to treat literal language as if it were figurative, constitute two of the greatest hindrances to understanding the meaning of the Bible. Furthermore, even when a passage is correctly identified as figurative, the meaning can be missed through using inappropriate principles or guidelines for interpreting the passage. We shall first consider the reasons for using figurative language, and then consider the necessary guidelines for understanding the meaning of nonliteral passages.

Reasons for Figurative Language

Why does the Bible use figurative language at all? Would not communication be much clearer if the whole of revelation were in straightforward, literal language? There are several reasons for the use of figurative language in Scripture.

Figurative language is often used because all human language contains nonliteral talk.

C. S. Lewis put it this way:

> Very often when we are talking about something which is not perceptible by the five senses, we use words which, in one of their meanings, refer to things or actions that are. When a man says that he grasps an argument he is using a verb (grasp) which literally means to take something in the hand but he is certainly not thinking that his mind has hands or that an argument can be seized like a gun. To avoid the word *grasp* he may change the form of expression and say, "I see your point," but he does not mean that a pointed object has appeared in his visual field. He may have a third shot and say, "I follow you" but he does not mean that he is walking behind

you along a road. Everyone is familiar with this linguistic phenomenon and the grammarians call it metaphor. But it is a serious mistake to think that metaphor is an optional thing which poets and authors may put into their work as a decoration and plain speakers can do without. The truth is that if we are going to talk at all about things which are not perceived by the senses, we are forced to use language metaphorically. Books on psychology or economics or politics are as continuously metaphorical as books of poetry or devotion. *There is no other way of talking.* . . . All speech about supersensibles is, and must be, metaphorical in the highest degree.

Anyone who talks about things that cannot be seen, or touched, or heard, or the like, must inevitably talk *as if they could* be seen or touched or heard (e.g., must talk of "complexes" and "repressions," *as if* desires could really be tied up in bundles or shoved back; of "growth" and "development" *as if* institutions could really grow like trees or unfold like flowers; of energy being "released" *as if* it were an animal let out of a cage.)[1]

All human languages are filled with talk that is not literal, but Eastern languages are especially full of figures of speech. Since those languages are foreign to us, that is all the more reason to work hard at understanding exactly what the author had in mind. There is the hurdle of distance in language and culture, and there is also the hurdle of figurative language. Consider the plight of a foreigner seeking to understand the English word *hang.* A literal definition is easy to come by, but what is he to think when he hears, as a foreigner, that he has many hang-ups; that he should indeed hang loose and allow his true feelings to hang out? If he searches out those idioms carefully, he still may be at a loss to know why someone is absent because of a hangover, or when he is told, in spite of all the obstacles to understanding, that he should not only hang on, but hang in there.

Figurative language is often used to emphasize a point. To say, "Tell that fox" (Luke 13:32), is considerably more forceful than to say, "Tell the king." "If a person does not hate his father and his mother" is stronger than, "You must love Me more than

1. C. S. Lewis, *Miracles* (New York: Macmillan, 1947), pp. 88-89.

you love your father and mother." Figurative language makes a stronger impression.

Figurative language can be used to move one to action. "Behold, I stand at the door and knock," gives an emotional impact far beyond the impact of saying simply, "I am waiting for you to respond." In the East, where dining together is the seal of friendship, great is the emotional impact of being shut out awaiting the invitation to come in. Figurative language is powerful in moving to action.

Figurative language may help the memory. "Don't hide your light under a bushel" or "bury your talent"; he is a "good Samaritan," or she is "the salt of the earth." Those expressions are now common to English usage, proof that figurative language emphasizes a point in such a way that it is not easily forgotten. It can even, as in those cases, become a part of the language.

Figurative language is effective in illustrating. When Christ said, "I am the bread of life" (John 6:48), He was illustrating a basic truth concerning His relationship with those who belong to Him. He satisfies and nourishes. "The kingdom of heaven is like leaven" (Matt. 13:33) immediately evokes the image of gradual, steady growth permeating the whole. When the Christian is told that he is a soldier or a farmer, the illustration helps in understanding his responsibilities. Thus figurative language is very effective in illustrating spiritual truth.

Figurative language is useful in clarifying. The familiar can be used to explain the unfamiliar. That is particularly helpful when the unlimited truth of God must be made simple enough for limited man to understand it. To speak of God as our husband or father brings within the range of our very limited understanding basic truths about the relationship He desires with us. How could God, who is infinite and without material being, explain to us His activity in creating a being who is limited, material, and yet designed on the pattern of His own nature? And so it is said that He breathed life into Adam (Gen. 2:7). Figurative language is helpful in clarifying, in making spiritual and infinite truth available to finite human beings.

In fact, as C. S. Lewis pointed out above, whenever the author wishes to speak of things not perceived by the senses, he may be forced to use nonliteral language. Some abstract truth can be communicated only with concrete models—we need models we can see to understand the unseen.

Figurative language may be used as a code. In the case of Christ's parables, we are told that parables were chosen as a medium for the very purpose of obscuring:

> And the disciples came and said to Him, "Why do You speak to them in parables?" And He answered and said to them, "To you it has been granted to know the mysteries of the kingdom of heaven, but to them it has not been granted. For whoever has, to him shall more be given, and he shall have an abundance; but whoever does not have, even what he has shall be taken away from him. Therefore I speak to them in parables; because while seeing they do not see, and while hearing they do not hear, nor do they understand. And in their case the prophecy of Isaiah is being fulfilled, which says,
>
> > 'You will keep on hearing, but will not understand;
> > And you will keep on seeing, but will not perceive;
> > For the heart of this people has become dull,
> > And with their eyes they scarcely hear,
> > And they have closed their eyes
> > Lest they should see with their eyes,
> > And hear with their ears,
> > And understand with their heart and return,
> > And I should heal them.'
>
> But blessed are your eyes, because they see; and your ears, because they hear. For truly I say to you, that many prophets and righteous men desired to see what you see, and did not see it; and to hear what you hear, and did not hear it." (Matt. 13:10-17)

Thus figurative language is sometimes used as a "code language." It gives light to those who have obedience, obscurity to those who do not. Not only is that a judgment for not obeying, but it is actually for their own good lest they have increased light that would bring increased responsibility and consequently increased judgment. Sometimes, then, figurative language is to obscure.

There is another reason for using obscure language. Sometimes prophecy is given obscurely so that it may remain hidden until the time of fulfillment. We will consider that more in detail when we consider guidelines for understanding prophecy. However, a clear example of that is found in the words of Christ to the Jews:

> Jesus answered and said to them, "Destroy this temple, and in three days I will raise it up." The Jews therefore said, "It took forty-six years to build this temple, and will You raise it up in three days?" But He was speaking of the temple of His body. When therefore He was raised from the dead, His disciples remembered that He said this; and they believed the Scripture, and the word which Jesus had spoken. (John 2:19-22)

There are many reasons, then, for the use of figurative language in Scripture, and it is our responsibility to study diligently that we may handle that kind of Scripture in an appropriate way.

Guidelines for Interpreting Figurative Language

The goal of studying figurative language in the Bible is the same as studying literal language: to discern the meaning intended by the author and to apply that meaning to life. However, in the case of figurative language, there is a prior step. We must first establish that the language is figurative rather than literal, and then identify the type of figurative language. After identifying the nonliteral passage, we are ready for interpretation and application. In other words, an intermediate step is necessary in the case of figurative language: identifying the fact that it is figurative and identifying the kind of figure being used.

IDENTIFYING FIGURATIVE LANGUAGE

Two guidelines will help to identify figurative language.

The first guideline. Biblical language, like newspaper language or any other ordinary human communication, should be taken as literal unless there is one of three compelling reasons for considering it nonliteral:

1. *If the statement would obviously be irrational, unreasonable, or absurd if taken literally, the presumption is that it is a fig-*

ure of speech. "I am the door," and "you are the salt" are obviously irrational if taken literally.

2. *The context may indicate that language is figurative.* When taken in isolation, the expression or statement might be either figurative or literal, but in the context the author indicates that he does not intend the meaning to be taken as literal.

   When Paul said, "I wrote . . . not for the sake of the offender" (2 Cor. 7:12), the immediate context and the context of the whole event reaching back into the early chapters, and on into the later chapters of 2 Corinthians, clearly show that he was exaggerating for effect. He wrote very much for the sake of the one who did the wrong and said so clearly and repeatedly. What, then, did he mean here? He meant, "I did not write *only* for the purpose of saving the one who did wrong."

3. *If there is a contradiction with clearer and more enduring emphases of Scripture, it is legitimate to ask whether or not the passage is to be taken as literal.* For example, to hate your mother and father (Luke 14:26) contradicts both Old and New Testaments in their plain, strong, and enduring teaching that parents are to be loved and honored. So it is not only permissible but necessary to look for a figurative meaning. This guideline actually depends not on the ordinary use of human language, but on the fact that the Bible is also a supernatural Book. We will consider that in greater detail when we study the relationships among various teachings of Scripture.

Although it is legitimate to look for an authentic, nonliteral understanding, the student must not force a figurative meaning on the language. Some passages are thought to be figurative by those who believe the Bible and try to find the harmony among all its teachings. They might seek to bring a specific difficult passage into harmony with other clearly literal passages and the predominant, clear teaching of Scripture, as we have just indicated. On the other hand, there are those who do not believe the Bible and who take literal statements to be figurative. Creation, unclean spirits, the resurrection, and the second coming are unacceptable to those who hold rationalistic presuppositions. So they look on them as figurative or mythological to avoid acknowledging the supernatural. Thus a person's presuppositions concerning the Bible will raise questions about whether specific passages are to be taken literally or figuratively.

With these exceptions in mind, one must still remember that the basic rule is to take every passage of Scripture as literal. Only compelling reasons makes the words figurative.

The second guideline. The viewpoint of the author and the original recipients, not our own perceptions, must control our understanding of what is appropriately literal or figurative. We may think that it is appropriate to use a lamb or a lion to designate something about Jesus Christ but resist using a thief or corpse to picture Him. But the appropriateness of a particular figure is not for us to evaluate. Rather, we must evaluate the language in terms of what the author intended. When people are compared to sheep, for example, it will not do to study present-day sheepherders and the behavior of sheep to determine what the author had in mind. Present-day sheep shed light on the possibilities for meaning, but the way the author and his contemporaries viewed sheep is what must determine the point of comparison. Indeed, an author may change the point of comparison in the same passage. "All of us like sheep have gone astray" (Isa. 53:6) uses a comparison different from another in the same passage, "Like a sheep that is silent before its shearers" (v. 7). Obviously, the author had something different in mind for each comparison.

Christ told us that we are the salt of the earth, and we are not free to choose our own preference as to what comparison was intended. We must search diligently to discern what comparison He intended. I once heard a fascinating sermon in which many characteristics of salt were used in analogy to exhort Christians toward more appropriate and more biblical behavior. Salt was used to preserve the Galilean fish on the journey to Jerusalem, arresting corruption. Speech seasoned with salt adds flavor to a tasteless society. In the Old Testament there was a salt offering, indicating that God is a covenant God, One who is faithful. Consequently, the witness of a miracle life, a transformed life, is the greatest evidence of God's existence, the speaker said. Furthermore, salt was not to remain isolated in a block but was to be ground down and sprinkled, thereby losing its own distinctiveness. Finally, salt has impact out of proportion to its size.

Is it legitimate to make all of those points of comparison with the assurance that Jesus had all of that in mind when He said, "You are the salt of the earth"? No, for the first task of the interpreter is to discern what the author had in mind by way of comparison, not what our own experience in another culture or our own ingenuity may devise. The guideline is this: the intent of the author must control our understanding of his meaning.

IDENTIFYING KINDS OF FIGURES

It is important before interpreting a figurative expression to identify the kind of figure being used. Often that identification itself will provide the key for interpreting the meaning, as we shall see.

Literary analysts have identified a large number of distinct figures of speech. In one publication for the use of Bible translators, twenty-eight figures of speech were identified, including such exotic kinds as antonomasia, asyndeton, hendiadys, oxymoron, and paronomasia. Rather than seeking to identify all possible figures of speech in our study, we will concentrate on a few that are used often and are of great importance for understanding Scripture.

Figures of comparison. By far the most common figurative language in Scripture is the figure of comparison. It may consist of a simple or a complex comparison, as in parables or allegories. The comparison may be used on a single occasion, or it may be used as a permanent comparison, as in a symbol. Prophetic symbols, called *types,* are basic to the understanding of much of Scripture. We will list the major categories of comparison separately, but the kind of figurative language indicated in this section is basically that of comparison.

A *simile* is a common figure of comparison in which two unlike things are explicitly compared. "All of us like sheep have gone astray" (Isa. 53:6) is an example, for the comparison is stated. On the other hand, in a *metaphor,* the comparison may simply be implied. For example, the psalmist says, "We are . . . the sheep of His pasture" (Ps. 100:3). Simply stated, similes and metaphors are expressions of similarity between two objects or concepts that are, in most respects, unlike.

In examining figures of comparison, remember that ordinarily only one point of comparison is intended. The comparisons are limited, and the reader is not permitted to improvise or decide what point of comparison he likes best or finds compatible with his doctrinal structure or sermonic outline. As indicated earlier, in the analogy between salt and people, the question is what Christ and His hearers had in mind, not what a fertile imagination can assign by way of additional meanings. If we are not careful, the Scriptures will no longer be an independent authority, sitting in judgment on our ideas, but rather, we interpreters will become the authorities, building unsound doctrine on misapprehension of a figurative biblical expression.

Another variety of figures of comparison is *representation* —one thing taken to represent something else. For example, symbols are one thing taken to represent sometling else, often a material object representing an intangible. Brass in Scripture seems to be symbolic of judgment, for example. A symbol is an implied comparison (metaphor), except that it is a special kind of metaphor. It is more universal and emblematic. The language of symbols is common in Scripture as in other languages, but because Scripture is also of divine origin, there is a great deal of prophetic symbolism. The technical term for a prophetic symbol is *type*. Symbolism and typology are so important for understanding Scripture that we will consider them more extensively later. But to get an overview of all the various kinds of figures of comparison, we introduce them at this point.

The diagram on the following page illustrates the relationships among the various figures of comparison.

Figures of association. Figures of association are different from figures of comparison in the following way: In figures of comparison unlike things are compared, whereas in figures of association the name of one object or concept is used for that of another to which it is related. That association is called *metonomy*. Christ gave us an example of the figure of association when He said, "He who swears by heaven, swears both by the throne of God and by Him who sits upon it" (Matt. 23:22). The Pharisee would not take God's name in vain, but he chose to use the place associated with

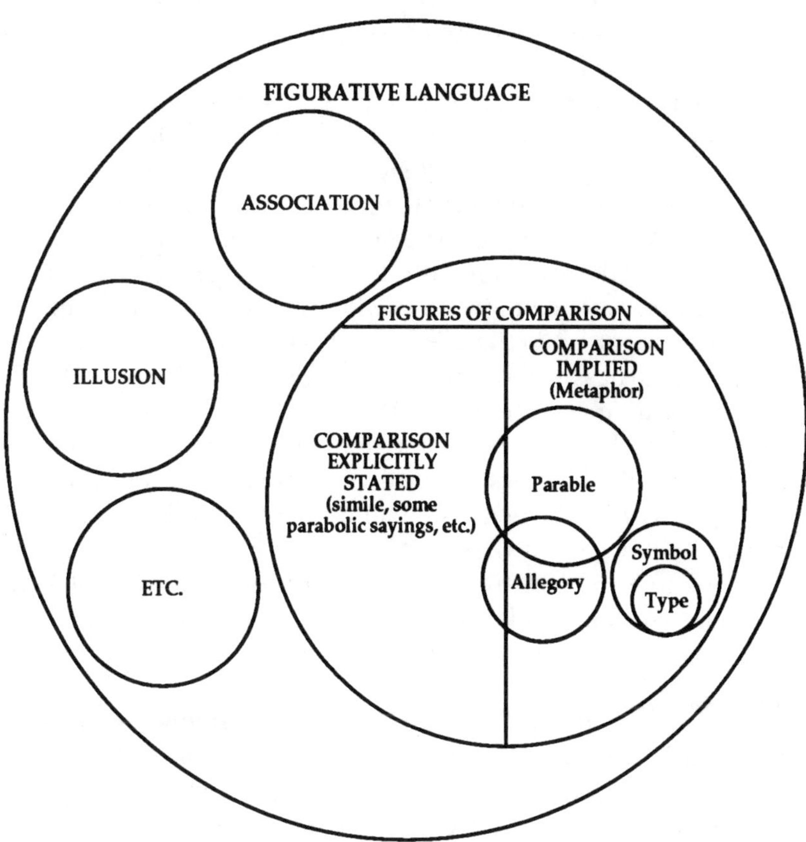
FIGURATIVE LANGUAGE
ASSOCIATION
ILLUSION
ETC.
FIGURES OF COMPARISON
COMPARISON EXPLICITLY STATED (simile, some parabolic sayings, etc.)
COMPARISON IMPLIED (Metaphor)
Parable
Allegory
Symbol
Type

God and swear by heaven. He used a figure of association to evade the requirement. But Christ disallowed that, pointing out that a figurative expression of association means the same thing as the object or concept for which it stands.

"All Jerusalem went out to be baptized of John" does not mean that the city itself moved, but rather, the people who lived in the city and were associated with the name *Jerusalem* went out to be baptized by John.

Sometimes the figure of association is *synecdoche,* in which part of something is spoken of as if it were the whole thing; or the whole thing may stand for only part of it. Often "the law" referred to the entire Old Testament. How could that be? The commandments were given by Moses, the lawgiver, who wrote the first five books of the Old Testament (the Pentateuch). Hence, both Moses and the law are associated with the Pentateuch, and are often used as a substitute or "shorthand" for that part of Scripture. The Pentateuch, in turn, is sometimes associated with the whole Old Testament, as the first section of it. So "the law," as a figure of association, came to be used either for the Pentateuch or for the entire Old Testament. The context must determine which was intended.

Figures of humanization. The Bible often will take a characteristic of people and attribute it to God to form an *anthropomorphism,* or to an object to form a *personification.* When it is said that God "stretched out His arm," that the "trees clapped their hands," or that the "hills skipped," we might call those figures of humanization.

In a sense, this kind of association is an implied comparison and might be treated as a figure of comparison, as described earlier. However, there is benefit in isolating this particular kind of figure in order to interpret certain passages of Scripture. For example, in the early chapters of Proverbs wisdom is spoken of as if it were a human being. Does that make the entire section messianic, as some hold? What was the author's purpose in personifying wisdom? Consider the way Scripture speaks of God, using physical and human characteristics. C. S. Lewis explained this graphically:

> God is basic Fact or Actuality, the source of all other facthood. At all costs therefore He must not be thought of as a featureless gener-

> ality. If He exists at all, He is the most concrete thing there is, the most individual, "organised and minutely articulated." He is unspeakable not by being indefinite but by being too definite for the unavoidable vagueness of language. The words *incorporeal* and *impersonal* are misleading because they suggest that He lacks some reality which we possess. It would be safer to call Him *trans-corporeal, trans-personal.* Body and personality as we know them are the real negatives—they are what is left of positive being when it is sufficiently diluted to appear in temporal or finite forms. Even our sexuality should be regarded as the transposition into a minor key of that creative joy which in Him is unceasing and irresistible. Grammatically the things we say of Him are "metaphorical": but in a deeper sense it is our physical and psychic energies that are mere "metaphors" of the real Life which is God. Divine Sonship is, so to speak, the solid of which biological sonship is merely a diagrammatic representation on the flat.[2]

In fact, "all, or almost all, of the language used by the Bible to refer to God is metaphor (the one possible exception is the word "holy")."[3] To interpret metaphors of God, it is necessary to discern the point of comparison intended by the writer and not to improvise some point of comparison felt to be a "fresh insight." When God "breathed" into the lifeless form of Adam, for example, what did He actually do? How important it is to discern what was intended by that figure of humanization, by that particular ascription of human qualities to God! The decision on what that means affects the whole theology of creation.

Figures of illusion. Many statements in Scripture would be untrue if they were taken literally. For example, irony is an expression that says the opposite of what is really meant. Exaggeration for making a particular impression is common in Scripture (from the Greek word *hyperbole*). Paul was speaking with irony or sarcasm when he said, "Forgive me this wrong!" (2 Cor. 12:13). From the context it is quite plain that he did not consider his making tents to earn a living something that was morally wrong. He was saying the opposite of the truth in order to bring the Corinthi-

2. Ibid., pp. 110-11.
3. G. B. Caird, *The Language and Imagery of the Bible* (Philadelphia: Westminster, 1980), p. 18.

ans to shame and repentance. Both Paul and the prophets of the Old Testament used sarcasm and irony. Those figures must be identified as illusory, or the meaning will certainly be misconstrued.

When the writer indicates that "all Jerusalem went out to be baptized," it may not be of great importance whether or not every single person in Jerusalem went out into the wilderness to be with John the Baptist. However, when Scripture says, "So all shall be saved," it is of tremendous theological significance to discover whether it is a literal statement or if it is figurative.

Exaggeration for effect (hyperbole) is common to all languages. But among Semitic peoples, and thus in the Bible, it is very common. It seems almost to come from a basic way of thinking. G. B. Caird quotes T. E. Lawrence, who was living among the Arabs during the First World War:

> Semites had no half-tones in their register of vision. They were a people of primary colours, or rather of black and white, who saw the world always in contour. They were a dogmatic people, despising doubt, our modern crown of thorns. They did not understand our metaphysical difficulties, our introspective questionings. They knew only truth and untruth, belief and unbelief, without our hesitating retinue of finer shades.[4]

As we approach the Bible, then, we must be constantly alert to the possibility of overstatement and not treat such figures of speech as literal statements of fact.

Questions intended to affirm a truth. In speech such questions are called rhetorical; the answer is obvious to the listeners. Consider the following:

> If God be for us, who can be against us? (Rom.8:31)
>
> Are all apostles? (1 Cor. 12:29)
>
> How can they hear without a preacher? (Rom 10:14)

4. Ibid., p. 110.

The answers to those questions are not in doubt. The author obviously put those truths in the form of questions to increase their impact. They must be treated as even stronger affirmations of the truths intended. If God is for us, *no one* can be against us. Certainly not all are apostles—nor prophets, nor teachers, nor do all speak in tongues. There *must* be a proclaimer if people are to hear the Word of God. Those are the affirmations implied, and the passages must be treated in that way.

Idiomatic expressions. There are many other figures of speech and idiomatic expressions. For instance, the author can use the *omission* from a sentence of a word or words that would complete it (Ex. 32:32), *riddles* (Judg. 14:14), *fables* (Judg. 9:8-15), and *understatement,* or *euphemism.* We will not deal with those extensively because they are not many in number, and both the figurative expressions and the interpretations are usually quite obvious. One example of a not so obvious occurrence, however, is the expression, "It is good for a man not to touch a woman" (1 Cor. 7:1). According to the context of the passage and the idiomatic usage of the time, that expression should be taken as an understatement, or euphemism, for sexual relations, and in that passage, marriage. "Uncover . . . nakedness" is a milder expression to describe immoral relationships (Lev. 18: 8, 12).

Such passages are not easily understood without word studies or investigating the cultural setting. But for the most part, those figures are not many in number and are easily understood. A figure must be identified before interpretation is attempted. In many cases the meaning will be quite obvious, once the figure has been identified. But there are some special guidelines that are helpful for interpreting particular figures.

INTERPRETING FIGURATIVE LANGUAGE

The author's intended reference in a figurative expression must be identified. The first step in interpretation is to translate the figurative expression into its literal meaning. Who were the "bulls," "lions," and "dogs" that surrounded David (Ps. 22:12-13, 16)? Once the figurative elements have been understood, the entire kit of interpretive tools should be used to translate the figurative expression into its literal meaning and to interpret the entire passage. At each stage, all the guidelines should be brought into play; the cultural setting, word studies, and consideration of the context are indispensable tools for understanding figurative language.

But let us consider three special guidelines for interpreting particular kinds of figurative language.

1. *Figures of comparison often require special guidelines.* The most useful guideline is to remember that when a comparison is made between unlike things, the points of comparison are greatly limited. In fact, usually only one point of comparison is in mind, as we have seen. Therefore, the interpreter should resist the temptation to impose from his own imagination comparisons that might be made. Rather, he should sort out through word study, contextual study, and cultural and historical setting the author's intended point of comparison. In complex comparisons, such as parables and types, additional guidelines are necessary. Those will be studied later in greater detail.
2. *It is important to distinguish between a figure of association and a figure of comparison.* David spoke of "the valley of the shadow of death" (Ps. 23:4). Is that a figure of comparison or a figure of association? Some interpreters tell us that the expression "valley of the shadow of death" was an idiom referring to danger. The comparison is with a deep ravine through which the traveler passes with fear for his life. On the other hand, it could be taken as a figure of association, where the place associated with death is used to indicate the fearful passage through death. That is the meaning given to the verse in many funerals.

   Which did David intend? By examining the context we find that David was making an extended comparison (allegory) between the shepherd/sheep relationship and the Lord's relationship with David. The natural meaning, then, would be another parallel between sheep and David. David can approach every unknown, fearful experience without fear because the Lord is with him. Of course, death itself could be one such experience, but the meaning would be much wider if the expression is taken as a comparison.

But other guidelines need to be applied. By examining the grammar of the passage, one can observe that David changes from the impersonal third person in the earlier verses ("*He* makes me") to the personal ("*Thou* art with me") in this verse. Does that imply a shift from the analogy of sheep to David's literal relationship with the Lord? If so, it might then be better to take the valley as referring to death, which would be a figure of association. Is that interpretation reinforced by the ancient symbolism of death as seen in another biblical author (Job 10:21-22)?

The latter part of the verse belies such an interpretation by returning to a comparison with sheep: "Thy rod and Thy staff, they comfort me." Comparing that with other writings of David, and examining the cultural setting (how the people thought of death) reinforces the idea that David had all kinds of danger in mind, not only death. Furthermore, the thought flow in this whole psalm would make death out of order in the passage, since it is followed by banqueting, anointing, "all the days of my life," and "the house of the Lord forever."

In that way, many of the guidelines are put to use in translating this figure of speech into its literal meaning. It would seem to be a figure of comparison in which David, like his own sheep, could face the most terrifying experiences of life without fear, because the Lord was present to protect him.

3. *Examine figures of illusion*. Sometimes an exaggeration is clearly a figure of illusion. When it is said that Christ did not speak to the people except in parables (Matt. 13:34), the writer obviously meant that parables were His chief means of communication. He did not mean that Christ never spoke in other ways, for even Matthew records many nonparabolic teachings of Christ, such as the Sermon on the Mount.

   When David said concerning his sin against Bathsheba and Uriah, "Against Thee, Thee only, I have sinned" (Ps.

51:4), he obviously was intending to emphasize that his ultimate and greatest sin was against God.

But not all exaggeration is so obvious. When the Bible says "forever," does it always mean without end? Scripture says, "[God] laid the foundations of the earth, that it should not be moved forever" (Ps. 104:5, ASV). And yet, two psalms earlier the psalmist said:

> Of old Thou didst found the earth; and the heavens are the work of Thy hands. Even they will perish, but Thou dost endure; and all of them will wear out like a garment; like clothing Thou wilt change them, and they will be changed. (Ps. 102:25-26)

Those passages are not at all incompatible when the interpreter bears in mind that *forever* sometimes means "without end" and often means "for a long time." We also use that term figuratively. ("He took forever to get here.") The Passover and the Levitical priesthood were forever (Ex. 12:14; 1 Chron. 15:2), but when Christ became our passover (1 Cor. 5:7) and our priest (Hebrews), "forever" came to an end. *Forever* usually means "without end," but not in every case.

The interpreter must always bear in mind that the people of Bible times were not committed to keep courtroom records in the modern way and that exaggeration for effect (hyperbole) was a common literary device. The context and other teaching in Scripture are sources that help identify whether a statement should be taken literally or understood as exaggeration.

Summary

The Bible is full of nonliteral language. Figurative language is very important and valuable for many reasons, as we have seen. But for Scripture to prove valuable in application to our lives, the intent of the author must be determined. We have studied the necessary steps: identify the language as figurative, identify what the figure is, and then use general guidelines and special guidelines to determine the meaning intended by the author when he chose to speak in "picture language."

Later we will consider principles for making application of biblical truths. However, at this point let's remember that *figurative* does not mean "untrue" or "less important." Figurative language teaches true and important matters. After one has determined the true implications of figurative language, it should be applied with confidence.

Selected Bibliography for Further Study

Bullinger, Ethelbert William. *Figures of Speech Used in the Bible: Explained and Illustrated.* Reprint. Grand Rapids: Baker, 1968.

Lamsa, George M. *Idioms in the Bible Explained.* New York: Harper & Row, 1985.

Terry, Milton. *Bibical Hermeneutics.* Reprint. Grand Rapids: Zondervan, 1974.

13
Parables

Guideline: Interpret parables strictly according to the special principles required by this type of literature.

When the eternal Word became human, God's self-revelation was both in the activity and in the words of Jesus Christ. Yet His activity must be interpreted by words—either His own or those of His appointed spokesmen, the apostles. Christ's verbal communication is crucial for understanding God and His truth. And for much of His verbal communication, Christ chose the parable. Therefore, it is of utmost importance that we understand this special kind of literary form.

A parable is a true-to-life short story designed to teach a truth or to answer a question. In Jesus' teaching the parable had an additional purpose. He told us, as we have seen, that one purpose was to obscure the truth from the unresponsive, while making it plain to the responsive. We noted in the last chapter that the parable is part of a distinct form of literature called "figures of comparison." It is kin to the metaphor, because usually the comparison is implied rather than stated.

We must distinguish a parable from a historic event. Historic events are often used as illustrations, but the parable is a special story-form designed specifically to teach a particular truth. Although a parable by definition is not the record of a historic event, to be a parable it must be true to life. Thus, a parable differs from other figures of comparison, such as allegory and prophetic symbolism, that may or may not be true to life.

We will explore six basic guidelines for understanding parables. They are: begin with the immediate context, identify the central point of emphasis, identify irrelevant details, identify the relevant details, compare parallel and contrasting passages, and base doctrine on clear literal passages.

Begin with the Immediate Context

In the parable of the prodigal son (Luke 15:11-32), who is the chief character? What do you consider to be the main point of the story? Certainly, the title we have given the parable indicates the chief character in the view of most Christians. But there are those who consider the father to be the chief character. The passage is normally used to convey this evangelistic message: no matter how far you have fallen, come home to God, and He will receive you. But is that the purpose Jesus had in mind when He originally told the parable? The first and most important guideline for understanding parables is to examine the immediate context. In a parable, two crucial elements are normally found in the context: the occasion for telling the story and the explanation of its meaning.

THE OCCASION FOR TELLING THE STORY

Virtually all parables have a clear historical occasion that gave rise to the telling of the story. Although it may be legitimate to apply the parable of the prodigal son (Luke 15) evangelistically, the situation to which Jesus originally spoke indicates very clearly another purpose. Jesus was speaking to religious people who objected to His ready acceptance of sinful people. Therefore, one might conclude that the chief character is the elder brother. Certainly it was the "elder brother" Pharisees to whom Jesus spoke. Actually the point of the story was the contrast between the elder brother and the loving, forgiving father as represented by Jesus Himself. The context of the parable in that case, as in every case, is of primary importance in discovering the occasion and identifying the point of the parable.

THE EXPLANATION OF THE MEANING

Sometimes the explanation of the parable's meaning is given in the form of *application.* Such application is found in Matthew 24:44, "For this reason *you be ready too;* for the Son of Man is coming at an hour when you do not think He will," and in Matthew 25:13, "*Be on the alert* then, for you do not know the day nor the hour" (italics added).

Not all parables have explanations of meaning, but when Christ does explain the meaning or make the application, that is the controlling factor in interpretation. We may not impose other meanings on the parable.

Identify the Central Point

Immediately following the parable of the prodigal son, Luke records the parable concerning the unjust steward in 16:1-15. It is apparent in this passage that the setting is described both before and after the parable, along with an explanation of the parable itself. What is the point of the parable? Since it is said of Jesus at the end of the story of the prodigal son, "Now He was *also* saying to the disciples" (v. 1, italics added), it would seem that Luke intended to link that story to the confrontation with the Pharisees in the earlier parable. That becomes even more apparent at the end of the account, where Luke writes, "Now the Pharisees, who were lovers of money, were listening to all these things; and they were scoffing at Him" (v. 14). So the confrontation with the Pharisees continues. But what is the point? Is He teaching people to cheat? Is He teaching His disciples to use other people? Kenneth Taylor, in paraphrasing that section, wrestled with this issue and came to the following conclusion:

> But shall I tell you to act that way, to buy friendship through cheating? Will this ensure your entry into an everlasting home in heaven? No! For unless you are honest in small matters, you won't be in large ones. If you cheat even a little, you won't be honest with greater responsibilities. (Luke 16:9-10, TLB)

Here, the translator has interpreted the passage to mean exactly the opposite of what it seems to say. Without doubt the passage has been confusing to many. Identifying the central point of emphasis is essential in this case and leads one rather quickly to a solution. The central point in this parable is clear because, in the context, Christ clearly explains. The point of the story has nothing to do with cheating.

In the parable, the cheating manager was not commended for cheating. He was commended because he "had done wisely"; that is, he had used his present resources to plan for the future. That is wise. Christ went on to explain that His disciples were to use their present resources to plan for the future. The "sons of the light," in fact, were not doing that. That is why they were not wise. They were using their material resources to "live it up," when they should have been wisely using their present material resources to prepare for eternal blessings in heaven. Jesus then explains in detail how that wise stewardship was to be accomplished.

Having a central point of emphasis is the chief feature that distinguishes a parable from an allegory. In an allegory a number of significant parallels between the story and spiritual truth are intended. In the case of a parable, it is not legitimate to treat each detail as having a spiritual application.

Identify Irrelevant Details

The parables contain many details that are not intended to teach truth at all. They do not have spiritual significance. Those details should be identified and set aside. Any attempt to interpret them could lead one far astray from the meaning intended by Christ.

> But which of you, having a slave plowing or tending sheep, will say to him when he has come in from the field, "Come immediately and sit down to eat"? But will he not say to him, "Prepare something for me to eat, and properly clothe yourself and serve me until I have eaten and drunk; and afterward you will eat and drink"? He does not thank the slave because he did the things which were commanded, does he? (Luke 17:7-9)

If you saw that story portrayed on television, how would you feel about it? Did Christ here sanction slavery? Did He give principles for labor/management relations? Did He teach what is generous, gracious, and courteous behavior? No, none of those concepts is of any significance to the meaning of the parable. He has constructed a story that was true to the life of His times to make a single point.

By examining the context we find that Christ had been instructing the disciples about rebuking a brother who sins and forgiving him when he repents. The point of the story is that we do not deserve credit for doing the right thing. The other details are irrelevant to that central purpose and should be set aside.

Identifying the Relevant Details

Relevant details are those that are intended to teach some truth and, therefore, may legitimately be interpreted and applied. But how can one tell which details are irrelevant and which are relevant? Relevant details will always reinforce the central theme.

In the parable of the prodigal son, the fact that the father stayed at home and did not go seeking the son is an irrelevant detail. Jesus was not teaching that the Father does not seek for sinners. He had already made that matter clear in the two preceding parables, in which the widow went in search of her coin and the shepherd went in search of his sheep. However, that the father ran to meet his son is a relevant detail and, therefore, has spiritual significance. How do we know? Because it reinforces the central theme, which was to reveal the heart of the father. The fact that he was eagerly waiting and that he responded with joy and eager acceptance is a significant detail. In considering this guideline, it may be helpful to contrast the approach toward parables and historic events on the one hand, and parables and allegories on the other.

PARABLES AND HISTORIC EVENTS

There is considerable disagreement as to whether the story of the rich man and Lazarus (Luke 16:19-31) is the record of a historic event or a parable. Some think that the historicity of the story must be maintained lest the truth concerning hell and eternal punishment somehow be weakened. But that is to misunderstand figurative language in general and parables in particular. The truth conveyed through a parable is just as true and important as the truth communicated through other literary forms.

Nonetheless, it is important to distinguish historic events from parables, because the guidelines for interpretation differ. The application of the story will differ in the case of historical narrative, for every literal statement is a fact and must be received as such. It has importance and significance independent of all the other facts in the story. That does not mean each fact has spiritual significance or can be applied to the present circumstance, however. The biblical author or the Lord Jesus Himself may use the historic event as an illustration and define what applications are legitimate.

If the story of the rich man and Lazarus is a historic event, every detail has meaning. People in heaven, at least sometimes, know the condition of people in hell and can communicate with them. That certainly has profound theological meaning. On the other hand, the fact that there is a rich man and a beggar may have no spiritual or theological implication. It is just a historic fact that the rich man wound up in hell and the beggar went to heaven. Of course, if you believe that all rich men go to heaven, as many did believe, the fact that even one went to hell would have great significance.

On the other hand, if the story is a parable, then the fact that there are a rich man and a beggar is no doubt a significant detail. This story is told immediately after the Pharisees' confrontation with Christ over the question of money and their love for it, and the unwise behavior of spending present resources without thinking of eternity. In this context, Christ is saying something additional about wealth and the preparation for the future. As a parable, then, the details of wealth and poverty would have specific meaning.

Both historical narrative and parables can contain figurative as well as literal language. For example, whether the above is taken as history or parable, Lazarus's reclining against Abraham does not have to be taken as the physical position from which he shouted across the abyss to the rich man. In either case it could be a figurative expression for the "place of the blessed." But the question of whether any detail has spiritual or theological significance will be decided on different principles, depending on whether the story is history used to illustrate, or manufactured to teach a particular truth. It would be a helpful exercise to list all the teachings about hell one could learn from that passage if it is a parable, and all the teachings about hell one could learn if it is a historic event. We would be certain of many more details about conditions in hell if this story were historical.

Is the story of the rich man and Lazarus a parable or a historical account? It seems to bear the marks of a parable. In the first verse of Luke 16 it is recorded, "He was also saying to the disciples, 'There was a certain rich man.'" Then follows the story of the cheating manager. In verse 19 He said again, "Now there was a certain rich man." And there follows the story of the rich man in hell and the beggar in "Abraham's bosom." Some have argued that Lazarus is named, and that that is not typical of parables. However, it would be a great assumption indeed to hold that a parable could not include names for the characters. After all, a parable is a deliberately constructed story, true to life, and the person telling it is free to use whatever elements he feels necessary to make his point. In this case, *Lazarus,* meaning "whom God helps," may have been one of those details that reinforce the basic teaching. (Guidelines for applying historical events to the contemporary situation will be studied in chap. 20.)

At any rate, it is important to notice that interpreting it as a parable should not weaken its meaning. A parable is not a myth or a fairy tale. It is true to life and constructed to teach full-orbed truth. In this case, the truth is probably a follow-up to that found in the earlier part of the chapter, that one should use his present resources to prepare for the future, and that if he does not, he will indeed suffer eternal loss.

PARABLES AND ALLEGORIES

Parables and allegories overlap (see diagram in chap. 11) in that both are designed to teach spiritual truth by comparing something to spiritual reality. Although they overlap, they differ in two ways:

1. A parable is realistic, but an allegory might not be. In an allegory, Christ might be a door or a vine; believers might be sheep or branches.

2. Though both might have a central theme, the parable is created to make one principal point, whereas the allegory often will teach many related or even unrelated truths.

When the distinction between parable and allegory is clear, it is important to follow the different guidelines for interpreting each. In Matthew 13:1-23 and Mark 4:1-20, we find Christ's parable of the four soils. It is called a parable, but the term is not equivalent to our technical use of the term *parable,* and it may well be an allegory. Indeed, in Christ's explanation of the four soils He makes a spiritual application of virtually every point in the story. The seed is the Bible, the birds are the devil, and the hard soil is a hard heart. How can we be sure? Because Jesus Himself explained the story that way. Nevertheless, the context that follows indicates clearly a single theme: the result in one's life depends on one's response to the Word of God. Many of the details were deliberately designed to reinforce that central message.

Although many of the details of the story have spiritual significance, that does not mean that all do. To use an allegory or a parable in that way is to abuse it. For example, one interpreter of the story of the sower has said:

> Did you know that only 25% will make it? Make what? Heaven. . . . But 25% of what? Of those who hear the Gospel, the Good News that Jesus Christ died for sinners, was buried, and raised bodily from the grave. Only 25% of those will get to heaven. Yes, that's the truth, according to the parable of the sower and the soils. Turn to your Bible and check it out.[1]

There is no hint in the parable or in the explanation of it that a proportion of response was predicted, but simply that different responses can be expected. The context must control, for there are virtually no limits to fanciful interpretation if the interpreter's imagination runs free.

In the case of a clear-cut allegory it is legitimate to draw many parallels to the points in the allegory. For example, the allegory concerning the Good Shepherd (John 10) is designed to have

1. Arnie Maves, "Only 25% Will Make It," *Come,* November-December 1975, p. 5.

many points of parallel. The shepherd, the thief, the hireling, the wolf—all may be characterized and identified in contemporary life. The relationship described between shepherd and sheep may be fully applied to the response to God's call by believer and nonbeliever today. Virtually every detail has meaning. Such is the way an allegory may be understood.

Compare Parallel and Contrasting Passages

This is a general guideline we will be studying later, but comparing and contrasting passages is also helpful in studying parables. Some parables are similar to one another and can be compared.

Luke 19:11-23 contains the parable of the pounds: a nobleman, going to a far county, gives the same amount of money to each of ten servants and rewards them differently on his return, when it was discovered that some had earned more than others. Matthew 25:14-30, on the other hand, is the parable of the talents, in which three different servants receive different amounts of money. The reward, so far as the story goes, does not differ except that the one who was unfaithful, as in the story of the pounds, is judged severely.

Other teaching concerning servants and preparation for the coming of the Lord is found in Matthew 24:45-51, in which the faithful, prepared servant is contrasted with the one who thought that his lord would delay his coming, and was unfaithful. That same teaching is given in greater detail in Luke 12:35-48, where the faithful manager who prepared is contrasted with the servant who did not prepare and was, indeed, unfaithful.

A central theme emerges in comparing the four parables: *be ready.* But each teaches different truths as well. For example, the parable of the pounds teaches that the one who has great faithfulness will be given greater responsibility. There is differing reward for degrees of faithfulness. The story of the talents assures us that reward is not based on degrees of success because of differing abilities. In fact, a fifth parable of the laborers in the vineyard (Matt. 20:1-16) assures us that the Lord rewards with eternal life all who come to Him, whether early or late in life.

Base Doctrine on Clear, Literal Passages

A parable may contribute toward the understanding of biblical doctrine; however, doctrine should rest on clear, literal passages. When an interpretation of a parable is given, it may be used legitimately as any other clear, literal passage in the building of doctrine. But, in general, figurative language is not the best ingredient for building doctrine.

For example, it would be a mistake to take the parable of the tares (Matt. 13:24-30), in which the laborers were instructed to let the true and the false grow together until the end, and conclude that church discipline is wrong. The doctrine of church discipline must be built on other teachings of Scripture. It is true that Christ interpreted that parable and indicated that in the Judgment Day there will be a great separation between the righteous (the wheat) and those who do iniquity (the tares, vv. 40-43).

However, in the explanation, Christ also said that the field is the world (v. 38), not the church. At any rate, neither the parable itself nor its explanation gives any direct teaching on the question of who should be baptized or whether there should be discipline of those in the church who sin. It is a grave error to use the parable, as many have, to teach that all who wish should be baptized indiscriminately and that no attempt should be made to judge applicants for membership or to discipline members of the church, no matter how grievously they sin. Christ taught instead that there are both good and evil people in the world, and at the final judgment all accounts will be settled.

A Case Study

Let's take the parable in Luke 11:5-13 and apply the six guidelines we have studied:

> And He said to them, "Suppose one of you shall have a friend, and shall go to him at midnight, and say to him, 'Friend, lend me three loaves; for a friend of mine has come to me from a journey, and I have nothing to set before him'; and from inside he shall answer and say, 'Do not bother me; the door has already been shut and my children and I are in bed; I cannot get up and give you anything.' I tell you, even though he will not get up and give him anything be-

cause he is his friend, yet because of his persistence he will get up and give him as much as he needs." (Luke 11:5-8)

BEGIN WITH THE IMMEDIATE CONTEXT

Christ had just taught the disciples a model prayer in answer to their request. Furthermore, in the verses immediately following the parable, an explanation is given of the meaning: "And I say to you, ask, and it shall be given to you; seek, and you will find; knock, and it shall be opened to you. For everyone who asks, receives; and he who seeks, finds; and to him who knocks, it shall be opened" (Luke 11:9-10).

In this case there is both an occasion for telling the story and an explanation of its meaning.

IDENTIFY THE CENTRAL POINT

An examination of the story, along with the explanation, reveals that it was given to teach that God answers prayer, particularly persistent prayer. The one who keeps on asking is the one who receives, and the one who keeps on seeking is the one who finds. (Note that the tense of the verb is of importance in understanding this particular passage: "keep on asking" is the force of the Greek verb, not a simple, one-time request.)

IDENTIFY IRRELEVANT DETAILS

Although the friend was unresponsive at first because of personal, selfish reasons, that does not reveal anything concerning God or His response to us. There are other irrelevant details, such as the fact that the request took place at midnight; that he asked for three loaves rather than four; and that it was for someone else, not for himself. Much has been made of those points, but they are simply supplied as part of the story to make it complete.

IDENTIFY RELEVANT DETAILS

On the other hand, some facts are essential. That the neighbor kept on asking is indeed the essence of the story. It will not do simply to ask God once and leave it there or to teach that one should not repeat a request to God. The explanation of the parable makes clear that we should persist in asking God for the supply of our needs.

COMPARE WITH PARALLEL AND CONTRASTING PASSAGES

Two passages can be beneficially compared with or contrasted to this passage. Since the setting for the parable is the request of the disciples that Christ teach them to pray and His responding with a model prayer (11:1-4), it is quite natural to compare the passage with Matthew 6:7-15, which gives the more commonly quoted version of the Lord's Prayer. In Matthew, He taught them to pray in that way rather than to pray with vain repetition. Thus, by comparing the two passages, we focus on complementary truths. Prayer with persistence is not to become mere empty repetition of the same request. On the other hand, although vain repetition is forbidden, that does not mean that a person should not persist in prayer. The two passages interpret one another.

Following Christ's explanation of the parable of the three loaves, He gave another illustrative explanation:

> Now suppose one of you fathers is asked by his son for a fish; he will not give him a snake instead of a fish, will he? Or if he is asked for an egg, he will not give him a scorpion, will he? If you then, being evil, know how to give good gifts to your children, how much more shall your heavenly Father give the Holy Spirit to those who ask Him? (Luke 11:11-13)

Here, additional truth is given concerning prayer. For example, if the reader would conclude from the story of the three loaves that God is a reluctant listener to the prayers of His children, this additional teaching would quickly end such a misinterpretation. And it is significant that the one thing we need above all else is identified not as bread for the body but as the Person of God the Holy Spirit. That is most reassuring.

BASE DOCTRINE ON CLEAR PASSAGES

By looking at the context and comparing it with other passages, the teaching of the parable falls into place in the overall doctrine of prayer. Several key elements in the doctrine of prayer are taught. As we have seen, it would be an error to build the doctrine of prayer on the story of the three loaves. But the central truth of the parable is a legitimate ingredient to be combined with other biblical teaching in building the doctrine of prayer: keep on praying; God will answer.

Summary

Parables have been the source of untold blessing in enlightening God's people concerning spiritual truth. At the same time, parables have been the source of untold confusion in both doctrine and practice in the church. That should not come as a surprise, since Christ Himself told us that the parables would both enlighten and confuse their hearers. So the first requirement in understanding the meaning of parables is, of course, that one belong to Jesus Christ and have the illumination of the Holy Spirit in a regenerate mind. However, that alone will not assure clear understanding and accurate interpretation, as the history of interpretation will attest. The simple guidelines outlined here will aid the serious Bible student in using parables legitimately and effectively.

Selected Bibliography for Further Study

Blomberg, Craig L. *Interpreting the Parables.* Downers Grove, Ill.: InterVarsity, 1989.

Capon, Robert Farrar. *The Parables of Grace.* Grand Rapids: Eerdmans, 1988.

———. *The Parables of the Kingdom.* Grand Rapids: Eerdmans, 1985.

———. *The Parables of Judgment.* Grand Rapids: Eerdmans, 1986.

Jeremias, Joachim. *The Parables of Jesus.* 2d ed. London: SCM, 1963.

Keistermacher, Simon. *The Parables of Jesus.* Grand Rapids: Baker, 1980.

Kissinger, Warren S.. *The Parables of Jesus: A History of Interpretation and Bibliography.* Metuchen, N.J.: Scarecrow, 1979.

Lockyer, Herbert. *All the Parables of the Bible.* Grand Rapids: Zondervan, 1963.

McQuilkin, Robert C. *Studying Our Lord's Parables.* 1935 reprint. Grand Rapids: Zondervan, 1980.

Pentecost, J. Dwight. *The Parables of Jesus.* Grand Rapids: Zondervan, 1982.

Trench, Richard C. *Notes on the Parables of Our Lord.* 1861 reprint. Grand Rapids: Baker, 1979.

Wenham, David. *The Parables of Jesus.* Downers Grove, InterVarsity, 1989.

14
Hebrew Poetry

Guideline: Use the parallelism of Hebrew poetry to gain insight into meaning.

Poetry is filled with figurative language, so we must use the guidelines we have studied for understanding the meaning of non-literal language.

Poetry differs from prose in another way—the structure of the language is different. For example, in English poetry is distinguished by the rhythm of the flow of words. A measured number of syllables gives a musical quality to the language. Traditionally, there is also rhyme so that word endings that sound alike can be matched at regular intervals. In Japanese, on the other hand, poetry is distinguished from ordinary prose by having a stated number of syllables. In the haiku, seventeen syllables constitute the verse—no more and no less. In English and Japanese, because poetry is distinguished by the form of the language, it is impossible to translate the poetic form itself. Poetry translated from those languages into other languages either becomes prose or must be recast in the poetic form of the other language.

Although a poem in Hebrew may have elements of meter, those elements are not the major characteristics. Rather, the distinguishing mark of Hebrew poetry is a correspondence in thought, or parallelism, between one line and the following line; or between one section and the following section. That is very helpful indeed, for it means that the poetic form of the Old Testament is almost fully accessible to us in the English language. An understanding of that correspondence, or parallelism, is the key to interpreting many passages.

We have been taught that it is good English to avoid redundancy. To the Hebrew, however, redundancy was a literary form to be cultivated carefully. In fact, structured redundancy was the epitome of the finest speech. That is what distinguished poetry from ordinary prose.

> Redundance is a measure of certainty and predictability—that is to say, the more redundant the form of the message, the easier it is for the recipient to guess what is coming next. So Schramm goes on to say, "In many cases, increasing the redundancy will make for more efficient communication." Nida and Taber state that there seems to be a relatively fixed tendency for languages to be approximately 50% redundant.[1]

Though redundancy is not unique to Hebrew thinking, the way it is formally structured in Hebrew poetry assists greatly in understanding its meaning. Equally important, the New Testament, though written in Greek, was written by people whose whole thought pattern was molded by the Old Testament and Hebrew ways of thinking. Thus, though the form or structure of the Greek language is different, the same kind of parallelism permeates the New Testament as well.

How significant is Hebrew poetry in the Old Testament? According to Milton Terry, almost half the Old Testament is poetry. However, some of that poetry is lost to us in most translations because not all poetic form in Hebrew has been translated into a poetic form in English. But it can be easily discerned by its parallel thought.

Parallelism in Hebrew Poetry

There are three basic kinds of parallel thought in Hebrew poetry: synonymous, synthetic, and antithetic parallelism. Let's look at each kind.

1. John Beekman and John Callow, *Translating the Word of God* (Grand Rapids: Zondervan, 1974), p. 43.

SYNONYMOUS PARALLELISM

In synonymous parallelism, *an idea is expressed a second or third time.*

Wisdom shouts in the street,
She lifts her voice in the square;
"How long, O naive ones, will you love simplicity?
And scoffers delight themselves in scoffing,
And fools hate knowledge?
Then they will call on me, but I will not answer:
They will seek me diligently, but they shall not find me.
They would not accept my counsel,
They spurned all my reproof.
So they shall eat of the fruit of their own way,
And be satiated with their own devices."
(Prov. 1:20, 22, 28, 30-31)

Noting the repetition of an idea in different words is often very helpful in discerning the author's intended meaning. It is also helpful in word studies. For example, wisdom is a theme found not only in the first chapter of Proverbs but throughout the whole book and in what has been called "wisdom literature." In other words, understanding wisdom is very important for understanding great sections of Scripture. In Proverbs 1:29 insight is gained into the meaning of wisdom, because "knowledge" is paralleled with the "fear of the Lord." "Wisdom" is speaking in this passage. We see knowledge linked with wisdom, with neither of them referring to intellectual comprehension of facts as much as to a right relationship with God.

The fear of God is true knowledge and wisdom. The Hebrew correspondence of thought makes that very clear in this passage.

SYNTHETIC PARALLELISM

In synthethic parallelism, *the poet adds to the original concept.* Consider the first two verses of Psalm 1:

How blessed is the man who does not walk in the
counsel of the wicked,
Nor stand in the path of sinners,

Nor sit in the seat of scoffers!
But his delight is in the law of Lord,
And in His law he meditates day and night.

There is a contrasting idea between verses 1 and 2; verse 1 speaks negatively of what the happy man does not do, whereas verse 2 describes what he does do. Each phrase in the verse adds an additional thought. To walk with the wicked may be the first stage; to stand with sinners is even worse; and to sit with scoffers would seem to be the ultimate. Again, the delight in God's law in the first phrase is expanded to show what real delight leads to—meditation on that law day and night. In that way additional ideas are given.

In Isaiah 55, we can see both simple and complex parallel thoughts combined.

Seek the Lord while He may be found;
Call upon Him while He is near.
Let the wicked forsake his way,
And the unrighteous man his thoughts;
And let him return to the Lord.
And He will have compassion on him,
And to our God,
For He will abundantly pardon.

(vv. 6-7)

Note that parallel thoughts can be simple and immediately follow one another, or they can be more complex and separated by other thoughts. Furthermore, the passage imediately above is a good example of how the author may combine different kinds of parallelism. For example, in the first sentence, *similar* thoughts are put side by side: "Seek the Lord" and "call upon Him" express similar ideas in different words, as do "while He may be found" and "while He is near." In the second sentence, "the wicked" and "the unrighteous" are similar.

The passage as a whole, however, presents a different kind of parallelism, one that *adds to* the basic idea. Isaiah built one thought on another, adding *repentance* to the idea of "seeking God." Furthermore, to the command for repentance he added the idea that this turning was not only a negative forsaking of evil but a positive returning to the Lord. To the concept of mercy he added the full meaning of abundant pardon. Thus, parallelism in Hebrew poetry often means adding to the original thoughts.

ANTITHETIC PARALLELISM

In antithetic parallelism, *the poet contrasts one idea with another*. Many proverbs contain such contrasts.

> The tongue of the wise makes knowledge acceptable;
> But the mouth of fools spouts folly.
>
> (Prov. 15:2)

That contrast helps in understanding the meaning of certain words. For example, *folly* is a key word in Proverbs—almost a theme. Note that it is not merely simple foolishness, but in this passage stands in opposition to true knowledge. And knowledge is far more than mere information. The fool, then, is one who rejects a right relationship with God (biblical "knowledge"), and, consequently, what comes out of his mouth is folly. It would seem that even knowledge, if it is godless, is ultimately foolish. Such is the contrast in this passage and throughout Proverbs.

In the Psalms is a verse that makes little sense as it stands alone:

> Who passing through the valley of Baca make it a well;
> The rain also filleth the pools.
>
> (Ps. 84:6, KJV)

What is the valley of Baca? An atlas does not help—no one knows where the valley was. A word study tells us that the Hebrew word meant "weeping." Is that thought similar to the thought in the second line? That is, was there something about that valley (literally or figuratively) that reminded the writer and his audience of wells and pools of water? Is there some subtle correspondence between tears and rain? Or is it a contrasting thought?

Because the guidelines on word study and physical setting have not helped, let us consider the context. Psalm 84 is the longing cry of one who wants to go to the Temple in Jerusalem. That journey is not always easy, given the arid climate and rugged terrain (physical setting guideline). Nevertheless, in verse 5, the psalmist says that to the one in whose heart are the highways (or footpaths) to Jerusalem, God gives special strength. In fact, in the verse immediately following our text (v. 7), he says, "They go from strength to strength" to appear before God at the Temple.

In that way, the context gives us a strong clue as to the meaning. The parallelism is *contrasting:* when a person is going through hard times ("the valley of weeping"), determined to get to God, the Lord makes that desert experience like a well; He sends rain till it stands in pools. Thus, He gives strength and enables the one who longs for Him to reach Him.

So the passage can be understood through the context. In turn, the verse sheds light back on the rest of the passage. But the key issue is the kind of correspondence in thought the writer uses. When contrast is inserted, it proves to be the key that unlocks the complicated puzzle and opens up the meaning of the whole passage.

Applying the Guideline

Isaiah said, "You will be like a watered garden, and like a spring of water whose waters do not fail" (Isa. 58:11). In describing the promise of an abundant life, is Isaiah giving a similar thought in different words; adding to the original thought; or contrasting a watered garden with a spring of water? If we take the form to be a similar idea, he is simply reinforcing the basic idea of a flourishing or abundant life. On the other hand, if there is a distinction between a watered garden and a spring of water, that would make a difference in the meaning.

How does one decide which interpretation is correct? Once again, we go to the other guidelines for interpreting Scripture. In studying the cultural background we learn that an irrigation system was used for watering gardens. It required a great deal of human energy working the treadmill to lift the water into the garden to make it flourish. On the other hand, there were also a few artesian wells, or springs of water that produced spontaneously. On first glance, the passage seems to offer a contrast.

For further light on the passage, consider another guideline: comparing one Scripture with another, or seeking for parallel passages. In this case, the Lord Jesus may have been referring to this passage in Isaiah when He said, "If any man is thirsty, let him come to Me and drink. He who believes in Me, *as the Scripture said,* 'From his innermost being shall flow rivers of living water'" (John 7:37-38, italics added). Where the Scripture says this is unclear. Perhaps the Isaiah passage is as close as we shall come. At any rate, the promise of the Lord Jesus is similar to the promise of God through His prophet Isaiah. God will give an abundant life in which there is a spontaneous flow of His own Spirit from within. (Note John's explanation: "This He spoke of the Spirit" [John 7:39].)

Using these guidelines for understanding a passage, we see in Isaiah a climactic building from the laborious, but fruitful, watered garden that might be good enough, to an even more abundant life, in which there is the endless supply of an artesian well of life. The parallelism here adds to rather than simply repeats the same idea in different words. Though there may be a slight element of contrast, the poetic form is not a contrasting thought, because both the watered garden and the spring are good promises. Furthermore, the connecting word *and* would seem to apply both blessings to the same people.

Summary

The three basic kinds of parallelism—similar thoughts, additional thoughts, or contrasting thoughts—may be found side by side in a single passage. The student of the Bible will benefit by becoming sensitive to the Hebrew idea of poetry: correspondence in thought. Actually, that way of thinking spills over into prose as well. The serious Bible student should cultivate a sensitivity to the Hebrew way of thinking, for through it he will find a helpful source for understanding the Word of God.

Selected Bibliography for Further Study

Alter, Robert. *The Art of Biblical Poetry.* New York: Basic, 1985.

Berlin, Adele. *The Dynamics of Biblical Parallelism.* Bloomington: Indiana U., 1985.

Bullock, Hassell C. *An Introduction to the Poetic Books of the Old Testament.* Chicago: Moody, 1979.

Kugel, James L. *The Idea of Biblical Poetry: Parallelism and Its History.* New Haven: Yale U., 1981.

Robinson, Theodore H. *The Poetry of the Old Testament.* London: Duckworth, 1947.

Yoder, Sanford C. *Poetry of the Old Testament.* Scottdale, Pa.: Herald, 1948.

DIVINE AUTHORSHIP: INTERPRETATION

PRINCIPLE:

Since Scripture is God-breathed and true in all its parts, the unity of its teaching must be sought, and its supernatural elements recognized and understood.

15
Unity of Scripture

Guideline: Compare Scripture with Scripture for light on each passage, and discover the unity of its teaching.

Introduction

Since the Bible is true in every part, when studying a specific passage the student must seek the unity of that passage with all other Bible teachings relating to it. It will not do to determine the meaning of a passage independent of the rest of Scripture. In some cases, to do so would leave one biblical teaching unnecessarily in conflict with other biblical teaching. Rather, the student should treat the Bible itself as the best commentary on the Bible. As the Reformers said, the Bible must be interpreted by the Bible. To compare a passage under study with other passages of Scripture will often clarify meaning, correct an initial misunderstanding, or bring the teaching to completion as part of the biblical whole.

For example, when it is discovered that "the kingdom of God" is used by one gospel writer, and in the same report another gospel writer speaks of "the kingdom of heaven," the meanings of both terms become clearer (see Matt. 13:31 and Mark 4:26-31). Those terms should not be made to mean something different when different Bible authors use them synonymously. The Sermon on the Mount, for example, cannot be relegated to some past or future "kingdom of heaven" different from the "kingdom of God." Again, one might take the teaching of Christ concerning answered prayer, "Whatever you ask of the Father in My name, He may give to you" (John 15:16), as being an unqualified promise. A study of other teachings concerning prayer, in other passages, will correct the initial, apparent understanding and put it in perspective as part of the whole biblical teaching on prayer and, specifically, on the conditions for answered prayer.

In seeking unity in Bible teaching, we should consider three kinds of Bible texts: parallel passages, similar ideas, and contrasting ideas.

Parallel Passages

Parallel passages are two or more passages that report the same event or give the same teaching. For example, when a discourse of Jesus is reported in two of the gospels, those passages would be considered parallel. The same event recorded in 1 or 2 Samuel and 1 or 2 Chronicles would be parallel.

We must combine all the elements of passages that record the same event to get a composite, whereas that is not necessary for passages that only have similarities. When passages simply contain similar ideas, we look for light on the interpretation of each passage but should not hold them to strict parallelism.

PARALLEL PASSAGES BY THE SAME AUTHOR

The first step in locating parallel passages is to seek parallel passages by the same author. An author tends to use similar terms and expressions and sometimes repeats the same teaching. For example, comparing one Pauline epistle with another can be of great help in identifying the meaning of words, expressions, and whole passages. Ephesians 6:5-9 and Colossians 3:22–4:1 throw a great deal of light on one another, as both passages deal with the question of servants and masters. The result of faithfulness or the lack of faithfulness on the part of either servant or master is treated only from a positive perspective in Ephesians, which is rather vague in its instructions for masters, whereas Colossians gives very forcefully the negative results of failure in that relationship and is explicit: "Grant to your slaves justice and fairness" (Col. 4:1). Each passage serves to illuminate and expand the meaning of the other.

PARALLEL PASSAGES BY DIFFERENT AUTHORS

Both historic events and similar teachings may be dealt with by more than one author in Scripture. A comparative study is often helpful in interpretation, and sometimes it is essential.

The Old Testament historical books frequently cover the same event. First and 2 Samuel and 1 and 2 Kings may be compared with 1 and 2 Chronicles at almost every point. First and 2 Chronicles were written to give greater emphasis to the spiritual meaning of historic events. For example, David's punishment for numbering Israel is often applied as a principle in contemporary life. Because David was punished for numbering Israel, some would hold that statistical studies in analyzing church growth are against the will of God. But that interpretation becomes very questionable when parallel accounts in 2 Samuel 24 and 1 Chronicles 21 are studied to gain a composite picture of all the elements involved.

In the New Testament, the gospels recount the life of Christ from different perspectives. When the same event is studied in more than one of the gospels, the significance of that particular event is enhanced. For example, combining the resurrection accounts yields tremendous insight and can serve to correct many potential false interpretations of those accounts considered in isolation.

SIMILAR IDEAS

Many passages are not parallel, in that they do not report the same event, but do have points of similarity. For example, Christ taught His disciples, "If anyone comes to Me, and does not hate his own father and mother and wife and children and brothers and sisters . . . he cannot be My disciple" (Luke 14:26). That is a difficult passage for people in any society, but it is especially difficult in an Eastern society, where God's will that children honor their parents is often the supreme command. Later we will consider guidelines for dealing with contrasting teaching, but at this point note that Christ's meaning is clarified when compared with other passages that have points of similarity. In Matthew 10:37, Christ says, "He who loves father and mother more than Me is not worthy of

Me; and he who loves son or daughter more than Me is not worthy of Me." When the two teachings are compared, the meaning of *hate* begins to become clearer. Apparently, the teaching has to do with the comparison, with choosing to give priority to God's claims on our lives.

Consider two other passages that have points of similarity. Luke 14 refers to hating oneself, and John 12:25 clarifies the idea. "He who loves his life loses it; and he who hates his life in this world will keep it to life eternal." It becomes increasingly apparent that *hate* does not focus on one's feelings but rather on one's choices and behavior.

With that background on some of the passages dealing with hatred, we gradually come to the conclusion that the term is used at least sometimes in Scripture as a description of a relationship that is deliberately chosen for a specific purpose. In the case of human beings, that purpose would be the higher glory of God, when a choice must be made between God's rights and the rights of someone in a human relationship. That, in turn, throws light on the teaching that Esau was "hated" of God (Mal. 1:2-3; Rom. 9:13). Passages that deal with the same theme, touching on ideas that intersect, often throw light on each other's meanings.

When a study is made of similar thoughts, life-focusing truths may be discovered. Following His resurrection Christ came back to that theme of the "great commission" over and over again. This is far from being an isolated proof text for missionary fanatics. Christ spoke of His purpose for His disciples on the night of His resurrection (John 20:21), on the mountain in Galilee (Matt. 28:18-20), on His return to Jerusalem (Luke 24:46-48), and at the time of His ascension (Acts 1:8). Even if the Luke passage is interpreted to have taken place at the same time as John's account (not likely), the responsibility to witness still seems to have been the central theme each time He met with them. Add to those passages the most famous Great Commission of all (Mark 16:15), and we have yet another reinforcement of the theme. How important it appears when all of these similar teachings are brought together in a united whole! Indeed, it seems that the parallel with Christ's own mission is the only adequate way to understand His purpose for us: "As the Father has sent Me, I also send you" (John 20:21).

Sometimes it is very important to know if two passages are actually two parallel accounts, or if two different accounts are intended but have points of similarity. For example, some commentators insist that the Sermon on the Mount recorded in Matthew 5-7 is a parallel passage to Luke 6 and that the two gospel writers are recording the same occasion. But the differences are not merely on the surface. On the occasion recorded in Matthew, Christ gave general principles to the disciples. But if the teaching recorded in Luke is considered a general principle, it would seem to teach that all poor people are happy or even that if you do not become poor, you cannot be happy. Neither of those is true, of course, in the light of a great deal of other biblical teaching. But it is true that some poor people, in spite of their poverty, are happy. And it was some of those people whom Jesus was addressing in Luke 6:20, "Blessed are you who are poor." From the world's point of view it is not reasonable that any poor people should be happy, but Jesus was teaching that it is quite possible.

We know Jesus spoke here of physical poverty, not spiritual, because He contrasted that condition with "woe to you who are rich, for you are receiving your comfort in full" (v. 24). On the other hand, in Matthew He gave a general truth that all who are poor in spirit are blessed. That is, God gives blessing on the condition of poverty of spirit. It is a state to be desired and fostered, whereas material poverty is never treated that way in Scripture.

How can the two passages be reconciled? There is no problem if they are taken as describing different occasions with different, though overlapping, teachings. The context indicates that when we are told in Matthew that Jesus went up into the mountain, and in Luke that He came down to a level place. It is common practice for a preacher to use parts of one message in another message; to take illustrations or phrases from one context and use them in another context. But some find difficulty in allowing that for our Lord.

In comparing similar ideas, the most helpful tools are cross-reference Bibles and topical Bibles. However, those tools will not enable one to discover all passages that have similar events or ideas. The lifelong student of the Bible will discover many such passages over the years and find fruitful comparisons that shed additional light on the passage under study. So it is important to keep a record of those passages that deal with themes of particular personal interest.

Contrasting Ideas

Many times a passage cannot be fully understood until the teaching has been contrasted with teaching in other passages. Since commitment to the trustworthiness of Scripture means that there can be no ultimate conflict, an attempt must be made to resolve apparent conflicts between passages. Guidelines for doing that will be considered in greater detail in the following chapter, when we study a method for building a systematic theology. However, at this point we should mention that there are many teachings in the Bible that do not stand alone. A. W. Tozer, ever the incisive critic of sloppy thinking, has stated it well:

> Truths that are compelled to stand alone never stand straight and are not likely to stand long. Truth is one but truths are many. Scriptural truths are interlocking and interdependent. A truth is rarely valid in isolation. A statement may be true in its relationship to other truths and less than true when separated from them.

Christ said, "Do not judge lest you be judged" (Matt. 7:1). Paul emphasized the same truth: "Who are you to judge the servant of another?" (Rom. 14:4). Many have taken that as an absolute norm for Christian conduct, insisting that no Christian may ever judge another human being. However, there are contrasting passages, one of which is also in the Sermon on the Mount: "Beware of the false prophets. . . . you will know them by their fruits" (Matt. 7:15-16). In fact, Christ said directly, "Judge with righteous judgment" (John 7:24), and John reinforces that: "Test the spirits to see whether they are from God. . . . By this we know the spirit of truth and the spirit of error" (1 John 4:1, 6). To understand all God would teach us concerning judging and refraining from judging others, a systematic study must be made of all biblical teaching on the subject. However, at this point, it is important to note that neither of those teachings can be rightly understood without reference to contrasting passages.

The classic example is the controversy concerning God's sovereignty and man's responsibility. When interpreting verses that seem to teach one of those truths rather than the other, it is necessary to consider the contrasting passages for a balanced and full-orbed understanding of biblical truth. In other words, a person might study God's sovereignty in Ephesians 1, John 6, and Romans 9 and come to conclusions that would relax a person's responsibility for his own choices. To do so would be to misunderstand the full truth. Since all of Scripture is true, the student committed to seeking the unity of Scripture must be diligent and study also what the Bible says of man's responsibility. But he should not study it in isolation or he will distort the balanced truth of God. Sadly, it seems easier to go to a consistent extreme than to stay at the center of biblical tension.

Many promises or commands seem to be unconditional, but it is important to check for conditions found elsewhere. Promises concerning David's descendants and throne often seem unconditional, but Psalm 132:12 says, "If your sons will keep My covenant, and My testimony which I will teach them, their sons also shall sit upon your throne forever." Often the condition is given in the same passage with the promise. Sometimes conditions must be searched out since *all* Scripture is trustworthy and authoritative. The harmony of biblical truth must be sought.

In a few instances, the contrast is found in the same Scripture passage. In Proverbs 26:4-5 the contrast is immediately apparent. "Do not answer a fool according to his folly lest you also be like him. Answer a fool as his folly deserves, lest he be wise in his own eyes." The interpreter is forced to interpret one teaching in the light of the balancing teaching.

But what about passages of contrasting teachings that are not found together? There are two ways to discover those. The first is to study systematic theologies that deal with the subject under consideration. A practical way to discover all passages that may be significant for the study in contrasts is to check those theologians who hold a view contrary to the apparent meaning of the text. For example, if the passage seems to teach man's ability to choose his own destiny, and one wishes to discover contrasting passages concerning God's sovereign purpose and control, theologians who advocate that position can be counted on to marshal all the evidence there is in favor of their own position. They may not be counted on to marshal all the evidence there is for the contrasting position, and therefore one would need to go to theologians of the opposing view to be sure of full identification of potential texts that emphasize man's responsibility for choice.

A second method for discovering all significant contrasting teachings on a given subject is for the student to develop a personal file on the subject. For example, in preparation of a thirty-minute sermon on biblical balance, it was necessary for me to accumulate biblical data over a period of almost ten years. If the Bible student begins to keep a file of materials and biblical references on every subject of particular interest to him, in the course of a few years, and after having read through the Bible a number of times, he can be confident of having pinpointed at least the major passages that touch on the subject.

The Bible itself is the best commentary on the Bible. That is not the natural way to approach a book written by many authors over a period of 1,600 years. You would expect it to be full of contradictions, and you would think it foolish indeed to try to reconcile those conflicting ideas. But the Bible is no ordinary human book. The right approach to a book that was inspired in its entirety by the Spirit of God is to search out its unity. God does not contradict Himself. He gave us a written revelation, not a disoriented conglomeration of disconnected or conflicting ideas. The Bible is harmonious, and we must interpret it accordingly.

Summary

The student should compare Scripture with Scripture, allowing the Bible to illuminate itself. He should search for passages dealing with the same event or giving the same teaching, for passages with similar teaching, and for passages with contrasting teaching. He does that to gain insight into the meaning of the passage under study and to be sure that his interpretation is in harmony with the rest of Scripture. The approach outlined in this chapter is the foundation for doing topical studies or building a systematic theology. We turn now to that study.

Selected Bibliography for Further Study

HARMONIES OF THE BIBLE

Crockett, William D. *A Harmony of the Books of Samuel, Kings, and Chronicles: The Book of the Kings of Judah and Israel.* Grand Rapids: Baker, 1951.

Daniel, Orville E. *A Harmony of the Four Gospels: The New International Version.* Grand Rapids: Baker, 1987.

Goodwin, Frank J. *A Harmony of the Life of Paul: According to the Acts of the Apostles and the Pauline Epistles.* Grand Rapids: Baker, 1973.

Newsome, James D., Jr., ed. *A Synoptic Harmony of Samuel, Kings, and Chronicles: With Related Passages from Psalms, Isaiah, Jeremiah, and Ezra.* Grand Rapids: Baker, 1990.

Pentecost, J. Dwight. *A Harmony of the Words and Works of Jesus Christ.* Grand Rapids: Zondervan, 1981.

Thomas, Robert L., and Stanley N. Gundry. *The NIV Harmony of the Gospels.* Grand Rapids: Zondervan, 1988.

______. *A Harmony of the Gospels: New American Standard Bible.* Grand Rapids: Zondervan, 1978.

UNITY OF THE OLD AND NEW TESTAMENT

Archer, Gleason L., and Gregory C. Chirichigno. *Old Testament Quotations in the New Testament.* Chicago: Moody, 1983.

Johnson, S. Lewis. *The Old Testament in the New: An Argument for Biblical Inspiration.* Grand Rapids: Zondervan, 1980.

Kaiser, Walter C., Jr. *The Uses of the Old Testament in the New.* Chicago: Moody, 1985.

TOPICAL STUDIES

Elwell, Walter A., ed. *Topical Analysis of the Bible: Using the New International Version.* Grand Rapids: Baker, 1990.

Geisler, Norman, L. *Christ, the Theme of the Bible.* Chicago: Moody, 1968.

The New Nave's Topical Bible. Rev. and enl. Grand Rapids: Zondervan, 1986.

Swihart, Stephen D. *The Victor Bible Sourcebook.* Wheaton, Ill: Victor, 1977.

16
Coherence of Truth

Guideline: Establish the coherence of revealed truth.

A necessary step in understanding God's revelation of Himself and of His will for man is to take the bits and pieces of biblical teaching and put them all together into a harmonious whole.

The first step in doing a topical study or building a systematic structure of biblical teaching is to analyze each passage, examining it to determine the author's intended meaning. However, as we saw in the last chapter, to study only one element of a revealed truth in a single passage may lead to a distortion of that truth. Inconsistencies, omissions, and wrong emphases may go undetected. For example, to begin and end one's study of God's character with passages that deal solely with His love will not give a complete or accurate understanding of the Person of God. Other characteristics of God, such as His holiness and justice, must also be considered.

The Bible was given, for the most part, by prophets and apostles relating only one part of God's truth to a particular person or group. Therefore, some have argued that the desire to organize all the bits and pieces into a united whole is not necessary and, indeed, may not be true to the Scripture as God gave it. Analysis is legitimate in such a view; synthesis is not. The attempt to systematize or synthesize (put together) the various elements of a doctrine or of all doctrine, it is held, comes from a Western way of thinking in logical categories. That is not the only way of thinking or, perhaps, even the best way of thinking, they say. If it were, why was the Bible not given in a systematic form?

Actually, as we have seen earlier (chap. 5), that contention is not well based. All of us think by relating new ideas to ideas we have already accepted. It may be possible for a rational human being to hold two contrary ideas simultaneously by keeping them isolated from one another in his own thinking, but it would be impossible to treat all of his perceptions and concepts that way.

All of us are systematic theologians. That is, we have various ideas about God that fit together in one way or another. The poor theologian is one who has an inadequate or limited view of God because he is aware of only some of the elements of revealed truth, or he is one who has a distorted view of God because he lacks an overall biblical perspective. A good theologian, on the other hand, is one who has taken into account all revealed truth about God and has related each part to a consistent whole.

If that is a good objective of biblical study, why did God not give truth to us in an organized way? Although no explanation is offered in Scripture, there are several possible answers. First, much of the truth of God is given in an organized fashion. The book of Romans is a classic example of an organized presentation of truth. But in the education of a child, not much communication would take place if the entire curriculum for his education were presented in a single block of organized material. It is necessary to begin where he is and to build his perception and understanding step by step. Likewise, God revealed Himself and His will in stages as people were prepared to receive the communication.

Although we cannot prove it, another reason the historical, anecdotal way that God has revealed His truth in Scripture is that this may be the way it is best understood by the widest spectrum of people. The revelation is given in many contexts and in many forms so that there is the built-in potential of speaking again and again to all the conditions of men in all ages.

There are, no doubt, other reasons. None of those reasons, however, relieves us of the responsibility of being sure that we have discerned everything God intends us to understand about Him and His will. He did not create the world with a large supply of finished products but provided the raw material and allowed man to mine the riches of His creation. In the same way, He has provided in the Word of God the raw material from which each generation may mine the riches of His truth.

A topical study is systematic theology in miniature. That is, one small segment of all biblical teaching is isolated and treated as a unit. For example, a systematic theology of the doctrine of God would organize in a single whole all that the Bible teaches concerning the Person and work of God. All of His characteristics would be exhaustively examined. But for a Sunday morning sermon or a Sunday school lesson, one cannot consider every attribute of God. So a topical study of God's unchangeableness (immutability) might be considered. An even narrower topic might be considered, such as the implication of God's unchangeableness for human ethical standards. Human moral behavior as a reflection of God's character would then be considered in the light of the fact that God's moral character never changes.

In doing systematic theology, Christians find their greatest differences. How can Bible truth be organized in a systematic way so that we are closer to God's truth as it is in ultimate reality and not actually find ourselves further from it? Are there guidelines that enable us to reach our goal of seeing God's truth as completely as possible with each of the parts harmoniously related? I believe such guidelines exist, but more important than any guideline is the approach one takes in the study of biblical themes, topics, or doctrine. Therefore, we will consider the approach necessary to achieving the goal, and then we will examine the guidelines for actually developing a proper theology.

A Proper Approach

As we approach the Bible intent on discovering all the truth God intends for us to understand, we should examine our expectations and attitudes, as there are limitations on what is possible.

GOAL OF THEOLOGICAL STUDY

First, theological study must not be a barren academic search for ultimate truth. God is not nearly so interested in what I know as He is in what I *am* and how I *behave*. As Andrew Murray once put it, "Scripture was not given to increase our knowledge but to change our conduct." The Bible was not given only to teach us what to believe and what not to believe; it was also given to show us how to behave and how not to behave (2 Tim. 3:16). All of our rigorous Bible study must be for the purpose of making the application to life, transferring the truth into day-by-day living.

For example, take the Bible doctrine of prophecy. The Bible tells us why prophecy was given—clearly not for the use commonly made of it. "I am telling you before it comes to pass, so that when it comes to pass, *you may believe* that I am He" (John 13:19; italics added). "And now I have told you before it comes to pass, that when it comes to pass, *you may believe*" (John 14:29). That is clearly the purpose of prediction after it has been fulfilled. But what about the great mass of unfulfilled prophecy—does it have any purpose for today? Prophecy is primarily forth-telling God's message, not fortelling the future. Of 164 predictive passages in the New Testament (excluding the book of Revelation, which is devoted exclusively to the subject), 141 are directly related to conduct, and apparently given to affect conduct—not to increase knowledge. Only 23 passages seem to be given primarily for information concerning the future.

The study of Bible prophecy should be, then, primarily for two purposes: (1) the study of fulfilled prophecy to confirm our faith, and (2) the study of unfulfilled prophecy to influence our conduct.

What a release from mental gymnastics and what godly profit would exist if prophecy were so studied, and if Bible students would refuse to study with the goals of satisfying curiosity and of detailing future events beyond the clear basic teaching of the Bible. What peace among the brethren if Bible students refused to base fellowship on adherence to certain strongly held prophetic minutiae! If God had purposed to satisfy our curiosity concerning the future, it surely would have been no more difficult to do than it was to give the great basic teachings on which His people agree. And for His primary purpose in giving prophecy—to influence our conduct—the clear teaching of the Bible is more than sufficient. "It is not for you to know times or epochs which the Father has fixed by His own authority; *but* you shall receive power . . . and you shall be witnesses" (Acts 1:7-8; italics added).

In the realm of Bible study, at least, a lot of knowledge can be a dangerous thing. Omniscience is not required, but faithfulness is. And that includes faithfulness with what we know. For we are responsible in a special way to live out what we know (Luke 12:47-48). The quest for theological truth, then, should never be an end in itself but a means for knowing and obeying God more perfectly.

MOTIVE FOR THEOLOGICAL STUDY

If all Bible students would make application to life a higher goal than academic propositional truth, would all doctrinal warfare cease and denominational division be healed? No, for there are other essential attitudes in a biblical approach.

What, then, is the cure for the deeply channeled divisions in the one Body of Christ? The answer Paul gave is simple: knowledge puffs up; love builds up (1 Cor. 8:1). In a nutshell, there it is. God is primarily interested not in what we know but in what we are and how we act. And His love embraces all His will concerning that. First Corinthians 13 was not given merely as a description of love. It was given primarily in direct condemnation of division in the Body of Christ. This is the positive answer: love. But that is not the whole answer. There is a negative part: knowledge puffs up. First Corinthians 1-3 and Philippians 2 provide the antidote: humility; that is, being of one mind by having the mind of Christ, who, having everything, became nothing.

The pattern is simple. After knowledge puffs up and divides, Christ enters, infinite in all things, and we are deflated, humbled, shorn of all pretended knowledge, personal ambition, jealousy, and exclusivism. Then love—not as sentiment, but as an all-consuming way of life—can operate, and the building up of the one Body moves forward (cf. Eph. 4). Biblical knowledge unapplied destroys; knowledge applied gives life.

ATTITUDE IN THEOLOGICAL STUDY

An essential element in studying Bible doctrine is humility. Humility must clear the way for love to operate. But rock-bottom humility—actually counting everyone else better than oneself (Phil. 2:3)—is not always easy. How is it realized? Humility in regard to Bible doctrine comes as the result of facing certain facts. The sincere Bible student recognizes: (1) revelation is only partial,

(2) we are finite, (3) we are fallen, (4) we need an open mind, and (5) we must be willing to obey.

Revelation is only partial. The very purpose and nature of the Bible is to reveal, not to obscure, hide, or divide. God could have clearly revealed many details. Yet for some reason God has chosen not to reveal the details as clearly as He has the great basic truths. It is the glory of God to conceal some matters (Prov. 25:2). "The secret things belong to the Lord our God" (Deut. 29:29). Surely the great biblical emphases and patent truths provide an inexhaustible store to challenge and satisfy; they are "to us and to our sons forever, that we may *do* all the words of the law" (v. 29). Yet, why is man not satisfied to leave it so? A humble mind is essential.

Why does God not reveal more than He does? Why does He leave our curiosity unsatisfied? There are some things we do not need to know. Jesus told the disciples "I did not say to you . . . because I was with you" (John 16:4). At that point in their spiritual pilgrimage the disciples did not need to know everything they might have wanted to know. Perhaps even more important, God does not reveal that which we are unprepared to receive: "I have many more things to say to you, but you cannot bear them now" (John 16:12). Apparently only those small bits of God's immensity that are necessary for our good have been unveiled.

Great divisions have often occurred because men reason out what they believe to be the balance of unrevealed truth. For example, many systematic theologies take the nature of God's sovereignty and the nature of man's responsibility beyond revelation on the wings of reason. The learned and saintly Bishop Moule commented on this problem: "Let us, like (Scripture), 'go to both extremes'; then we shall be as near, probably, as our finite thought can be at present to the whole truth as it moves, a perfect sphere, in God."[1]

We are finite. Even if revelation were full, we could not fully comprehend it, for we are finite and truth is infinite. God's thoughts are as far above ours as heaven is above the earth (Isa. 55:9). Every judgment we make is out of perspective. We are near-

1. H. C. G. Moule, *Romans* (London: Pickering & Inglis, n.d.), p. 306.

sighted, limited drastically in time, space, knowledge, experience, and mental ability.

The first time I flew over the Blue Ridge Mountains I realized a little of the great difference a person's point of view makes in his perspective. The heavens indeed are far above the earth, and those familiar mountains that had seemed so great when I had climbed them or driven over them could hardly be distinguished from one another. I actually asked the pilot, after we had crossed the range, when we would reach it! Big and little took on entirely different meanings. I came to wonder if we really see anything in divine perspective—as God sees it and as we will see it one day. We certainly see nothing in completeness. Our depth of field is very shallow. When we focus on one thing, other things seem to get out of focus with reality. Only God in His infinite scope of vision can keep all reality in focus. C. S. Lewis put it this way:

> Five senses; an incurably abstract intellect; a haphazardly selective memory; a set of preconceptions and assumptions so numerous that I can never examine more than a minority of them—never become even conscious of them all. How much of total reality can such an apparatus let through?[2]

A. W. Tozer also wrote on the subject:

> The soul of man, says Matthew Arnold, is a mirror suspended on a cord, turning in every breeze, always reflecting what is before it but never reflecting more than a small part of the whole.
>
> The size of the mirror varies from man to man, but no one is able to comprehend the vast panorama that lies before and around us. The mental giant has a larger mirror, to be sure, but even the largest is pathetically small.
>
> As long as we know that our view of truth is partial we can preserve that humbleness of mind appropriate to the circumstances; but let us once get the notion that our view is total and we become intellectually intolerant. Let us become convinced that ours is the only sensible view and our ability to learn dies instantly, . . .
>
> Unity among Christians will not, in my opinion, be achieved short of the Second Advent. There are too many factors working

2. C. S. Lewis, *A Grief Observed* (London: Faber and Faber, 1961), p. 51.

> against it. But a greater degree of unity might be realized if we all approached the truth with deeper humility. No one knows everything, not saint nor scholar nor reformer nor theologian.[3]

We know only in part—as a child (1 Cor. 13:9-12). I once came upon my four-year old daughter and a friend building with blocks.

"It isn't chimbley. It's chimley."

"It is not chimley. It's chimbley."

And so the argument went on and on. I smiled to myself and then began to wonder. How often does our Father smile on us and our dogmatic declarations that so often go beyond the realm of our knowledge? The children were both right within their field—how to build a chimney of blocks. But they became foolish when they dogmatized outside the realm of their very limited experience.

The good news is that we will not remain children. We will become adults. We will not become infinite, but we will know more fully, even as we are fully known, when we no longer see dimly in a mirror, but face to face. "They shall see eye to eye, when Jehovah returneth to Zion" (Isa.52:8, ASV).

The humble, yielded mind is satisfied when, in the study of a doctrine, it comes to the place of parting, and God's infinite truth slips on out of the realm of finite sight beyond the veil into the infinite. To run after it or to fret at its departure is not wise. When one truly sees his own finitude against the backdrop of infinity, humility is inevitable and dogmatism impossible.

We are fallen. Not only are we finite; we are fallen. Sin has dimmed and warped our understanding of the revelation we do have, and therefore, we are subject to error. "It is to be expected that the Holy Spirit should not completely clear from error the minds of those whose hearts He does not completely clear from sin."[4]

We choose the interpretation that lets us do what we want to do. We twist and turn and rationalize until the Scripture means what we want it to mean. And we are so stubborn about our theo-

3. A. W. Tozer,"Our Imperfect View of Truth," *The Alliance Witness,* 11 March 1959, p. 2.
4. George Salmon, *Infallibility of the Church* (Grand Rapids: Baker, 1957), p. 285.

logical opinions. Our sinful desires and our arrogance distort our understanding of God's Word.

These first three elements of humility in Bible study should remind us that humility and love are more becoming than dogmatism. A healthy agnosticism concerning all that goes beyond certain fact will preserve the unity of the Spirit among God's children and peace in one's own heart. Nothing is more likely to disrupt unity among brethren or the calm of one's own soul than a dogmatic difference of opinion in questions of Bible doctrine.

Augustine has said, "In essentials, unity; in nonessentials, liberty; and in all thing, charity." The problem comes, of course, in dividing between essentials and nonessentials. If everyone could only be satisfied with the great clearly revealed truths of God's Word and refuse to move any mere opinion from "nonessential" to "essential" standing, what unity and harmony and consequent blessing would result!

Humility in regard to knowledge should be inevitable when one faces the above facts. However, I have not found it to be inevitable. It would be if humility were the product of reason alone. But it is not. Humility is a fruit of the Spirit, and rational facing of the facts is possible only to one who belongs to the order of the broken and contrite heart, to one with a totally yielded will.

We need an open mind. Total surrender is both passive and active. Passively, it means complete openness of heart and mind. But in its full development, this openness of mind is not merely a mental nod of assent to an idea that is proposed. It is, rather, a deliberately and difficultly acquired attitude that becomes a controlling factor in a person's thinking. Such a mental attitude cannot be summoned on occasion and then dismissed when it has served its purpose. Instead, it is a deep-seated integrity and mental honesty that is passionately concerned with objectively examining all the evidence to discover facts and exclude all else.

Openness is a very difficult frame of mind to develop, even though few are deliberately closed in mind, and almost all will claim openness of mind. The most difficult thing in the world is to be absolutely, rigidly, and lucidly honest in one's own thinking. That is because dishonesty is not usually deliberate. We see things through the glasses of our experiences, by what we have read and heard, through our way of life, or through a previously settled system of doctrine.

That fact is illustrated by an interesting experiment conducted by a research psychologist. He placed two different pictures in a stereoscope. The left eye was to see a bullfighter; the right eye, a baseball player. Then he asked some Mexican subjects and some Americans subjects to peer through the instrument. Most of the Mexicans saw the bullfighter, most of the Americans saw the baseball player. What is behind our eyes often has more to do with what we see than what is before our eyes.

Therefore, we must develop a healthy suspicion of ourselves and of our own ideas, and a view of the Bible that separates it from our own past thinking and experience (insofar as humanly possible) to let it speak not what we already believe or want to believe, but what it says. A suspicion of our own ideas will lead to a willingness to reject even lifelong and deeply cherished opinions, ways of living, friendships, and associations without hesitation, once God's Word has come into clear focus.

The surrendered heart wants to know what the Bible says, not what it can be made to mean. The acceptance of the possible, rather than the certain, meaning is often done to make a self-consistent scheme. But the system must not force the Bible into its logical mold. The Bible gives the system all it can legitimately have. If it needs more to complete it, it must wait for the fuller light of eternity. Charles Simeon of Cambridge said:

> My endeavor is to make out of Scripture what is there, and not to thrust in what I think might be there. I have a great jealousy on this head [point] never to speak more or less than I believe to be the mind of the Spirit in the passage I am expounding. I would run after nothing, and shun nothing.

We must be willing to obey. Surrender is not merely a passive openness of mind, but it is also a willingness to believe and to obey. It is seen in an active, positive attitude: a hungry heart that is eagerly seeking. When one comes to the Bible with a willingness to learn and obey only when cornered, or with fear and cringing lest it change his opinions and reprove his conduct, that one gives evidence of a stubborn, unyielded heart and cannot be sure he is discovering God's truth.

The aggressively seeking mind proposes new hypotheses, and then tests them mercilessly in the clear light of what the Bible actually says. It is constantly testing and reexamining, perfectly willing to discover the truth in conflict with the sanctions of tradition. It purposefully ousts opinion—even widely held opinion—and demands that it return only with the authorized credentials of solid Bible evidence. It fears the bog of semantic stagnation—traditional statements and terms that hide or obscure the pure biblical statements, or those that have lost their vitality and accuracy through common use or misuse.

The eager search for basic truth is evidence of an active surrender of heart, which is a parent indispensable in the birth of humility. This spirit of unconditional surrender coupled with an honest facing of the facts produces humility. The humble mind does not aspire to omniscience, nor to any measureable degree thereof. It has sought out the facts with an open, yielded mind, recognizing the difference between established fact and matters of conviction or opinion. It keeps them separate, content to leave outside the realm of certainty those things that are not clearly revealed. As the psalmist wisely declares:

> O Lord, my heart is not proud, nor my eyes haughty; nor do I involve myself in great matters, or in things too difficult for me. Surely I have composed and quieted my soul. (Ps. 131:1-2)

In summary, three attitudes are essential for building a theological system:

1. The full assurance that knowledge is only legitimate as it leads to being and doing
2. Awareness that love sums up the being and doing
3. Deep, unaffected humility born of unconditional surrender and honest facing of the facts of one's own limited, finite, fallen point of view

Because of the partial character of revelation, our own finitude and susceptibility to error, and our sinful hearts, we should not aspire to the total understanding of all truth. On the other hand, we believe that the essential things are clear. Terry has said: "By far the greater portion of the Old and New Testaments is so clear in general import that there is no room for controversy, and those parts which are obscure contain no fundamental truth or doctrine which is not elsewhere set forth in clearer form."[5] To discern that truth, we will now learn the guidelines that should be followed.

Guidelines for Builing a Systematic Theology

BASE DOCTRINE ON A SOUND EXEGESIS OF EACH TEXT

All of the guidelines studied thus far must be employed in determining the meaning intended by the author in each text. This work of exegesis forms the building blocks for constructing any doctrine. That is the first and essential guideline for building an authentic doctrine or system of doctrines.

The popular idea about topical sermons is that they are much easier to prepare than expository sermons, which are based directly on the analysis of particular passages. However, a legitimate topical sermon or lesson, or a paper dealing with a single theme of Scripture, is actually much more difficult to prepare, for it must be founded on a solid exegesis of each of the passages that are used. In other words, a topical sermon, to be authentic, must represent a very broad understanding of many passages of Scripture. For the mature Bible student who has already done a thorough study of most of the passages, the preparation of a topical sermon may not be so difficult. However, until such a thorough work has been done, great care should be exercised in developing a theme from many texts.

BASE DOCTRINE ON THE ENTIRE BIBLE

The second guideline for building a sound doctrinal structure utilizes the guidelines indicated in the last chapter. It will not do to build a doctrine on a single passage or on a few of the passages that speak to a particular topic. Although the basic approach was

5. Milton S. Terry, *Biblical Hermeneutics* (Grand Rapids: Zondervan, 1974), p. 583.

presented in the last chapter, several guidelines need to be reinforced.

Data must he assembled and organized. All data on the subject under consideration must be identified. Then the data must be organized into a coherent whole so that the relationships among the various elements in the doctrine may be seen clearly. To do that, all parallel passages must be considered, all passages with similar teaching must be examined, and all contrasting passages must be integrated. In other words, everything the Bible says on the subject must be taken into account. To leave out some crucial passage or some elements of the truth God is revealing is to distort what is left.

When all the data is assembled, it should be organized into a coherent whole so that inconsistencies may be spotted, omissions recognized, and biblical balance maintained. For example, when identifying and relating all teaching on the subject of living the Christian life, it is necessary to study at least three major subject areas: God's standard for Christian living, God's provision for Christian living, and man's responsibility for appropriating God's provision. God's standard might deal with two major divisions: biblical personal ethics and biblical social ethics.

Under biblical personal ethics, love would be among the many standards that should be considered. But the topic of love itself is treated in Scripture extensively and requires thorough study. To fully understand the biblical concept of love, we must identify all the following: the relationship of the noun *love,* describing how a person feels; the verb *to love,* describing how a person should behave; how love should be defined; the basis of biblical love; the objects of biblical love; the evidence of love; and the limits of love.

In turn, that becomes one among many elements in the theologian's consideration of biblical personal ethics, which is part of the larger subject of biblical ethics or moral standards. The entire subject of biblical standards is, again, only a part of the larger subject of the Christian life (the doctrine of sanctification). Eventually, the Bible student begins to build, with the building blocks of individual truths discovered in various passages, a harmonious whole.

If love is not considered as part of God's standard for Christian living, or if the teaching on love considers only part of the biblical data on the subject, a warped standard may be incorporated into one's teaching on Christian living. The whole scope of biblical teaching on a subject must be included. *All* data must be incorporated.

A specific doctrine must be systematized. A specific doctrine or theme must be related to all other teaching that might affect that particular doctrine. In this way, the various areas of doctrine are combined into what might be called a systematic theology. For example, in the doctrine of Christian living mentioned above, a full understanding cannot be achieved without considering other areas of doctrine, such as the doctrine of salvation (soteriology). How do forgiveness, justification, regeneration, and other doctrines of salvation relate to biblical Christian living? Or consider the nature of God. If God's will is that His moral likeness be restored in those He saves, is it not necessary to consider the moral nature of God to fully understand what He desires the Christian to be and how He desires him to behave?

For a fuller understanding of a particular topic, theme, or doctrine, we should relate it to all other biblical themes that affect it.

Data varies in importance. Not all the data is of equal importance in building a doctrine. All data on a given subject should be considered, and that subject should be related to other relevant subjects; however, equal weight should not be given to every text that provides a building block for the doctrine. Four criteria apply in assessing the importance of the data.

1. *The clear passage is to be preferred above the obscure.* If the author's intended meaning is not altogether certain, and interpreters are at odds as to its meaning, the text is not an ideal building block for doctrine. The weight of a doctrine or teaching should rest on the solid foundation of clear teaching. For example, 1 Peter 3:19 is very difficult to understand, and it is found in a passage difficult to understand: "In which also He went and made proclamation to the spirits now in prison."

   Many interpreters have despaired of identifying a certain meaning, and few interpreters have agreed fully on its meaning. Therefore, to base so important a doctrine as the idea of purgatory on such an obscure text is not building on a solid foundation.

Note, however, that *obscure* does not mean "incompatible with my system." Obscure passages are those in which the meaning is unclear, even with diligent use of the guidelines for interpreting Scripture. Passages with this kind of obscurity should not be the basis for building doctrine.

2. *Greater weight is to be given to teaching often repeated.* It is not wise to build an important doctrine on an isolated text, even though it is true that God does not need to speak twice to make His statements authoritative. Greater weight should be given to that which is often repeated and emphasized in Scripture.

> The argument from each text may be nullified or largely set aside when taken singularly or alone; but a great number and variety of such evidence, taken as a whole, and exhibiting a manifest coherency, may not thus be set aside.[6]

Acts 22:16 may seem to teach baptismal regeneration: "And now why do you delay? Arise, and be baptized, and wash away your sins." However, the great bulk of New Testament teaching concerning the ground for our salvation would seem to identify faith as the sole criterion. A doctrine, particularly a major doctrine, should be built on a broad foundation of many texts and biblical emphases. The unanimity of the testimony of many passages provides a solid foundation.

3. *Direct, literal teaching should be given preference.* The structure of Bible doctrine must be built on the sure foundation of literal passages containing direct teaching. It should not be built on figurative, poetic, or historical passages, unless that picture language or those historical passages are literally interpreted by Scripture. Historical and figurative passages are not necessarily excluded from con-

6. Ibid., p. 587.

sideration in building a biblical doctrine, but they must be used with great care. Guidelines for their use will be considered later.

4. *Later revelation takes precedence over earlier revelation in building doctrine.* It is true that the New Testament may not legitimately be used as a foundation of a doctrine independent of Old Testament teaching. Actually, New Testament revelation grows out of the Old, and even the terms used are derived primarily from Old Testament usage. Nevertheless, many Old Testament teachings are superseded in the New Testament because of the progress of redemption in history and the progress of revelation in Scripture. Therefore, greater weight should be given to later revelation, particularly when New Testament revelation supersedes Old Testament revelation, as in the case of the redemptive work of Christ.

   That does not mean that an Old Testament teaching may be set aside without New Testament authorization. It does mean, however, that a Christian doctrinal structure must rest squarely on the New Testament and on those Old Testament teachings and passages that underlie and provide the foundation for New Testament teaching. Christ states this explicitly in Matthew 5:21-22:

> You have heard that the ancients were told, "You shall not commit murder" and "Whoever commits murder shall be liable to the court." But I say to you that everyone who is angry with his brother shall be guilty before the court; and whoever shall say to his brother, "Raca," shall be guilty before the supreme court and whoever shall say, "You fool," shall be guilty enough to go into the fiery hell.

   Nevertheless, New Testament teaching can be adequately understood only with the earlier revelation, as Christ affirmed: "Do not think that I came to abolish the Law or the Prophets: I did not come to abolish, but to fulfill. For truly I say to you, until heaven and earth pass away, not the smallest letter or stroke shall pass away from the Law, until all is accomplished" (Matt. 5:17-18).

BASE THE DOCTRINE SOLELY ON THE BIBLE

Scripture makes the claim of truth and authority only for itself. It does not ascribe either of those qualities to other writings. Only the Bible may bind the conscience of the believer. The Bible alone must be the foundation of all theological building.

Do not build on inference. Rational powers are God-given, and our commission is to study thoroughly so that we may handle correctly the Word of God with no need to be ashamed. Furthermore, since revelation is very limited, it is inevitable that many gaps will appear in any system that aims at wholeness or completeness. It may be legitimate to logically deduce the missing elements. But if Scripture is our sole authority, we may not invest logical deduction with divine authority.

For example, Scripture teaches that God the Father is the one and only God. It also teaches that Jesus Christ is the Son of God and that the Holy Spirit is Deity. How do those teachings relate to one another? It is necessary that we seek a coherent unity and that we build theories as to how the threeness and oneness of our God might be related. In fact, the doctrine of the Trinity is such an inference. But the way in which the three ultimately relate is not revealed in Scripture, and thus our theories for relating them should be held tentatively.

In building a systematic theology, few have been able to resist the temptation to bridge the gap with logical deductions. But to build a superstructure on inference from the limited data of Scripture and then to require allegiance to that as certainly the truth of God is not to allow the Bible itself to be the final authority. Terry states this well:

> Most of the great controversies on Christian doctrine have grown out of attempts to define what is left in Scriptures undefined.[7]

> The Holy Scriptures contain all things necessary to salvation; so that whatsoever is not read therein, nor may be proved thereby, is not to be required of any man, that it should be believed as an article of faith, or be thought requisite or necessary to salvation.[8]

7. Ibid., p. 585.
8. Ibid., p. 583.

I do not decry the inevitability and even the value of "filling in" a system constructed on biblical data with bits and pieces of logic. We must insist, however, that they not be invested with biblical authority.

Do not build on tradition. It is very helpful to study the history of doctrine or of a particular doctrine. Most heresies have already been invented and refuted. Furthermore, it is not necessary for each Bible student, nor even for each generation, to reinvent the wheel. It is legitimate and wise to build on the efforts of those who have gone before. If an attitude of humility characterizes the Bible student, he will never take lightly the efforts of others or fail to recognize the work of the Holy Spirit in His church. But in the final analysis, doctrine must be based solely on the Bible, not on some tradition, no matter how hallowed by time or how widely accepted.

> The systematic expounder of Scripture doctrine is expected to set forth, in clear outline and in well defined terms, such teachings as have certain warrant in the Word of God. We must not import into the text of Scripture the ideas of later times, or build upon any words or passages a dogma which they do not legitimately teach.[9]

Do not build doctrine on other extrabiblical sources. As we have seen earlier, the Bible is given for a specific purpose—to reveal God's salvation—and is not designed to teach us all there is to know of God or even of man. Therefore, man, created in the image of God and commissioned to participate in superintending part of God's creation (Gen. 1:28), finds it his glory to search out knowledge (Prov. 25:2). Such empirical investigation and theorizing cannot be invested with the same authority as a revelation from God, but it certainly can be of practical benefit to mankind.

How does that relate to constructing a theology? It is quite legitimate to look to human experience and scientific investigation to question traditional interpretations of Scripture. Traditional interpretations of Scripture that taught that the earth was the center of the universe were challenged scientifically, and Scripture was reexamined.

9. Ibid.

Again, it is quite legitimate for man to study his own mental processes and social relationships to discern better ways of effective living. But it is not legitimate to use extrabiblical sources such as nonbiblical historical records, scientific theory, or human experience to set aside the clear teaching of Scripture. Those concepts from extrabiblical sources may not be intermixed with the doctrinal structure as if they were part of the authoritative revealed truth of God. Some subjective blending is inevitable, but the careful student will stay alert to screen out as much of that as possible. For an authoritative system of divinely revealed truth, we must keep the doctrinal structure distinct from scientific, cultural, traditional, or other thought structures.

It is legitimate for us to ask questions of Scripture that derive from our human experience. For example, I may have derived from Scripture a doctrine that physical healing will always result for the one who has faith. An examination of the experience of Christians in general and of people who teach that doctrine most strongly reveals that those who seem to have the strongest faith often are not healed. That fact alone should not cause a person to reject the doctrine, for human experience is not the final court of appeal. However, it is quite legitimate for the Christian to reexamine Scripture to see if the position he has held is, indeed, the teaching of Scripture.

Bible doctrine should reflect Bible emphases. A preaching and teaching ministry should emphasize those elements of biblical truth that are most needed by the hearers. Strong biblical teaching against legalism may not be appropriate to an audience that is already against law (antinomian). Rather, the emphasis may need to be on the law. But to a fearful, guilt-ridden person, teaching against legalism may be just the emphasis needed.

It may be impossible to completely separate the work of interpreting Scripture from that of applying Scripture. The present context of the Bible student inevitably influences his work of digging out the meaning of Scripture from its ancient context. Interpretation and application constantly influence each other. This influence should result in an upward spiral toward more fully understanding and obeying the will of God. The present situation may suggest questions to ancient Scripture, and the very form of the question affects the way the answer appears, even to the most objective and careful student. Then, to one committed to the authority of Scripture, obedience to the truth discovered in Scripture immediately changes his own situation, so that the kind of question addressed to Scripture next will differ from that addressed to Scripture earlier. Ideally each round of interaction will lead one closer to the truth.

Thus, the present context legitimately influences one's emphasis. However, in one's doctrinal structure the student must follow the guidelines of emphasizing what Scripture emphasizes. In fact, it is not only easy but common to distort the teaching of Scripture simply by emphasizing one aspect of truth and failing to emphasize another. Actually, that is one of the greatest sources of sectarianism or denominational difference. For example, Paul remonstrated with the Christians in Corinth because they were so emphasizing the gift of tongues as to distort the whole doctrine concerning Spirit-given abilities and the ministry of the church. Any minor teaching of Scripture, or even an inference based on scriptural data, may be so emphasized as to become the basis for division in the Body of Christ.

Consider another example. For the Christian who is behaving as a non-Christian, several things are necessary. He needs to return to the relationship he once had of trusting Jesus Christ as Lord of his life. Such a return has been called a "crisis experience." Such a turnaround is certainly necessary, but it is possible to so emphasize that necessary commitment, surrender, or repentance that the whole doctrine of Christian growth is neglected and the overall force of the teaching on Christian living is distorted. On the other hand, it is possible to emphasize Christian growth and neglect the fundamental relationship with God, so that people assume they are growing when, in truth, they are in no position to grow at all.

In those illustrations, no false teaching has been incorporated into the system of doctrine; yet the emphasis, not being the emphasis the Bible itself gives the teaching, has the same end result—a distortion of biblical truth.

Doctrine, then, should be built on the solid foundation of what the *Bible* teaches, for that alone has the authority of God to support it. Inference, tradition, human experience, nonbiblical historical records, and scientific theory are all valuable sources of knowledge. But all of those are fallible and may not legitimately be incorporated as part of a doctrinal structure purporting to have authority as God's revelation of truth.

Summary

We may, with confidence, gather together all that Scripture teaches on a subject or all that Scripture reveals of divine truth, and organize it into a coherent whole. We do that by basing our doctrine (1) on sound exegesis of each passage, (2) on the entire Bible, and (3) on the Bible alone.

Theological study in earlier centuries was considered "the queen of the sciences." Perhaps the designation is not far off. Topical or theological study may not be demanded by Scripture, but it is certainly permitted by Scripture and seems to be demanded by our human condition. It helps us understand the truth of God and His will for us more fully. It even helps us interpret more accurately individual passages, because Scripture is examined in the light of Scripture. "In Thy light we see light" (Ps. 36:9). Although topical and doctrinal studies do not solve all problems, they do solve many of the apparent problems of Scripture.

Selected Bibliography for Further Study

Davis, John Jefferson. *Handbook of Basic Bible Texts: Every Key Passage for the Study of Doctrine and Theology.* Grand Rapids: Zondervan, 1984.

Elwell, Walter A., ed. *Evangelical Dictionary of Theology.* Grand Rapids, Baker, 1984.

Johnston, Robert K., ed. *The Use of the Bible in Theology: Evangelical Options.* Atlanta: John Knox, 1985.

17
Approach to Alleged Discrepancies

Guideline: Since we hold that the Bible is God-breathed and true in all its parts, when a statement appears to be in error, we are committed to seek an explanation.

We approach the Bible with confidence because Jesus had confidence in it. The attitude of Jesus toward the holy Book is very different from His attitude toward the holy place (the Temple) and the holy people (religious leaders). He had no difficulty in pronouncing woe on those who were considered the most righteous of all people, nor did He hesitate to predict the destruction of the Temple. But the Scriptures He held to be indestructible and wholly trustworthy.

The defense of Scripture is not the responsibility of our present study—that belongs to apologetics or biblical introduction. We will not study alleged discrepancies in depth, yet we must determine an approach for handing such discrepancies as we learn guidelines for the interpretation of Scripture. (For further study, see the selected bibliography at chapter's end, which deals with the various kinds of Bible problems, including alleged discrepancies.) We will use actual biblical examples, but will not necessarily seek a final solution to each problem. Rather, we will point out the path that leads to a possible solution.

Because our presupposition is that the Bible is true in all its parts, we seek solutions when there appears to be error. When we cannot solve a problem, we admit it. We do not conclude, however, that it cannot be solved. Rather, because of loyalty built on the solid foundation of strong evidence of trustworthiness, and honestly facing the alternatives with which disloyalty would leave us, we hold in abeyance problems yet unsolved. We do not grant that a problem is unsolvable and then proceed to interpret the passage as if it were in error. Furthermore, we hold that a possible solution is all that is demanded. We do not have to prove that a possible interpretation is the correct solution but simply that there is a reasonable solution to the apparent problem. Since the Bible has proved itself trustworthy through the ages, we hold it innocent until proved guilty. The accuser must prove error. When problems are unresolved, it is not the Bible that is wrong, but rather our understanding of it. We wait either for more evidence or for a better theory to more coherently explain the evidence.

Alleged Internal Discrepancies

INTERNAL HISTORICAL PROBLEMS

Certain parallel accounts in both the Old Testament and the gospels seem to give contradictory accounts. The resolution of each such problem must be handled individually. However, a general approach to this category of problem is helpful. We must remember five guidelines.

First, to *say that Scripture is inspired even to the word and that there is no error does not mean that verbal identity is necessary.* It is only necessary that the words convey the truth. For example, when one gospel writer quotes Christ as speaking of the kingdom of God and another quotes Him as speaking of the kingdom of heaven, that is in no sense an error. *The kingdom of God* and *the kingdom of heaven* refer to the same thing, so each told the truth about what Christ said. A clear-cut example of that is found in the account of Jesus' prayers in the Garden of Gethsemane: "My Father, if it be possible, let this cup pass away from Me; yet not as I will, but as Thou wilt" (Matt. 26:39). A second time He prayed, "My Father, if this cannot pass away, except I drink it, Thy will be done" (Matt. 26:42). The two prayers do not contain exactly the same words, but they convey the same thought, so it is quite proper for Matthew to then say, "He . . . prayed a third time, saying the same thing once more" (Matt. 26:44). That indicates clearly the approach to quotations in the biblical culture. Words did not need to be verbatim duplication; they only needed to convey the truth accurately.

Consider Peter's confession of Christ:

Thou art the Christ, The Son of the Living God (Matt. 16: 16).	Thou art the Christ (Mark 8:29).	The Christ of God (Luke 9:20).

Are two of those quotations in error? No, for the confession is the same. Matthew apparently gave a more complete quotation, Mark the crucial element, and Luke a summary But all three told the truth.

Another example indicates even greater variation—but no discrepancy.

And when they came to the multitude, a man came up to Him, falling on his knees before Him, and saying, "Lord, have mercy on my son, for he is a lunatic, and is very ill; for he often falls into the fire, and often into the water. And I brought him to Your disciples, and they could not cure him" (Matt. 17:14-16).	And one of the crowd answered Him, "Teacher, I brought You my son, possessed with a spirit which makes him mute; and whenever it seizes him, it dashes him to the ground and he foams at the mouth, and grinds his teeth, and stiffens out. I told your disciples to cast it out, and they could not do it" (Mark 9:17-18).	And behold, a man from the multitude shouted out, saying, "Teacher, I beg You to look at my son, for he is my only boy and behold, a spirit seizes him, and he suddenly screams, and it throws him into a convulsion with foaming at the mouth, and as it mauls him, it scarcely leaves him. And I begged Your disciples to cast it out, and they could not" (Luke 9:38-40).

Which of those statements did the man actually make? He may have made all of them, with one gospel writer selecting part of his conversation and another writer selecting another part. On the other hand, it might be said with equal accuracy that he did not say any of them. Without doubt he spoke in Aramaic, and we are reading an English translation of a Greek translation of what he did say. In that sense verbal exactitude is not possible. However, the import is the same.

We do not hold that every record has to be an explicit, verbatim account. As a matter of fact, if witnesses in court give verbatim testimony, they immediately become suspect. The very fact that the gospel writers differ is further evidence of their independent integrity and authenticity. Verbal identity is not necessary to verbal accuracy. That is not to divide between words and meaning—true meaning expressed through words. There can be no true meaning without accurate words to convey that meaning. But, there may be more than one way to express the same meaning accurately.

Second, *one author's purpose may be different from that of another.* For that reason, many details are not relevant to his purpose and so may be left out. In reconstructing Christ's birth, passion, and resurrection, it is necessary to add together the various accounts to get a complete record. Matthew mentions both thieves as speaking against Christ (Matt. 27:44), whereas Luke mentions only one thief as speaking against Him (Luke 23:39ff.). Matthew's purpose seems to have been to highlight the opposition, and therefore, he only mentioned the initial attitude of both thieves, which, in the course of the hours on the cross, changed. Luke's purpose, on the other hand, was to highlight the repentance and salvation of one of the thieves. The biblical author did not add things that did not take place but, quite legitimately, was selective in what he did record.

Third, *Christ said similar things on different occasions* (as we noted in chap. 15). Not only did He say similar things, He also did similar things. I am confident that if He Himself had not referred to the feeding of the 5,000 and the feeding of the 4,000 as two separate events, some interpreters would have assumed that they were the same event and would have noted a conflict between the two accounts.

Fourth, *the rules for writing history were not the same in the Hebrew/Greek culture of biblical times as they are today*. The natural language of everyday life was used, and there was not often a felt need to have an exact transcription such as we would require for court records today. The biblical writers used what has been called "phenomenal language," everyday language that speaks of things as they appear. Precise scientific terminology was not the medium of communication. When the Bible writer describes the sun rising, he is not speaking scientifically any more than we are in speaking of a sunrise or a sunset. Likewise, the Bible speaks of the ends of the earth without implying that the earth is flat and square.

When Christ referred to the mustard seed as the smallest of all seeds (Matt. 13:32; Mark 4:31), He was not teaching botany. It would be similar to our speaking of basketball players as being the tallest of all men. That does not mean that there is not another taller man somewhere who does not play basketball. It is simply the natural language of everyday life speaking of things as they appear and are experienced by the people who are speaking and hearing.

Fifth, *there are transcription errors*. A number referred to in one Old Testament account sometimes differs from that recorded in another account. The Hebrew language is particularly susceptible to that kind of transcriptional error, since letters are used for numbers. To grant that there are differences in the hand-copied manuscripts still in existence does not automatically mean that there must be an error of transcription. Rather, a solution to the conflict should be sought first in other ways.

Although these transcriptional errors are very few in number, there are known differences among the manuscripts that are still in existence. That means that one manuscript or the other is in error. The task of the textual critic is to compare those manuscripts and seek to determine as closely as possible what the original must have been. Most textual differences, such as spelling differences, do not affect the meaning. It has been said that all of the New Testament differences in the text that affect the meaning of a passage could be printed on one page of the Greek New Testament, and that none of those affect a major doctrine. We do not have large numbers of ancient manuscripts for the Old Testament, and so textual comparison cannot always be made. But when parallel texts are not in agreement, it is reasonable to assume that there might have been an error in transcription.

NEW TESTAMENT QUOTATIONS OF THE OLD TESTAMENT

Earlier we considered the occurrence of Old Testament passages in the New Testament. As noted, more than 250 Old Testament quotations appear in the New Testament. Often those do not correspond with the exact wording of the Old Testament. Why is that?

1. Most of the quotations are from the common Bible in the time of Christ, a Greek translation of the Hebrew Old Testament. The New Testament quotation of that version (the Septuagint) would be similar to our quoting a contemporary version in English, for often the Greek translation was more a paraphrase than a literal translation.
2. Often there is no attempt to make a direct quotation. The Old Testament passage is abbreviated, or just the thought is conveyed.
3. As we have previously indicated, God, as the Author, has the right to give His own meaning or the interpretation of His intent in the original revelation.
4. There are a few quotations or references that come from books not in our canonical Bible, or perhaps from writings that are no longer in existence. For example, Enoch is quoted as saying, "Behold, the Lord came with many thousands of His holy ones" (Jude 14 quoted from I Enoch). Michael is quoted as saying, "The Lord rebuke you" (Jude 9), a quotation from a writing not known to us.

DOCTRINAL PROBLEMS

An approach to apparent discrepancy among Bible teachings was outlined in chapter 16.

Alleged Discrepancies with Other Historical Records

The Bible is one of many books of ancient history. When the Bible and another book of ancient history do not agree, an enemy of the Bible may assume that the other record is more accurate. But given our presuppositions, we hold the biblical record to be the more accurate. Even from an antibiblical perspective, the Bible is the most accurate historical record of ancient history available. Archaeology has consistently validated biblical records thus far. For example, critics of the Bible long held that Moses could not have written the Pentateuch because there was no writing in the time of Moses. Now archaeologists have discovered writing dating long before Moses. When Scripture, then, is in conflict with other ancient records, we simply respond that the data is not all in and that we will wait. In the meantime, we are confident in the record we have.

Alleged Scientific Discrepancies

MIRACLES

The greatest conflict between people who consider themselves scientifically minded and people of faith is the question of miracles. Miracles are a stumbling block to the naturalist. What approach do we take to the skeptic? Three elements are worth noting in responding to critics.

First, it should be noted that the problem is philosophical, not scientific, in nature. A person's presuppositions concerning the nature of reality determine his view of the possibility of miracles. If God exists, then He is free to work. If such a God exists, and He chose to visit the natural world, it would be incredible if He did not possess more than human power. On the other hand, if one's presuppositions rule out the realm of the spirit or a God who is free to intervene in the affairs of man, no amount of historical or even "scientific" (empirical) evidence would bring such a person to faith.

Second, the question of miracles is an historical one, not scientific in the sense of empirically demonstrated. The scientist observes, tests, and experiments. Proof is empirical. Historical proof in this sense simply does not exist. Historical evidence depends on the credibility of witnesses. Are those who witness an event qualified to evaluate it and trustworthy to report it with fidelity? Historical evidence for a miracle in Scripture is of the highest level, inasmuch as the witnesses were many, well qualified, and of the highest integrity. The question is one of history, not science.

Third, the miracles in the Bible were not constant and frivolous as in mythology. They had meaning and were related to the message. Furthermore, they are recorded as having occurred in clusters. It seems that miracles were clustered at the introduction of an era to validate God's intervention: miracles attended Abraham, Moses, Joshua, the prophets in the divided kingdom, Christ, and the apostolic church. That does not mean that miracles could not have been constant events. However, the significance of divine intervention would be eroded if it became the norm. Even remarkable events that occur frequently are not remarkable for long. Soon the extraordinary would become ordinary and the supernatural the natural expectancy.

A seriousness and meaning mark the biblical miracles. The provision of bread for the hungry crowd pointed to the Bread of Life. Raising the dead demonstrated the power of God and pointed to the final victory of life over death. All the miracles of Christ were signs showing who He was—His divinity and His character—the compassionate One. He refused the temptation to use His power to feed Himself or to perform a magical stunt to gain the acclaim of men. Biblical miracles were filled with meaning.

SCIENTIFIC THEORIES

What about scientific theories that are in conflict with biblical statements, and scientific facts that are in conflict with biblical interpretations? Two guidelines to remember when considering the biblical record and scientific theories are:

1. *The Bible was not given as a textbook on science.* To use it in that way is to abuse it. We should not try to create an adequate biology text from the data related to biological matters in Scripture. When the Bible touches on biology or other scientific matters, it is accurate. But to teach those subjects is not the purpose of revelation.
2. *Not every scientific theory has been proved.* It is erroneous to make a comparison between Galileo and the question of a flat earth, and Darwin and the question of organic

> evolution. Evolutionary origins for mankind are hypothetical, and the theories of scientists are in radical disagreement. On the other hand, the shape of the earth has been proved conclusively. So when a resolution between biblical data and scientific data is sought, one must begin not with scientific theory but with the proved facts of our natural world.

If a resolution is to be found when Bible and science disagree, we must be certain that our interpretation of the Scripture that seems to be in conflict with empirically derived data is a final and authoritative interpretation. For example, passages of Scripture that seem to indicate a flat earth or a three-story universe do not represent the only legitimate interpretation of the passages involved. Nor does the interpretation that dates creation at 4004 B.C. recommend itself as the only legitimate interpretation of the biblical data.

Most important, scientific fact and biblical fact cannot be in conflict, for God is the God of all truth, and both "the book of nature" and "the Book of divine revelation'" are from Him. When they appear to be in conflict, either the facts of nature are misunderstood, or the interpretation of Scripture is in error.

Apparent Discrepancy with Human Nature

Some teaching of Scripture seems to be in conflict with the possibilities of human nature. The disciples thought that when Christ told them that they should forgive 490 times in a single day. Mark Twain has given us the solution to most problems of that kind: "My problem is not with the parts of the Bible I don't understand but with those I do!" Actually most problems of that kind are not problems of understanding but problems of faith or of the will.

When we trust God for the resources necessary to obey Him and choose the path of obedience, most problems of understanding His will are resolved. "If any man is willing to do His will, he shall know of the teaching, whether it is of God, or whether I speak from Myself" (John 7:17). However, there is indeed a great deal of conflict between certain interpretations of Scripture and human experience. If a person believes that Scripture teaches the possibility of living a life wholly without sin, the call may not be to trust God more fully or obey Him more perfectly but to reexamine the biblical data. We must be certain that our interpretation is beyond question before demanding obedience to it from God's people.

Summary

The Bible is from God and thus without error. Therefore, we approach the problems of Scripture in the confidence that there is some solution, and refuse to interpret any passage as if it were in error. Although we do not feel obligated to solve every problem, we do need to seek diligently for solutions to problems of alleged discrepancies involving historical records, scientific data, and our understanding of human nature. In seeking those solutions, we use approaches appropriate to each kind of problem. When a possible solution is not forthcoming, we should withhold judgment, awaiting further light on the problem rather than treating the passage as if it were in error. The acceptance of error in the Bible is too high a price to pay for the satisfaction of resolving a problem the easy way by declaring the passage to be mistaken. If error is admitted, authority shifts at that point to the person who decides what is true.

In listing some of the general approaches to particular biblical problems, I do not intend to imply that most problems can be solved easily. Nor do I want to imply that all problems can be solved with diligence and intelligence. We give our minds to diligent search, yet no matter how we may labor, "now we see but a poor reflection; then we shall see face to face. Now I know in part; then I shall know fully, even as I am fully known" (1 Cor. 13:12, NIV). In the meantime, a person's love commitment will determine how he handles the data. For a document written long ago in an alien culture and foreign tongue over a period of 1,600 years by more than forty authors, dealing with matters of infinite truth, the miracle is that there are so few problems!

Selected Bibliography for Further Study

Archer, Gleason L. *Encylopedia of Bible Difficulties.* Grand Rapids: Zondervan, 1982.

Brauch, Manfred T. *The Hard Sayings of Paul.* Downers Grove, Ill.: InterVarsity, 1989.

Bruce, F. F. *The Hard Sayings of Jesus.* Downers Grove, Ill.: InterVarsity, 1983.

Haley, John W. *Alleged Discrepancies of the Bible.* Grand Rapids: Zondervan, 1977.

Kaiser, Walter C., Jr. *Hard Sayings of the Old Testament.* Downers Grove, Ill.: InterVarsity, 1988.

O'Brien, David E. *Today's Handbook for Solving Bible Difficulties.* Minneapolis: Bethany House, 1990.

Sire, James W. *Scripture Twisting: Twenty Ways the Cults Misread the Bible.* Downers Grove, Ill.: InterVarsity, 1980.

Stein, Robert H. *Difficult Passages in the New Testament: Interpreting Puzzling Texts in the Gospels and Epistles.* Grand Rapids: Baker, 1990.

18
Biblical Prophecy

Guideline: To understand predictive prophecy in Scripture, faithfully observe biblical guidelines.

A prophet in Scripture could be any authorized spokesman for God. Any direct revelation from God in Scripture could be called a prophecy. Because all of Scripture is of divine authorship, the whole of Scripture could be called a prophetic word, and every author a prophet. However, there is a special use of the terms *prophecy* and *prophet.* Predictive prophecy in a special way bears the mark of divine origin. And much of Scripture is predictive prophecy.

As we have seen earlier, there are two purposes for predictive prophecy. The chief purpose is to affect the conduct of those who hear the prophecy. Another purpose is met only when the prophecy is fulfilled. That purpose is to build faith, to establish confidence in the God who miraculously foretold events (John 13:19; 14:29; 16:4).

Fulfilled prophecy is the mark of God. In fact, we are invited to evaluate the authenticity of the prophet on the basis of whether his prophecy is fulfilled (Deut. 18:22; Isa. 41:23; 44:6-8; Ezek. 33:33).

In the early 1970s I received a written prophecy as follows:

> The State of Georgia is in danger of a very strong earthquake before the end of October, 1972. This earthquake will affect South Carolina greatly.

> Thus said the Lord, It will snow here in Columbia, South Carolina in May 1972.

The author understood the implications of making such a prophecy. He said:

> I feel I have been called of God to be a prophet and I am asking that you keep this letter on file as a matter of record until you have seen evidences of these.

Inasmuch as 1972 passed with neither of those prophecies proving to be true, one did not need to take seriously the additional prophecy, "God says the United States will be destroyed by an enemy in about 10 years." Had it snowed in South Carolina in May, one would have been well-advised to take seriously any other prediction from that source!

The purpose of fulfilled prophecy is to establish the authenticity of the prophet, and thus, to build faith in God, who has done the impossible, revealing events before they came to pass. Thus, the Old Testament prophecies that were fulfilled in the New Testament concerning the birth, life, death, and resurrection of Jesus Christ are of enormous value in establishing faith, not only in the God who revealed those events hundreds of years before they came to pass, but also in the person whose coming was foretold.

But what of unfulfilled prophecy? A great deal of predictive prophecy of Scripture is yet unfulfilled. In the time before a prophecy comes to pass, it is designed to affect present thought and conduct, not to satisfy curiosity concerning the future. Yet, in order for any prophecy to have an impact on our thinking or actions, its meaning must be understood. Are there any special characteristics of predictive prophecy in Scripture that must be considered? Predictive prophecy is a special and unique form of communication, and there are guidelines that will assist us in understanding this part of God's revelation.

Literal Language

The first guideline for understanding predictive prophecy in Scripture is a principle that guides in the interpretation of all Scripture: take the passage in its most simple, direct, and ordinary meaning unless there are compelling reasons to do otherwise. In other words, predictive passages, like any other human communication, should be taken as literal unless there are compelling reasons to understand them in some figurative sense. We will review those compelling reasons, which are legitimate, but first it is important to begin with the principle of looking at the straightforward, ordinary meaning of language. Consider the following prediction:

> Also I will restore the captivity of My people Israel, and they will rebuild the ruined cities and live in them, they will also plant vineyards and drink their wine, and make gardens and eat their fruit. I will also plant them on their land, and they will not again be rooted out from their land which I have given them, says the Lord your God. (Amos 9:14-15)

There is no indication in that passage that the language is to be taken figuratively. Though many interpreters do so, there are no compelling reasons, either in the ordinary rules of human language or in subsequent biblical revelation, for taking this passage figuratively. We must begin with the assumption that a prediction is to be understood literally. Nevertheless, to begin there does not mean that we end there. A great deal of prophecy is indeed figurative, and we must be able to distinguish between the literal and the figurative.

Figurative Language

The second guideline for understanding prophecy is to identify figurative passages by following the ordinary rules of language in making the distinction between literal and nonliteral. By way of review (see chap. 12), let us apply the three basic guidelines to the specific question of prediction in Scripture.

1. *Some language is obviously figurative because it would be absurd to understand it literally.* The moon might literally be turned into a vast pool of blood (Joel 2:31); a branch could conceivably grow out of a human being (Isa. 11: 1); a literal mountain could be removed (Zech. 4:7) —but none of those things is likely. On the surface, they

do not seem to be literal predictions of literal events to come. They were intended by the author and understood by the original readers just as we understand them today: as picture language. The task of the interpreter is to discover the literal meaning intended in the picture.

Dreams are one of the ways of revelation in the Bible, particularly in prophecy. When Pharaoh dreamed that seven healthy ears of corn would eat up seven blasted ears of corn, neither Pharaoh, his courtiers, nor his wise "prophets" understood that as a prediction of something that would literally come to pass. On the surface, it was intended to refer to an ordinary human event. So the search was on to interpret the prophecy, to find the literal meaning of an obvious figure. Daniel and Revelation are both filled with marvelous imagery of fantastic animal-like creatures that have never existed. To take those as prophecies of the appearance of literal beasts fitting such descriptions would not only trivialize the work of the prophet, it would be an unforgivable putdown of human intelligence. Many predictive passages are figurative on their face.

2. *Other figurative language is so identified in the context itself.* Daniel tells us of four great beasts that appeared from the sea. The first was like a lion with eagle's wings; the second was like a bear; the third, a leopard with four wings and four heads; and the fourth, so extraordinary that it could not be defined in terms of an animal known to the reader. What do those things signify? In the context itself, Daniel said, "These great beasts, which are four in number, are four kings, who will arise from the earth" (Dan. 7:17).

   When Christ stood before the Temple He predicted, "Destroy this temple and in three days I will raise it up" (John 2: 19). That could be a prediction of a literal event, and His hearers took it that way. But in the immediate context there is an explanation. "But He was speaking of the temple of His body" (v. 21). The result was that the disciples remembered His prediction after the prophecy was fulfilled "and they believed the Scripture, and the word which Jesus had spoken" (v. 22).

John explained many of the symbols of Revelation. The seven stars are the angels of the seven churches and the seven candlesticks are seven churches (1:20). The golden bowls full of incense are the prayers of the saints (5:8). This same passage identifies "the Lion that is from the tribe of Judah," "the Root of David," and "the Lamb" as references to Jesus Christ.

Those who are arrayed in white robes are the ones who come out of great tribulation, and the white robes symbolize their forgiveness in Christ (7:13-14). Jerusalem is figuratively called "Egypt" and "Sodom" (11:8). The great dragon, the old serpent, is identified as the devil, Satan, and the deceiver (12:9). The seven heads are seven mountains (17:9). The ten horns are ten kings (17:15). The waters are peoples, multitudes, and nations (17:15). The woman is the great city, the capital of the whole world (17:18).

Symbolic and typical language is often defined in the context quite clearly. The interpreter must not impose literal or other meanings on those symbols.

3. *Other Scriptures may identify an apparently literal statement as having a figurative meaning.* This is not a normal rule for understanding human language. It is only valid because all Scripture is God-breathed. As we have seen earlier, later Scripture may legitimately interpret earlier, because the Holy Spirit is the Author behind the authors. This does not mean it is legitimate for contemporary interpreters to take a literal passage and impose on it a figurative meaning. We hold that Scripture alone is inspired in this unique way. Only the biblical writers are authoritative spokesmen for God in giving wholly true revelation. Present-day interpreters are illuminated by the Holy Spirit, but their interpretation is subject to error and should have as its object the identification of the author's own intended meaning. But that which is not legitimate for the contemporary interpreter is quite legitimate for

> the Son of God or for His authorized spokesmen of divine revelation, the apostles in the New Testament.
>
> For example, when God predicted that there would be war between the descendants of Eve and the descendants of the serpent (Gen. 3:15), a literal understanding of that would lead one to expect a continuing war between men and snakes, with men crushing snakes' heads and snakes biting men's heels. However, subsequent Scripture does not reveal any such battle between people and snakes. On the other hand, it does reveal, as its main theme, the war between Satan and the powers of evil, and God's forces, with Eve's descendants as the battleground. The serpent is used in Scripture as a symbol of Satan (Rev. 12:9; 20:2). In fact, in the Genesis account, it was not the animal that was the focal point but rather the satanic power of darkness embodied in the serpent. Furthermore, the seed of the woman, although ordinarily a figure of the descendants of the woman, has gradually come to have a special meaning, culminating in Paul's interpretation: "He does not say, 'And to your seeds,' as referring to many; but rather to one, 'And to your seed,' that is, Christ" (Gal. 3:16). The promise to Eve was fulfilled in the New Testament person of the Descendant, the Man, the Deliverer who would vanquish Satan and crush his power.
>
> All of subsequent revelation seems to flow out of that original prediction. Subsequent revelation then interprets the prediction in its profound meaning, with cosmic implications.

Note again that *figurative* does not mean "mythical." The most profound of all truths may be expressed in nonliteral language. The goal of interpretation is to discern what the figure points to because the thing figured is to have a literal fulfillment in history. Predictions in Scripture, therefore, should be taken at their face value. If there are no compelling reasons to understand a nonliteral meaning, the literal meaning is to be accepted. Since the compelling reasons are limited to the above, present-day interpreters are not free to assign figurative or "spiritual" meanings to prophecy. Scripture itself is the authority, not the interpreter.

Yet, not all interpreters hold to those limitations.

> The biblical spiritualization of any item, connected with the typical Old Testament kingdom, includes any special import, or broadening meaning or richer implication that the Holy Spirit gives to this item, with a view toward realizing the fulfillment of the typical, Old Testament kingdom, in the anti-typical, New Testament kingdom, as identified with the church, both here and in eternity, hereafter.[1]

Wyngaardern's "principle" is nowhere enunciated in Scripture and is, in fact, an allegorizing approach (see chaps. 3 and 12). This particular approach does not treat all Scripture allegorically, for only selected prophetic passages are allegorized and all are treated as the same allegory: Israel typifying the church. As we have seen, for this "spiritualizing" approach to be valid, the author himself must identify his own teaching as figurative or subsequent Bible authors must so identify it.

Even if the New Testament seems to allegorize a specific Old Testament passage, that does not free the interpreter to treat other passages in the same way. If a New Testament author establishes a whole category explicitly designating something in the Old Testament as figurative, other Old Testament references to the same thing may have figurative characteristics. For example, the Tabernacle is explicitly cited as typical, so it is legitimate for the interpreter to examine every reference to the Tabernacle with this in mind. But without such biblical authorization, literal passages must be interpreted literally.

Typology

In considering figurative prediction, we need to give special attention to typology, a major category of prophecy. Types are common in Scripture—and commonly misunderstood. People, rites and ceremonies, acts and events, objects, offices (e.g., prophet, priest, and king)—all are used in Scripture as types. As we have seen in chapter 12, a type can be defined as a "prophetic symbol."

1. M. J. Wyngaardern, *The Future of the Kingdom in Prophecy and Fulfillment* (Grand Rapids: Baker, 1955), p. 85.

So to understand biblical types, it is helpful to compare them with ordinary symbols.

A symbol is something used to represent something else; it is often a material object representing something immaterial. For example, there are many symbols representing the Bible. It is referred to as meat, milk, bread, fire, water, seed, sword, and light. Symbolic language, like other figures of comparison, does not attempt to make a full-scale comparison of many points of likeness, but uses an object to designate one characteristic held in common by the symbol and the thing symbolized. The task of the interpreter is to identify, not from his own experience or culture, but from the biblical culture, what that point of reference is.

Understanding symbols is important, for they are abundant in Scripture. For example, there are symbolic numbers in the Bible. That does not mean that every time such a number is used it has a symbolic meaning. However, numbers often have a particular meaning, such as forty being used to symbolize testing, six to symbolize man, and seven to show completeness or perfection. There are material symbols such as brass, water, and leaven. Animals such as sheep, dog, and serpents may also be used symbolically. Places such as Babylon or Egypt are often used symbolically. People may be symbolic; for example, Abraham came to stand for faith. Events such as the Exodus and rituals such as circumcision are constantly used symbolically.

Symbols in the Bible are to be understood according to the same rules by which any symbolic language is understood. However, when a symbol is used to predict something future, it assumes a supernatural character and partakes of the nature of prophecy. The principles for understanding prophecy apply when prophetic symbols are used in Scripture.

Before considering an approach for understanding types, it might be helpful to note the distinction between symbols and types.

Symbols Versus Types

Symbol	*Type*
DEFINITION	
Something taken to represent another thing; often a material object representing something immaterial.	Prophetic symbolism
ESSENCE	
A symbol normally represents something different in essence from itself. A book and bread are quite distinct in essence, but bread is used to symbolize the Bible.	A type may be different in essence from the thing typified, as an ordinary symbol, but it may be something similar or even the same. Animal sacrifice and the sacrificial system were designed to foretell the sacrificial, redemptive work of Christ. Death is similar in both the type and the thing typified. Melchizedek and David are seen as types of Christ. Both the type and the object typified are human beings.
TIME RELATIONSHIPS	
A symbol is timeless. It can symbolize something past, present, or future.	A type, by definition, points to the future. It is usually an Old Testament type prefiguring something about redemption in the New Testament.
REFERENCE	
The thing symbolized may vary with a single symbol. Seed can refer to the word (Matt. 13:19)	A type points to *one particular fulfillment,* or antitype. Usually biblical typology relates to

or to sons of the kingdom (Matt. 13:38). Water can refer to cleansing, satisfaction, the Bible, or Jesus. A sheep can symbolize meekness or stupidity, vulnerability or sacrifice. A dove can symbolize peace, harmlessness, God's people, or the Holy Spirit. A serpent, on the other hand, can symbolize evil, Satan, or wisdom.	redemption. The Tabernacle is so used in the book of Hebrews.
PARALLEL ELEMENTS	
Usually a single parallel is intended between a symbol and the thing symbolized. As noted above, a single symbol may be used to parallel a variety of other things.	A type may parallel many points in the antitype. The Passover is a detailed picture of many elements of redemption. Likewise, the sacrificial system and the Tabernacle both contained many parallels to New Testament truth.

Note that a type often *contains* symbols. The Tabernacle is treated in the New Testament as having foreshadowed the redemption of Christ. Yet in the Tabernacle were many symbols, such as water, that pictured spiritual cleansing. A type, by definition, is an explicitly divinely planned prophecy. When items not designated as typical in Scripture are so named by the interpreter, he rather than Scripture tends to become the authority. Restraints are broken so that "spiritualizing" and using biblical language typically are doors opening to almost unlimited abuse. To call any illustration or application a type is to vest it with biblical authority. Debate is no longer possible, because "God has revealed it." This approach should be rejected. It is quite legitimate to see parallels and to use illustrative material, but in such a case the interpreter should clearly designate the authority as his own, not Scripture's.

We are often tempted to ignore symbols and types. But the problem is that the Bible is full of symbols. The opposite temptation is to delight in making use of the idea of typology and to improvise freely. We must reject both of those temptations, accept types as God's good and purposeful gift, and work hard to understand the meanings intended by the authors. Note that I am using symbol and type in their technical meanings. If we speak of symbolizing or typifying, the meanings are much broader, perhaps designating the same ideas for which we have used *allegorize* and *spiritualize* in chapter 3. There we concluded that the only valid way to spiritualize or allegorize (here we might add typify and symbolize) is when the author himself or some later Bible author gives a second or hidden meaning. Otherwise, we are restricted to using words in their ordinary, literal sense. When the interpreter finds the Old Testament full of typical language and symbolic references that the Bible itself does not identify, he has undermined the authority of Scripture.

Once a statement is identified by *Scripture* as a symbol or type, how do we identify the meaning? What meaning was intended by the author or, in the case of types, by the Holy Spirit? We may follow three guidelines.

1. *Consider the context.* The context is especially important in the case of symbols and types, because in different contexts a symbol may have different meanings. The context of Matthew 16:6 clearly says that leaven symbolizes wrong teaching. Yet what does the context of Matthew 13:33 indicate about leaven? Is the spread of the kingdom of God wrong? The context points, rather, to an expansion of a good thing.
2. *Refer to other Scriptures.* As we have learned, later revelation may identify something as symbolic that was not so identified in the Old Testament passage. Since Joseph is not identified as a type of Christ, one should not call him such. It is quite legitimate to see parallels to Christ in his sojourn in Egypt, his betrayal, his being sold, his advance to royal domain, and his forgiving spirit. Such parallels exist, yet there are other elements that cannot be made to parallel the experience of Christ, such as his marriage to the daughter of a pagan priest, the assignment of pagan names to his children, his arrogance with his brothers,

and his bringing his family out of their Promised Land. In addition, Joseph inaugurated one of the most oppressive regimes in human history. It is much safer to use Joseph as an illustration rather than a type.

If other Scriptures use a word symbolically, it is legitimate to try that symbolism in passages in which the meaning is not clear. But the context must determine whether the symbol can be carried over. For example, six is said to be the number of man (Rev. 13:18), but does it always have that significance? The context must determine. In Isaiah 53, sheep symbolize (by their straying) human beings and, in the same passage (by their meek docility) the Lord Jesus. Thus, when the term *sheep* is used in a symbolic way, it is legitimate to ask if either of those meanings is intended, or if yet another meaning was in the mind of the author.

3. *Let the author's intention control.* In identifying the meaning of a symbol, we must draw a parallel compatible with the nature of the object, as viewed by the author and the immediate recipients.

Since the relationship described in the Song of Solomon is nowhere identified as a type of Christ and the church, the interpreter should not assume that Solomon and the Holy Spirit intended it as a type. On the other hand, both the Old and New Testaments use the imagery of marriage to reflect the ideal relationship between God and His people. Therefore, it is quite legitimate to find in the Song of Solomon parallels to and illustrations of the spiritual relationship between God and His people. However, the interpreter should approach the text with the central purpose of determining what the author intended to communicate. If Solomon intended to write a song of human love, that is the meaning the interpreter should seek in all of the rich symbolism. Afterward, if need be, parallels to divine love may be pointed out and used as illustrations, but not as interpretations, of the meaning intended by Solomon.

This rule of language can be seen clearly in the case of symbols. When Scripture tells us not to cast our pearls before swine nor give that which is holy to dogs (Matt. 7:6), it jars the sensibilities of many contemporaries. How could this passage refer to giving spiritual truth to people who are not prepared to receive it wisely? How could we call people "swine" or "dogs"? The answer to such questions does not lie in the symbolism *we* find in a particular object, but in the point of parallel seen by the original hearers. In this case, Jesus' listeners would not analyze the many characteristics of a pig and apply them all to a person, but would rather take the overall image of incongruity and foolish wastefulness of giving an expensive jewel to an animal who was interested only in food. The earlier guideline of interpreting by the cultural understanding of the original recipient is clearly necessary in the case of symbols, inasmuch as symbolism represents a normal use of language. The same guideline also applies to biblical types.

Did Jewish people see their history as a typical prototype of the personal pilgrimage of every believer in subsequent generations? Is the wilderness symbolic of the normal Christian life, or is it a picture of a defeated Christian life? Is Canaan symbolic of the victorious Christian life or of heaven? The wilderness wanderings, particularly because there is a great deal of revealed interpretation of the significance of the event, may legitimately be used to *illustrate* various aspects of the Christian life. However, those historical events are not identified as *typical* in the same way that the Passover, the sacrificial system, and the Tabernacle are identified as being designed to foreshadow particular events. Therefore, it is not wise to use those applications as if they were interpretations of the meaning intended by the author. To call them types is to imply such an intended meaning or divinely revealed, and thus authoritative, interpretation. If the Bible does not identify something as being typical, it may still be legitimate to draw parallels and use the object, the event, or the person as an illustration, but it is questionable to designate it as a type.

We have considered in some detail guidelines for distinguishing figurative language in predictive prophecy and guidelines for understanding figurative language, especially types. This has been necessary because so much of prophecy is figurative, and this part of Scripture has been abused and misunderstood more than any other. We turn now to a special feature of prophecy, the time reference.

Special Time Features

Much of biblical teaching is timeless. For example, moral commandments apply to all people in all times. Symbols, as we have seen, are not time-related. But predictive prophecy relates to the future. That presents no problem when a specific event is predicted, such as the death of Jesus Christ. However, the New Testament made one thing clear about Old Testament predictions: the prophesied Messiah came, left, and is coming again. Old Testament prophecies that relate to the coming of Messiah could refer to either His first coming, His second coming, or both. Furthermore, some Old Testament prophecies that refer to an event in the near future are also applied by the New Testament to the Messiah many centuries later.

> Now all this took place that what was spoken by the Lord through the prophet might be fulfilled, saying, "Behold, the virgin shall be with child, and shall bear a son, and they shall call his name Immanuel," which translated means, "God with us." (Matt. 1:22-23)

Matthew is saying that Isaiah's prophecy (7:14) was of the virgin birth of the Messiah, even though the passage seems to most interpreters to speak of the prophet's own child (7:16; 8:3, 18). How could the prophecy refer to both future events at the same time? It is one of the special time-related features of predictive prophecy.

Multiple Reference

As we have argued earlier (chaps. 1, 3), it is quite legitimate to have more than one meaning in a statement. That is a common literary device. It is the essence of humor and of code language.

However, if a person is not trying to deceive, the secondary meaning must become clear either in the immediate context (as in the case of a joke, lest it become a lie) or in a larger context. For example, a code may be given to the recipients so that they can understand the secondary meaning. A subsequent explanation, either verbally or in action, may be given.

There is some debate as to whether the prophets actually had both the initial fulfillment and the larger fulfillment in mind, or whether the Holy Spirit revealed to later prophets a second or third reference. Nevertheless, all should agree that there is in some biblical prophecy a multiple reference and that any larger fulfillment or second reference must be made by the Holy Spirit through an inspired author of Scripture. The interpreter today does not receive infallible revelation or additional information not revealed through the biblical author.

Some call this multiple referencing "partial fulfillment"; the prophecy is one, but has both a partial and a more complete fulfillment. In the one view, there is only one meaning; in the other view, there are two or more meanings. Proponents of both views agree that the Holy Spirit must indicate any additional reference. Others call this "progressive fulfillment," emphasizing that the prophecy is one, with a larger or greater fulfillment at a later time. That time-related phenomenon in prophecy might be pictured as indicated in the illustration below.

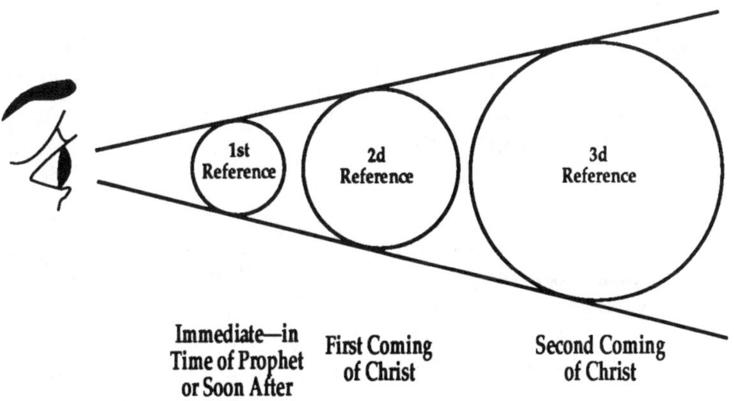

Consider some examples of multiple reference.

> The Lord your God will raise up for you a prophet like me from among you, from your countrymen, you shall listen to him. This is according to all that you asked of the Lord your God in Horeb on the day of the assembly, saying, "Let me not hear again the voice of the Lord my God, let me not see this great fire anymore, lest I die." And the Lord said to me, "They have spoken well. I will raise up a prophet from among their countrymen like you, and I will put My words in his mouth, and he shall speak to them all that I command him." (Deut. 18:15-18)

If the initial reference is to Joshua, the ultimate reference is to Christ (John 1:21,45; 6:14; Acts 3:22-23; 7:37). Similarly, David's messianic psalms often referred to his own experience, but the final, complete fulfillment was to be accomplished in his descendant the Messiah. Matthew 24 seems to be a New Testament example of multiple reference in a single prophecy. The destruction of Jerusalem seems clearly in mind, but the final fulfillment is certainly future.

SPLIT REFERENCE

A second and similar time-oriented feature of prophecy is what might be called split reference. Part of the prophecy might refer to one future event and another part to a second, later event. In multiple reference or "partial fulfillment," the same prediction refers to more than one fulfillment. The second is a more complete and final fulfillment of the same prediction, whereas in split reference, part of the prediction refers to one future event (near at hand) and another part of the prediction to another future event (more distant). The most celebrated example of split reference is the prophecy in Isaiah 61:1-3:

> The Spirit of the Lord God is upon me, because the Lord has anointed me to bring good news to the afflicted; He has sent me to bind up the brokenhearted, to proclaim liberty to captives, and freedom to prisoners; to proclaim the favorable year of the Lord, and the day of vengeance of our God; to comfort all who mourn, to grant those who mourn in Zion, giving them a garland instead of

> ashes, the oil of gladness instead of mourning, the mantle of praise instead of a spirit of fainting. So they will be called oaks of righteousness, the planting of the Lord, that He may be glorified.

Both the year of the Lord's favor and the day of vengeance are predicted in the same passage. When the Lord Jesus read that passage (Luke 4:16-21), He stopped midway and commented, "Today this Scripture has been fulfilled" (v. 21). Obviously, the balance of the passage was not yet fulfilled and lies in the future. That is a typical example of a split reference.

Similarly, consider Isaiah's prophecy of a coming Messiah:

> For a child will be born to us, a son will be given to us; and the government will rest on His shoulders; and His name will be called Wonderful Counselor, Mighty God, Eternal Father, Prince of Peace. (Isa. 9:6-7)

Here again, the first coming and the second coming of Christ are combined in a single prophecy. It is quite understandable that biblical interpreters before the time of Christ should see no time difference between the prophecies that spoke of the coming of a meek and mild, even suffering Messiah, and those that spoke of the coming of a conquering king. It is not simply that one naturally prefers a physical deliverance from bondage and the victory of a conquering king. The predominant view of prophetic Scripture at the time of Christ was based on the emphasis in the prophetic Scriptures concerning what we now know to be the second coming of the Messiah.

The elements of multiple reference and split reference should not come as a surprise. When the future is predicted and a whole series of events are anticipated, a summary view may legitimately combine a number of elements, which at a later time may be distinguished. So it is with biblical prophecy. Those characteristics should be borne in mind when interpreting a specific prophecy, whether already fulfilled or yet to be fulfilled. Ours is the advantage of standing between the first and second comings of Christ so that certain distinctions can easily be made. On the one hand, we should be prepared to discover that what may appear in prophecy to be a single event, upon fulfillment may break into consecutive elements. On the other hand, if we believe that we discern separate events and a specific time sequence that are not so clearly seen by other interpreters, the experience of interpreters before Christ should caution us to modesty concerning the authority we invest in our particular interpretation.

One problem with dogmatically detailing future events is that the very dogmatism, if misplaced, may lead us astray when events other than those we anticipated unfold, as in the case of first-century students of the Old Testament prophetic Scriptures. In fact, when strongly held opinions prove to be false, the misunderstanding that results can undermine faith rather than establish it.

Summary

The great body of predictive prophecy in Scripture can be understood when reasonable guidelines are followed: begin with the assumption that the prediction is intended as literal; use guidelines for identifying and interpreting the figurative; and be alert to the special time features of possible multiple or split references.

Having considered in some detail guidelines that would help in interpreting the large body of prophecy found in Scripture, it is well to return to the original statement of purpose. The primary purpose of unfulfilled prophecy is to condition the way we think and behave today. For that reason, in our interpretations, let us concentrate on discerning what the Holy Spirit originally intended as the response to a particular prophecy. If Christ said that the gospel of the kingdom shall be proclaimed in all the world for a witness, and then the end shall come, what profit is there in wrangling over the future sequence of events? Is it not far more profitable to look at the great body of New Testament teaching concerning the proclamation of the gospel, and get on with the job assigned us? The fact that both the living and the dead will participate in the glory of Christ's coming (1 Thess. 4:16-17) is intended to give us great comfort, not to divide us over precise delineation of the sequence of events.

The other purpose of prophecy, that it should establish one's faith upon its fulfillment, is another reason to diligently study prophecy. Those prophecies that already have been fulfilled should strengthen the faith of Christians and challenge the skepticism of unbelievers. Prophecies not yet fulfilled should be identified, particularly in their broad, clear outline, so that as the events themselves unfold, we may be established in our confidence and respond in obedience to their instruction.

Selected Bibliography for Further Study

OVERVIEWS

Clouse, Robert G., ed. *The Meaning of the Millennium: Four Views.* Downers Grove, Ill.: InterVarsity, 1977.

Erickson, Millard. *Contemporary Options in Eschatology: A Study of the Millennium.* Grand Rapids: Baker, 1977.

Ludwigson, R. *A Survey of Bible Prophecy.* Grand Rapids: Zondervan, 1973.

SURVEYS OF SCRIPTURE TEXTS

Beiderwolf, William E. *The Second Coming Bible.* Reprint. Grand Rapids: Baker. 1977.

Payne, J. Barton. *Encyclopedia of Biblical Prophecy: A Complete Guide to Scriptural Predictions and Their Fulfillment.* Grand Rapids: Baker, 1980.

PREMILLENNIAL

Feinberg, Charles L. *Millenialism: The Two Major Views.* Rev. ed. Moody: Chicago, 1980.

Kaiser, Walter C., Jr. *Back Toward the Future: Hints for Interpreting Biblical Prophecy.* Grand Rapids: Baker, 1989.

Ladd, George Eldon. *The Blessed Hope.* Grand Rapids: Eerdmans, 1956.

AMILLENIAL VIEW

Hokema, Anthony A. *The Bible and the Future.* Grand Rapids: Eerdmans, 1979.

POSTMILLENNIAL VIEW

Boettner, Lorraine. *The Millennium.* Phillipsburg, N.J.: Presb. and Ref., 1957.

SPECIAL TOPICS

Hengsenberg, E. W. *The Christology of the Old Testament.* 2 vols. Reprint. Grand Rapids: Kregel, 1970.

Morris, Leon. *Apocalyptic.* Grand Rapids, Eerdmans, 1977.

DIVINE AUTHORSHIP: APPLICATION

PRINCIPLE:

Since Scripture is God-breathed, it is absolute in its authority for doctrine and life.

Introduction

> The Holy Scriptures are able to give you the wisdom that leads to salvation through faith in Christ Jesus. All Scripture is inspired by God and is useful for teaching the truth, rebuking error, correcting faults, and giving instruction for right living, so that the man who serves God may be fully qualified and equipped to do every kind of good work. (2 Tim. 3:16-17, TEV)

Any teaching derives its authority from that inherent in its source. Paul here identified God as the source of all Scripture. In that way the whole Bible, and the Bible alone, is of ultimate authority for doctrine and practice. To acknowledge this basic truth concerning the authority of Scripture does not ensure that the Scripture will actually function as the authority for a Christian or a group of Christians. The purpose of Scripture is to lead to salvation (2 Tim. 3:15) and to equip the Christian for life and service (v. 17). In doing so, the Bible teaches what to believe and what not to believe, how not to behave and how to behave (v. 16). But it is quite possible to swear allegiance with great fervor to the Bible as one's final authority while believing and behaving contrary to the teaching of Scripture. The Bible can thus become a "constitutional monarch," enjoying the pomp and affection of adherents whose real authority is some long-held tradition, a sectarian system of doctrine, a cultural pattern, or even personal preference. How does the Bible become the functional authority in the life of a Christian or a church?

The degree to which the Bible actually functions as the ultimate authority depends on answers to the following questions:

Who said it?
What did he say?
What did he mean?
For whom is it intended?
What response does God desire?

Theology and literary criticism seek answers to the question, "Who said it?" If God is not the Author behind the author and if the writer or speaker is not an authorized spokesman for God, that word does not have the authority of God.

Textual criticism and, in a secondary way, translation seek answers to the second question, "What did the author say?"

Exegesis, using the principles of interpretation, must answer the third question, "What did the author mean?" If one's understanding of a passage differs from the author's intended meaning, the interpretation is not God's authoritative word to the interpreter or to those who follow him. The answer to this question has been the subject of our study thus far.

The church has marshalled an impressive array of scholarship and literature to answer those three questions. But who is charged with the responsibility of answering the fourth question, that is, to determine the intended recipient? We do not even have a discipline assigned to the task or guidelines to help the Christian or his pastor determine this crucial issue. This chapter will seek to outline guidelines for answering this crucial question: "For whom is it intended?"

The final question, "What response does God desire?" does have such a discipline. We call it theology (see chap. 16). But it deals almost exclusively with what God intends us to know and believe. At that most crucial point of all biblical studies, what God intends us to *be* and *do,* we stammer and improvise and go astray. We train theology students in criticism, exegesis, doctrine, and methods of preaching and counseling but offer few if any ways for them to know with certainty to whom any specific passage is addressed and to tell their people with authority what God intends them to be and do. That is the root cause of the yawning gap between classroom exegesis and pulpit proclamation. Much application can be done intuitively because of the clarity of Scripture—it is to reveal, not to obscure. And so the disciple and his discipler often have done quite well. But it would be much better were we to include the task of application in the assignments of the exegete and the theologian; or to introduce some new discipline (call it application) and require that it formulate principles for designating God's intended recipients (chap. 19) and for making the application of truth to life (chap. 20). For that neglect the church is paying dearly with confusion resulting in false doctrine and, especially, false living.

My first premise is that the Bible itself must answer each of those five questions about itself; the meaning of Scripture must be the controlling factor in our conclusions. To impose from other sources answers to the question of authorship, text, interpretation, intended recipient, or God's desired response is to place that source above the authority of Scripture.

John Warwick Montgomery has written,

> A passage of Holy Scripture is to be taken as true in its natural, literal sense unless the context of the passage itself indicates otherwise, or unless an article of faith established elsewhere in Scripture requires a broader understanding of the text. . . . Extra-biblical linguistic and cultural considerations must never decide the interpretation of a text; and any use of extra-biblical material to arrive at an interpretation inconsistent with the truth of a scriptural passage is to be rejected. Extra-biblical data can and should put critical questions to a text, but only Scripture itself can legitimately answer questions about itself.[1]

1. John Warwick Montgomery, "Whither Biblical Inerrancy?" *Christianity Today*, 29 July 1977, p. 42.

19

Identifying the Audience God Intended

Guideline: Every teaching of Scripture is to be received universally, unless the Bible itself limits the audience, either in the context of the passage itself or in other biblical teaching.

After the meaning of a passage is established, it must be applied to life. In our final chapter we will consider guidelines for applying Scripture. But before that can be done, a prior question must be answered: "Is the message of the passage to people of all time, or is it to some specific person or group that does not include me?"

To answer that crucial question, we now turn to criteria based on the presupposition that the Bible alone is the final authority for faith and living. Therefore, we must look to the Bible itself to decide the recipients God intended for any given passage. There are several ways to determine the audience God intended: the context, the audience designated by the author, history, and other Scripture.

Context

The immediate context of a passage may indicate a limited audience. The author may plainly state his intended recipient, or it may be implied in the context.

AUDIENCE DESIGNATED BY THE AUTHOR

Matthew designated his recipients when he recorded these words of Jesus: "Blessed are the poor in spirit" (Matt. 5:3). All who are poor in spirit qualify for blessing. When Luke recorded Jesus' words, "Blessed are you who are poor" (Luke 6:20), he designated his recipients from among all the materially poor of the world. Those Jesus addressed were blessed. Certainly not all poor people are blessed, and much confusion has arisen over confounding the two passages, in which the recipients are clearly designated.

Both Jesus and Paul were single and taught reasons for the superiority of that state (Matt. 19:12; 1 Cor. 7:8). However, both Jesus and Paul, in the contexts of those passages, restricted the application of that teaching. Jesus said, in response to the disciples' observation that it would be better to remain single (since divorce is out), "not all men can accept this statement, but only those to whom it has been given." Paul said that though it would be well if all men were unmarried like he, not everyone had the ability to remain single. So the teaching is addressed not to all Christian men but only to those so gifted. It is important to determine from the context, not from one's theological, cultural, or personal preference, the author's intended audience, whether all people or just believers; whether Old Testament Jews or New Testament Christians; whether first-century Christians or all Christians; or whether the designated addressee or others as well.

HISTORY AS REVELATION

An inspired record of redemptive history is recorded for our example and admonition (1 Cor. 10:11). Whatever the Bible records is true; history took place the way it is recorded. But to be authoritative as a model for behavior—a God-given norm for all people of all time—any historic event must be so designated by an authorized spokesman for God. That an event was reported to have truly happened does not necessarily make it a revelation of God's universal will.

Historical events are often reported without comment as to God's approval or disapproval, as in the case of Lot's daughters and their incest (Gen. 19:34). Even when a moral evaluation is made—an act commended or condemned—the reason for that evaluation may not be recorded. For that reason, perhaps, Scripture nowhere hints that any event, by its inclusion in the Bible, is made normative for all people of all times.

How much less evidence there is that activities not recorded should be forbidden. And yet zealous students of Scripture constantly set norms from the book of Acts, for example. Principles for indigenous mission activity, including what must be done and what must not be done, are deduced from what the apostles did and did not do. Immediate baptism of converts, banning of musical instruments in church buildings, and many other specifics are made normative on the basis of whether or not they were a part of the apostolic church. Many use Acts in that way to build a doctrine of speaking in tongues as a necessary sign of being Spirit-filled. That is not a legitimate use of history recorded in Scripture. (There is a legitimate use, which will be considered later.) Consider two kinds of history-related teaching: historic events and teaching directed to a specific individual or group.

Historic events. Elihu's speech to Job may or may not make sense, but it does not have authority as revealed truth. The inspiration of the book of Job means only that the record of his speech is accurate.

We consistently make normative Paul's response to the jailer, "Believe in the Lord Jesus, and you shall be saved" (Acts 16:31), but we consistently refuse to make normative Christ's response to a similar question of the rich young ruler, "Sell your possessions and give to the poor . . . and come, follow Me." We resist this even though Christ repeats it in Luke 12:33 as a normative statement. Why is it that we tend to feel Paul's behavior is always exemplary and that Peter's behavior is (almost) always the opposite? Maybe some of what Paul did was bad, and maybe some of what Peter did was good!

An event or specific behavior should not be considered normative for today solely on the basis that it is recorded in the Bible. It must be evaluated in the light of direct biblical teaching.

Teaching directed to a specific individual or group. There are many passages in Scripture addressed to an individual or a group. When those injunctions to a specified individual or group parallel general teaching found elsewhere, they may be viewed as normative, but not on their own strength. When God said to Moses, "Remove your sandals . . . for the place on which you are standing is holy ground" (Ex. 3:5), or when Christ said to the disciples, "Untie them [the donkey and her colt], and bring them to Me" (Matt. 21:2-3), all will agree that those commands were historic-specific, not to be applied to anyone other than Moses or the disciples. But that principle can be abused so that all the teachings of Christ or those found in the epistles are made historic-specific rather than normative. Some hold that Christ was speaking to His disciples or to certain people, and therefore, such teachings do not necessarily apply to us today. And some seek to distinguish among the epistles, calling some "letters" and others "epistles." The letters are regarded as less authoritative than the epistles because they are judged to be addressed to specific situations and not to the church universal. Therefore, they are not considered to be authoritative for us today.

A similar question is raised concerning the imprecatory psalms: Is the example of the psalmist right or wrong?[1] The imprecatory psalms call upon God to curse the psalmists' enemies. They are authentic revelations of the feelings and the experiences of the authors. But some wonder whether it is legitimate to assign them the status of inspired testimony. Once again we must insist that any approach to Scripture must be the approach that Scripture takes to itself; otherwise, Scripture is no longer the ultimate authority. The apostles treated the teachings of Christ as the ultimate authority. Furthermore, there is nothing internal that suggests a distinction between epistles and letters or between the testimony of the psalmist and the revelation of God's will. The New Testament consistently treats the psalms as revelations of God's will. Peter treats Paul's writings in the same way (2 Pet. 3:15-16).

We must take the psalms, the teachings of Christ, and the teachings of the epistles as universal in their application and normative for us today because that is the way the early apostles took those teachings. That should remain true unless the context indicates an obvious historic limitation to the person or people addressed. For example, when Paul gave a list of specific greetings and instructions at the end of a letter, the context obviously limit-

1. See T. Norton Sterrett, *How to Understand Your Bible* (Downers Grove, Ill.: InterVarsity, 1974), p. 176.

ed the application of the command to a specific person and occasion. In cases where the distinction is difficult to make, in the interest of maintaining the independent authority of Scripture, we should assume the normative nature of the teaching rather than dispensing with it too easily. To broaden the scope of this principle would be far too costly for the independent authority of Scripture.

In summary, Scripture itself may limit the audience in the immediate context through a specific statement of the author or through an obvious requirement of the historical setting.

Subsequent Revelation

Subsequent revelation may clarify the recipient of any given teaching. For example, not all Old Testament teaching applies to the New Testament Christian. The most obvious case is the entire sacrificial system that was done away in Christ (Heb. 9-10). But the Bible itself must designate any change in the recipient intended by the author. Otherwise, Scripture loses its independent authority to the one who sets aside any teaching without biblical authorization.

Some disallow the entire Old Testament as normative. They believe that no teaching in the Old Testament is mandatory for the Christian unless it is repeated in the New Testament. However, to require a New Testament repetition is a dangerous mandate that is nowhere given in the New Testament. The New Testament authors and Jesus Himself treated the Old Testament (the only Bible they had) as the authoritative Word of God. It is not legitimate to set aside any Old Testament teaching without the authorization of subsequent revelation in the New Testament. Many Old Testament commands, such as those against bestiality and rape, are not repeated in the New Testament. Are they no longer normative? We must treat the Bible as it treats itself, as the Word of God, with absolute authority for the Christian life.

Of course, the New Testament may set aside a whole class of teaching, for it is not necessary for each specific teaching to be set aside. For example, all teaching that outlines God's way in relating to His people as citizens of the state (Israel) are modified by the New Testament teaching on the church. "My kingdom is not of this world," said Christ, a condition not true in the same way in Old Testament times. Specifics within that class may be spelled out as in Christ's commands to put away the sword. The church should not advance by force as did ancient Israel. But there are many other teachings in the Old Testament that are of this same class and which may not be specifically set aside in the New Testament. They are, nevertheless, no longer in effect because the whole class of teaching has been modified. For example, laws concerning the succession of kings are restricted in application to Israel and do not apply to the church or civil government today, because Christ's "kingdom is not of this world."

In Galatians, Paul not only disallowed circumcision as a necessary sign of a covenant relationship with God, but the entire system, along with circumcision, seems to have been set aside. All foods are reclassified as legitimate for Christians (Mark 7:13; Acts 10:15), so the dietary laws, though perhaps instructive, are no longer normative for Christians today. In that way, specific areas of teaching in the Old Testament—the ceremonial function of the law, the covenant relationship of a specific people signified through circumcision, civil government, dietary laws—have been specifically set aside in the New Testament.

The phenomenon of subsequent modification is also seen within the New Testament. In Matthew 10:9-10, Christ was not telling twentieth-century Christians to travel without money. We know that because He later rescinded the initial instruction (Luke 22:36). But the notoriously weak arguments from silence must not be introduced here. To hold that speaking in tongues is no longer valid on the basis that New Testament authors stopped talking about it after Paul wrote to the church at Corinth is to impose external criteria for changing the recipient of a clear Bible teaching.

But what if doctrine or behavior taught in one part of Scripture appears to contradict what is taught in another? How can both teachings be addressed to the contemporary church? Many times two or more passages in Scripture appear to make conflicting statements. Since we are committed to the basic tenet that all Scripture is inspired of God, and therefore that it is all true, apparent discrepancies must be resolved if at all possible. Use all the principles of interpretation in order to be sure of the meaning. Examine the purpose of the author, the audience intended, the grammar, and the historical and cultural setting of the writing. Should the meaning, the recipient, or the application remain uncertain, one may apply what has been called the "analogy of faith" (see chap. 16 for details on this concept). M. Cellerier defines this in his classic manual on hermeneutics:

> The method of interpretation called Analogy of Faith appeals to the general character of truth for the explanation of a special passage. This evidence and this authority vary according to the number, unanimity, clearness and distribution of the passages upon which they are founded.[2]

In other words, the teaching to be accepted for faith and obedience when the apparent discrepancy is unresolved is that which has the greater emphasis and clarity.

All of these approaches are legitimate when seeking to resolve apparent discrepancies among Bible teachings. A legitimate approach in reconciling conflicting teachings is to see if both were intended for the same audience. For example, Paul seemed to indicate that long hair for men was wrong by nature (1 Cor. 11:4). But uncut hair was the sign of holiness for the Old Testament Nazirite (Judg. 13:5; 1 Sam. 1:11). The audiences in the Old Testament and the New Testament were different. That helps to relieve the tension between the two teachings. Of course, it does not resolve the question of which of those commands, if either, is applicable today. Many of the guidelines we have studied should be employed in seeking to answer that question. But the comparison is helpful, indicating that long hair as such is not an intrinsically moral issue for all men of all times.

Note that application of any teachings that have not been reconciled should be made tentatively, not with dogmatic authority. The theme of this chapter is clear: all Scripture should be received as normative for every person in all societies of all time unless the Bible itself limits the audience. That limitation may take place in the immediate context or in other parts of Scripture.

But there are many who limit the audience to biblical times on other grounds. If one accepts the final authority of Scripture,

2. M. Cellerier, *Biblical Hermeneutics,* trans. Charles Elliott (New York: Randolph, 1881), pp. 172-81.

any such approach is not legitimate. Therefore, before going on to study guidelines for making the application of teaching intended for us today, consider some of these approaches, which are not legitimate.

Wrong Approaches for Limiting the Audience and Determining Application

Some hold that if the Bible is correct it must be believed and obeyed, but where it errs it is not normative. When the Bible speaks of the creation of the first couple, when Christ treated demons as if they existed, when Paul gave a distinct role in marriage to the husband, those teachings were in error and therefore are not binding for faith and behavior. An even more radical approach is taken by liberation theologians, who do theology by beginning with what God is doing in the world today. This activity of God in history, such as in social revolution, is the revelation of His will. The Bible is then used only as a source book for other examples of God's activity in history. Although those approaches set aside the authority of Scripture, each has been advocated by people who call themselves evangelicals.

Other approaches exist that are not so obviously nonbiblical. We cannot consider all of them, but we should identify those that seem to have the greatest influence among Bible-believing people. We will examine briefly two approaches that use cultural factors to define meaning, limit the audience, or determine application. Then we will consider two that use certain principles to define meaning, limit the audience, or determine application.

USE OF CULTURE TO DEFINE MEANING, LIMIT THE AUDIENCE, OR DETERMINE APPLICATION

The response God desires today. This approach examines the words of Scripture to determine the meaning. The intent is to get behind the meaning of a passage, however, in order to discern what response the author desired from his original audience. When that response is identified, through a process called "dynamic equivalence interpretation," the present-day interpreter then asks, "How can I reproduce that response in my audience today?"

The answer to this question will be the revelation of God's will. It will be the authoritative message for today.

To those who take this approach, the concepts are, as they say, culture-bound. The task of the interpreter is to discern the cultural universal in the biblical data and reproduce, in contemporary society, the impact God intended.

In this approach, all Scripture—as all other human writing—reflects the culture of the writer. Therefore, the task of the Bible student is to set the truth free from its cultural wrappings so that it can be applied to contemporary life. To do this, all the tools of cultural anthropology are used. When it is clear what the author intended to happen in his cultural setting through his writing, we are then prepared to seek the same response in our audience today in a way that fits our culture.

For example, Paul taught that spiritual leaders should have only one wife (1 Tim.3:2; Titus 1:6). That is what he said. In fact, that is what he seemed to mean. But what was he trying to accomplish? One interpreter will say he was trying to make sure that the church had leaders who were qualified, in the eyes of their fellow believers, to lead. He was setting criteria for leadership that were culturally relevant to their society. What about today? Well, in a particular African tribe, the requirements for leadership are just the opposite. A man is not fit to lead until he can afford and acquire at least a second wife. So how is one true to the command of Paul to Timothy and Titus? In this tribe, he must require that to serve as elders of the church, men must have at least two wives. No matter that this is the opposite of what Paul said. The purpose of the command must be discovered through cultural analysis and applied today in some culturally equivalent way.

In this approach to Scripture, current cultural understanding has displaced the apostle as the authority for church life. The end result is not merely that the church is free to baptize or not, as the culture may demand, or that one may arrange church government in accordance with local cultural norms. Far more basic theological teaching is modified through cultural understanding. For example, it is taught that people can be saved without knowledge of Jesus Christ through faith in what they do know of God and that which their culture will permit them to receive.

Universal cultural pattern. Only Bible teaching that reflects a universal cultural pattern is normative for all people in all societies. This position accepts for application today (with authority as God's certain will) only those teachings in Scripture that reflect universal cultural norms. The command "You shall not steal" (Ex. 20:15) is sometimes given as an example. The rest of biblical teaching is culture-bound, speaking to cultural specifics.

The task of the interpreter is to set the teaching free from its cultural bondage to determine a universal truth or principle. Depending upon the interpreter, Christ's teaching against divorce, Paul's teaching against homosexuality, and biblical norms for the role of the woman in marriage are all culturally bound teachings and not normative. Therefore, they do not demand obedience in every culture of every age.

This position is similar to the preceding one except that the interpreter does not try to get behind the meaning of a passage to discover the impact intended by the author; instead, he seeks the enduring principle in the meaning itself. In this position, the meaning itself is valid, but is normative (applicable universally) only when a culturally universal truth is being taught.

I once was seated across the luncheon table from a leading biblical linguist. We were discussing the question of what teachings in Scripture are normative.

"What do you think," I asked, "should be required of all people in every tribe and culture?"

He responded immediately, "Those teachings which are culturally universal."

"For example?"

"Well. . . " He hestitated. "I'm not altogether sure."

"Something like the forbidding of murder?" I suggested.

"Why, yes," he said, "that would be a cultural universal."

"I am surprised to hear that," I replied. "I would have thought that killing, and perhaps even eating the victim, would be a virtue in some societies."

"Well, I guess you're right."

The conversation continued in the same vein with considerable uncertainty as to whether there were any universally valid cultural norms. Since the Bible itself makes no distinction between cultural universals and cultural specifics, for us to seek to make that distinction and undertake the enormous task of positively identifying any cultural universals is well nigh impossible. And to attempt the distinction will result in making culturally relative teaching out of most Scripture. Thus, the independent authority of Scripture is set aside.

In chapter 8 we discussed the use of the cultural context in understanding the author's intended meaning, and earlier in this chapter we suggested an approach that limits the audience by recognizing the historical setting. How do those approaches differ from the cultural relativism we have just criticized?

LEGITIMATE AND ILLEGITIMATE USES OF CULTURE

Another incorrect approach in limiting the audience and the application is the wrong use of culture. Consider the distinction between the legitimate and illegitimate uses of culture.

History and culture. Is there a legitimate distinction between history and culture? Is history not the record of behavior as well as of events? Is culture not a part of history? The two overlap and exhibit great interplay, so that they are sometimes hard to distinguish. But I believe the distinction is crucial for biblical interpretations.

What is culture? Although many definitions exist, contemporary interpreters are using the term *culture* in the technical sense of all human language, behavior, morals, values, and ways of doing things in any particular group of people.

Let us agree at the outset that unevaluated and uninterpreted cultural elements in Scripture may be no more normative than unevaluated and uninterpreted historic events. But the difference between the two is vast. Much of history in Scripture is unevaluated and uninterpreted and, therefore, should not be made normative for other people in other times and places. However, virtually all the teachings of Scripture give cultural evaluation. Human behavior, morals, values, and ways of doing things are constantly evaluated, prohibited, or commanded. It is not too much to say that the purpose of divine revelation is to create a culture, a special people of God. He is out to change culture; although, at the same time, He uses human culture as a vehicle for revealing Himself and His truth.

The teachings of Scripture are not often "aimed at" history. True, historical events are often demonstrated to be the acts of

God, but revelation simply records the setting, whereas most biblical teaching is directly "aimed at" culture, for human behavior is the object of revelation.

My contention is that the historical context of teaching is normative only if Scripture treats it that way, whereas the cultural context is normative unless Scripture treats it as limited. As we have seen, history is often recorded without any evaluation as to whether the behavior is good or bad. God must take the initiative through revelation to make it normative. David's polygamy, uncondemned in Scripture, should not be taken as a normative model today, nor should Paul's taking a Jewish religious vow. But the apostles' response, "We must obey God rather than men" (Acts 5:29), although unevaluated in the immediate context, is obviously viewed as a model to follow because of abundant teaching in other parts of Scripture.

It is true that culture may also be recorded without an evaluation as to whether it is to be taken as normative. In such cases, culture is no more normative than a historical record. Was the behavior of the slaveholder in making his slaves serve tables after working the fields all day—and giving them no thanks—a normative model to be followed in labor-management relations (Luke 17)? We cannot conclude that. Unevaluated cultural behavior, however, is much less common than unevaluated historical events because the purpose of revelation is to create a way of behavior, a culture. Therefore, value-free or culturally relative records of behavior are not typical. Rather, cultural change is the point of revelation, and God must take the initiative through revelation to make cultural teaching not normative.

Thus the teachings of God concerning human behavior are final in authority and are to be set aside only if Scripture itself limits the audience intended or the response God desires. If anyone else sets such "cultural" teaching aside, he has become the authority sitting in judgment on Scripture.

Most of us might agree that washing another's feet at mealtime, leaving ladies' hair uncut, and other such commands are culturally specific and therefore do not apply universally. Specifically, they do not apply to us! However, we have discovered that the same principle can apply to virtually any teaching of Scripture. But to set aside any Scripture simply on the basis that it is cultural and therefore valid for only one specific cultural setting, is to establish a principle that can be used to set aside any or even all biblical teaching. With such a view, the interpreter becomes the authority over Scripture, establishing as normative for human belief or behavior only those elements of Bible teaching or those principles deduced from Bible teaching that prove universally valid according to some cultural criteria.

Because of the difference between historical record and culturally based teaching, we can say that historic events that Scripture does not evaluate should not be made normative. But of teaching concerning human behavior (what *should* happen as distinct from what *did* happen) we must conclude that the behavior is normative unless Scripture itself limits the recipient or application. No, Scripture is not a prisoner of culture. Rather culture, in the language of biblical authors and the context in which they wrote, is the vehicle of revelation, and at the same time, that very culture is the object of change demanded by Scripture. To disallow any teaching of the Bible because it is cultural is to make all Scripture vulnerable to this relativistic approach.

Valid cultural argument. Is the cultural context of no value at all? Can culture never be used to determine the audience or the response God desires? Perhaps culture is significant when the *Bible itself* gives a culturally based reason for a particular teaching. For example, Paul used a cultural argument to support his injunction to work with one's hands (1 Thess. 1:11). Scripture may not give a reason for a teaching, but if it does, the reason becomes a part of the teaching. Here, the reason given is not some eternal moral principle, but a cultural argument: "so that you may behave *properly* toward outsiders and not be in any need" (4:12; emphasis added). In other words, the enduring principle is given that Christians should earn their livelihood as a testimony to non-Christians. It reflects the cultural pattern ("properly") that, for Christians in Thessalonica, would mean manual labor. Since the argument is based on culture, if that cultural situation is not present, only the principle (not the command) should be made normative. In this case, the cultural factor is not imposed externally but is part of Paul's argument. Paul does not make the cultural context of the command a universal norm, and we are not obliged to duplicate the cultural context of the command to work.

There is another case in which the cultural factor may be considered in designating the recipient without usurping the authority of Scripture. The Bible may address people in cultural settings or historical situations that are not present in other cultures. If Scripture expresses no moral injunction that the situation be recreated, the generic principle that undergirds the biblical injunction rather than the culturally or historically limited injunction itself should be applied to other situations. That is a legitimate guideline to follow unless the cultural form itself is treated by Scripture as having enduring significance. For example, biblical commands requiring kind treatment for animals or slaves do not require a person to have either animals or slaves. The principle of kindness must be applied to any people or sentient beings that are dependent on the twentieth-century believer. But he does not need to become a farmer or slaveholder to obey the command.

Discerning the meaning intended by the author. Understanding cultural factors that provide the setting of a biblical text may be helpful in clarifying the meaning of a passage if it is unclear or contains an apparent inconsistency with other clearer biblical teachings (see chaps. 8 and 15 for discussion of this). But cultural insight may not be used to modify the plain meaning intended by the author; nor may it be used to determine the God-intended recipient of a passage. The data of Scripture must control those decisions because the Bible itself is our authority.

Current culture. An understanding of current cultural forms is helpful in two ways. First, present realities challenge the Bible student to reexamine accepted interpretations. For example, scientific theory has driven us to take a closer look at traditional understandings of Genesis. A sociological movement has forced reexamination of the role of women, just as a movement required our forefathers to reevaluate God's will concerning slavery.

Second, an accurate understanding of present cultural factors is essential if one is to make correct application of eternal truth to his culture. But contemporary customs and anthropological theory may not be used as the norm to which the plain meaning of Scripture is forced to adapt. For example, the command to love and cherish one's wife (Eph. 5:25, 28-29) must be applied differently in different cultures. In America, if a man never praises his wife before others and refuses to embrace her when saying goodbye in the lobby of an airport, he is probably disobeying the apostolic command. But for the Japanese husband to do those things might not be so much an expression of love as a public scandal bringing shame on the name of the family. The truth must be applied authentically in each cultural context, but in doing that the plain teaching of Scripture may not be set aside.

Finally, we must exercise modesty in using cultural tools, as we are far removed by language, history, culture, and geography from the setting in which the original revelation was given. We must use these tools but refuse to be used by them.

USE OF CERTAIN PRINCIPLES TO DEFINE MEANING, LIMIT AUDIENCE, OR DETERMINE MEANING

Only principles are valid. Only principles are valid, not the specific teaching itself. This position is the opposite of a commonly held view that only direct commands and injunctions are authoritative for present Christian behavior. Of course, that latter contention is invalid, since the Bible is filled with teaching in the form of general principles, rather than specific commands. In fact, far more than a collection of maxims, formula, and specific rules, the Bible is a book of principles. However, the opposite contention seems to be gaining ground: specific teaching and direct commands are not universally applicable, but only the principle that lies behind the direct teaching.

This approach is very appealing, not only because it makes life easier, in a sense, but because there is a strong element in the approach that is true to the authority of Scripture. The approach of limiting normative teaching to principles derived from biblical specifics need not be an attempt to subvert or get around Scripture but can serve to implement the authority of Scripture.

However, where in the Bible is such an approach taught? Where in Scripture are we told that the specific declarations of God's truth and God's will for men are not normative, but only the principles that lie behind them? The explicit declarations of Scripture are treated as normative both in the Old Testament and the New. To disallow the authority of explicit statements on that ground is not to permit Scripture to make the choice. The Bible gives both specifics and generic principles.

To derive generic principles from specific teaching is legitimate. But the principle must not then be turned on the specific teaching to modify it or disallow it for application today. To set aside any specific teaching of Scripture, allowing only the principle deduced to be normative, is to impose an extrabiblical notion and violate the authority of Scripture.

Only teaching based in the nature of God is normative. Only teaching that is based on the nature of God or on the order of creation is universally normative. Other teachings may be transient, that is, not applicable to the believer today. The problem here is the same as in the preceding case: Scripture itself does not enunciate such a principle for discriminating among its teachings. Therefore, the interpreter becomes the authority, sitting in judgment on the teachings of Scripture, which he may not deem to be based on the nature of God or the order of creation.

Furthermore, there is a problem in applying this principle. Is the Fall of man based on the nature of God or on the order of creation? It does not seem to be based on either, although it is inherently theological. Or is it? Is teaching concerning the Lord's Supper and its observance grounded in anything other than the authoritative word of Christ? It does not seem to be grounded in the nature of God or in the order of creation. It was a cultural form that He made normative. What of the command that the wife should be in subjection to the authority of her husband, or that homosexual behavior is wrong? If all explicit teaching not limited by Scripture itself is taken as normative, those teachings are normative. However, if only those teachings that can be demonstrated to be theological in nature or to be certainly grounded in the nature of God or in the order of creation are considered normative, those teachings, along with many others, become legitimate questions for debate.

Seeking the theological basis of any teaching or searching for its foundation in the nature of God or in the order of creation is very helpful in several ways. To demonstrate that kind of foundation may reinforce or clarify specific teaching. It helps in discerning general principles lying behind specific teaching. This approach may be used along with other indicators in the text itself to ferret out that which Scripture did not intend as a universal norm. But to set aside any specific teaching simply because its theological nature cannot be proved is to introduce an extrabiblical hermeneutical principle that violates the independent authority of Scripture.

Summary

Scripture itself must determine whom God would have believe and obey a given teaching. If the context itself does not make that clear, appeal may be made to other passages. But in the end, external criteria may not be imposed on Scripture to disallow its applicability to contemporary life.

The Bible is God's revelation of His will for all mankind; therefore, any teaching of Scripture should be taken as normative for contemporary faith and living unless Scripture itself indicates otherwise. Yet, to identify the intended recipient of a teaching does not automatically indicate the specific implications for faithful discipleship. What response does God desire? Chapter 20 will address that question.

Selected Bibliography for Further Study

Carson, Donald A. *Biblical Interpretation and the Church: Text and Context.* Grand Rapids: Baker, 1988.

Larkin, William J., Jr. *Culture and Biblical Hermeneutics: Interpreting and Applying the Authoritative Word in a Relativistic Age.* Grand Rapids: Baker, 1988.

20
Identifying the Response God Desires

Guideline: *God desires the response of faith and obedience to both the direct teachings and the principles of Scripture.*

The goal of all Bible study is to apply the truth of Scripture to life. If that application is not made, all the work put into making sure of the author's intended meaning will have gone for naught. In fact, to know and not do doubles the offense of disobedience.

Unfortunately, many Bible students "get a blessing" from the Bible through subjective impressions suggested by what they read without any serious attempt to determine the author's meaning. If they are taught merely to carefully search out the meaning along the lines given in the earlier portions of this book, they may feel dry or academic, inhibited from freely taking off from some text and soaring in imagination. That can be tragic, because it bypasses the purpose of Scripture, and it can open the door for doing almost anything one pleases to do with a passage, while feeling that the impression is an authoritative message from God. Through the prophets and apostles God spoke truth He intended us to understand, believe, and obey. So we must work hard at understanding Scripture so that what we believe and obey is truly His will and not our own ideas.

In contrast, others are very careful to search out the exact meaning intended by the author, yet do not follow through by making serious application to life. They study carefully but do not spend much time in reflecting on the response God desires. That failure is even more deadly than failing to understand the author's meaning. The application for faith and obedience in my life and in the lives of those for whom I have spiritual responsibility is the purpose of Bible study.[1]

How do we go from understanding to application? As we saw in the last chapter, we must first determine whether a given teaching is intended for contemporary obedience. Our premise is that all of Scripture is for us unless, in one way or another, Scripture itself limits a teaching to others. Once the recipient of a given passage has been determined, we must next inquire: What response does God desire from me or from those to whom I have a responsibility to communicate God's truth? The response God desires is faith and obedience. Yet the content of doctrine and the way of obedience are not always immediately apparent. God reveals His will in two ways through Scripture: explicit declaration and generic principle. Consider both, because the initial response differs.

Explicit Declarations and Directives

When the doctrine of Scripture is explicitly declared, the only response acceptable to God is faith. God's existence and character, the incarnation of His Son, and the sinful nature of man are explicitly revealed to be received by faith. Again, the declaration of what I and my fellow believers are to be and do often is explicitly revealed—follow Jesus, pray always, forgive our neighbors. The response to the explicit directives of Scripture is obedience.

When a doctrine is clearly taught, we are called to faith. That means more than simply agreeing that a doctrine is true. For example, to apply the truth of God's sovereign control over all things means to think through the implications of that truth for applicability to present circumstances. Am I fearful? Is some Christian friend constantly worrying about the future? Application means that we clearly face the implications of each doctrine we say we believe, and learn to respond to it in faith.

1. A book that is very helpful in identifying guidelines for making application is *Toward an Exegetical Theology: Biblical Exegesis for Preaching and Teaching*, by Walter C. Kaiser (Grand Rapids: Baker, 1981).

The Bible is filled with promises for all of God's people. Our responsibility is not merely to make sure of the meaning by analyzing the text and relating the promise to other teachings of Scripture, such as those that might qualify the promise. No, God has promised to supply all our needs, but until my mind is tranquil and my life reflects contentment, I have not fully applied that promise.

Not only are there truths to believe and promises to claim, there are commands and instructions to obey. For example, it might be difficult to actually consider others better than myself. But until I examine my attitude toward each person in my life and ask God's assistance in obeying such a command, I have not begun to apply it to my life. Are there those in your congregation who hold a grudge? Is there a formal relationship among the members that does not go deeper than friendly church suppers? God says we must forgive one another if we desire His forgiveness, and that we should love one another with fervency. The leader of the church who does not search out all the biblical teaching on relationships among believers and does not constantly seek ways to correct wrong or inadequate relationships has stopped short of the final and indispensable step in Bible study—application.

In the case of explicit declaration of doctrine or some directive for life, the implications for faith and obedience are usually clear enough, though perhaps difficult to follow. But what of teaching that is not explicit? Does it have less authority? Are the demands of faith and obedience weaker when the teaching is not in the form of an explicit command? No, for the Bible is a book of general principles as well as of explicit directives. Note that principles of Scripture have the same authority as explicit directives. For example, one should refrain from saying not only "Raca" (Matt. 5:22) but any other derogatory term as well. However, the specific teaching itself is normative as is the principle behind it, unless the condition of the teaching is not mandated in Scripture and it does not exist in the situation at hand. In 1 Timothy 2:2, to pray for the king is the specific teaching. To pray also for the governor or the U.S. president is the principle applied. You do not have to anoint a king to obey the command—just obey the principle. But if you do have a king, obey the specific command and pray for him. Wash your brother's feet if they are dirty (John 13) but serve him in other ways if he does not need such help at the moment.

Note one other guideline for relating explicit commands to principles in Scripture. No general principle, such as love, can be used to set aside an explicit directive of Scripture, as situationists would do. If the Bible commands a person to stay married, he cannot seek a divorce by appealing to the principle of love. He has no authorization to deduce a principle from an explicit directive forbidding polygamy and then apply that principle to violate the specific command itself. In this case, that would not only permit polygamy but require it under certain circumstances. No, both the specific teaching and the principle inherent are normative, requiring faith and obedience of all people of all times.

Discerning God's desired response is not always as clear in the case of principles as in the case of explicit directives. So the task is to recognize the full authority of each biblical principle; to carefully determine what it is; to reflect seriously on the implications of that principle; and to put it into practice.

Generic Principles

A generic principle is a biblical norm or standard that may be applied to more than one type of situation. Yet the response to such principles should be the same as to explicit declarations: faith and obedience. Because general principles are not always immediately apparent, faith and obedience have special characteristics: diligence, openness, and courage; that is, diligence to probe, openness to change, and courage to challenge traditional interpretations.

Where do principles come from? Basically, there are four sources of biblical principles. Let us consider each in some detail.

EXPLICITLY STATED PRINCIPLES

"You shall love your neighbor as yourself" (Lev. 19:18) is an explicit directive in a sense, and yet it is also a generic principle. How love is to be expressed is described in specific detail in Scripture. Yet the specifically revealed applications are in no way intended to be exhaustive. It is imperative to ferret out the full implications of that command for contemporary life, for the Bible does not apply its related principle to all contemporary problems. For example, how does this principle work out in labor/management relations or in a multinational corporation policy? The implications of neighborly love must be rigorously pursued in all of life.

GENERAL PRINCIPLES DERIVED FROM EXPLICIT DECLARATION

A principle may be derived through logical deduction from a teaching or a combination of direct teaching. For example, there is a network of explicit teaching concerning sexual purity. "You shall not commit adultery" (Ex. 20:14), "Everyone who looks on a woman to lust for her has committed adultery with her already in his heart" (Matt. 5:28). The principle behind that pattern of commandments relates to sexual purity. Behind it is no doubt another principle, that of fidelity, and behind the principle of fidelity is yet another principle, love.

To derive a general principle concerning purity is not only legitimate but necessary to make the Bible the functional authority in contemporary life. For example, neither pornography nor voyeurism is explicitly condemned in Scripture. For that reason, some evangelical counselors use pornography to treat troubled marriages. But that is not possible if the scriptural pattern of commands yielding a very clear principle is applied faithfully. Sexual purity in mind and body is a biblical principle derived from many teachings on the subject of human sexuality, on the nature of sin (cognitive as well as physical), on fidelity, on love, and no doubt on other teachings as well.

GENERAL PRINCIPLES DERIVED FROM HISTORICAL PASSAGES

A historic event always has some implication. Otherwise, it would not be included in Holy Writ. And often there is more than one implication. That implication may be no more than to provide necessary historical setting. The event could be used as an illustration of some important truth. But if it is to be used to derive a general principle, it must be so interpreted by Scripture itself. If an event is not interpreted by Scripture, it may not be used to derive a doctrine or principle of conduct.

Scripture leaves many historic events uninterpreted, but of many it renders a judgment: the behavior is either commended or condemned. In some of those instances Scripture goes even further; it gives a reason for the commendation or condemnation. Such interpreted events are the legitimate raw material for refining general principles. For example, if Abraham is held up as an example of faith in the sacrifice of Isaac, then we are safe in considering his act commendatory, although we might not have thought so on our own. If Scripture commends the deception of the Egyptian midwives and condemns the deception of Abraham and Sarah, we are pressed to search for the principles lying behind the commendation and the condemnation before applying those illustrations to current conduct. However, if Scripture does not say whether or not the event is commendable, I may not derive a principle or make application to what I may consider parallel circumstances, using the biblically recorded circumstances as the authority for establishing a norm.

We shun the error of evil men and take warning from their punishment (1 Cor. 10:11). We follow the example of righteous men when their actions illustrate the basic will of God. Paul repeatedly tells us to do that—to imitate him as he imitates Christ. Nevertheless, was Paul's pattern of splitting synagogues to establish churches a universal norm that we should take as an example to follow? Those historic events must be interpreted in the light of clear, direct teaching, and be used to illustrate principles for current application only with that validation. If the Bible did not render a verdict on whether God approved of the conduct, we are not free to use it authoritatively as a model to follow or to expect others to follow.

Consider the story of Job. It is illegitimate to derive the principle that all temptation is of the devil. A historic event such as Job's experience can yield only the principle that at least some temptation is of the devil, and, therefore, any specific temptation might be the work of the enemy. If one advocates the doctrine that all temptation is the direct work of Satan, he will need to prove it from some other source.

Paul said to the Philippian jailer, "Believe in the Lord Jesus, and you shall be saved." This is a report of a historical event, yet we rightly infer that it has an application to others as well as to the jailer. And yet the jailer asked, "What must I do?" He did not ask, "What must anyone, anywhere, anytime do?" Paul answered his question as to what *he* must do. We cannot prove from this passage a doctrine—that this is all that ever must be done to gain salvation. The doctrine must be proved elsewhere. Peter said, in answer to a similar question, "*You* particular people must repent and be baptized." Christ, in answer to a similar question said, "Sell what you have, give to the poor and come, follow Me." We may not be selective among these and choose what we please. We must examine all the data of Scripture and establish the validity of a universal norm seen in any specific historical context from the affirmations of Scripture.

Historic events occur in books that are not devoted to history and those also may be fruitful for deriving principles that can be applied today. For example, in Romans 15 and 16, Paul reported personal details about himself, gave specific instructions for people then living in Rome, and included many greetings. That passage is primarily limited to specific people and events in history and much of it is not directly applicable to us. But interspersed is teaching that is universal. Paul had a policy of not preaching the gospel where it had already gone (Rom. 15:20). That is not a principle that all Christians or even all missionaries must follow; it was Paul's specific "job description." But when he said that the Gentile churches had a duty to help materially the Christians at Jerusalem because they had benefited spiritually through those Christians (Rom. 15:26-27), he seemed to imply a general principle. Why? Not only because that teaching is given explicitly elsewhere, but also because Paul gave, in the passage, the reason for the duty. And that reason is given as a basic principle: they should give because they had benefited spiritually.

Other historical passages from which we may legitimately draw principles are prayers and songs. If they reflect godly responses of godly people, we should feel free to pray those prayers and sing those songs. But they have authority as infallible truth only if they were given by an inspired author of Scripture, such as David or Paul. Even then, care must be exercised. For example not every prayer of Christ is suitable for us to pray. A pastor may legitimately pray for his people in the words Christ prayed for His disciples, "The words which Thou gavest Me I have given to them;

and they received them. . . . I do not ask Thee to take them out of the world, but to keep them from the evil one" (John 17:8, 15). He might even go on to pray, "As Thou didst send Me into the world, I also have sent them into the world" (v. 18). But he could hardly pray, "Father, I desire that they also, whom Thou hast given Me, be with Me where I am, in order that they may behold My glory" (v. 24). Although there are pastors who behave in that way, it would hardly be an appropriate prayer!

In summary, historical passages have three levels of authority when used as sources for deriving general principles to be used for contemporary application.

1. When Scripture itself evaluates an event and gives the reason for that evaluation, the historical event has the highest authority for being normative.
2. If Scripture evaluates a historic event as worthy of commendation or condemnation but does not make the reason clear, it is legitimate to use that event, along with clear teaching of Scripture, in deducing a principle. But the principle so derived does not have the same level of certainty.
3. On the lowest level of usefulness are those historic events on which Scripture does not render a judgment. Although those passages may be used to illustrate truth clearly taught elsewhere, they may not be used independently to establish normative Christian doctrine or behavior.

GENERAL PRINCIPLES DERIVED FROM PASSAGES THAT DO NOT DIRECTLY APPLY TO CONTEMPORARY LIFE

As we have seen, many commandments or teachings (1) are qualified in the context as to whom and under what circumstances they apply; (2) are modified by later revelation; or (3) appear to conflict with teaching that is clearer or receives greater and more enduring emphasis in Scripture. Nevertheless, those teachings in some way reflect God's will since they originated with Him. Therefore, some universal truth compatible with God's character must lie behind the teaching, even if it is not God's desire that everyone follow that particular teaching. How can it be of any value if it was limited at the time or modified later?

If the purpose of a command or teaching is given in Scripture, its applicability has the force of principle even if the teaching itself is not universal. The same approach suggested for deriving principles from historical passages applies. That is, since the purpose is given, that purpose becomes the basis of an enduring principle. For example, God commanded Joshua to drive out the people of Canaan to make room for Israel. Does that mean God intends the church to launch a crusade against the Muslims who occupy the same land? No. But why did God do it? Because, we are told, He loved Israel. And that reason is an unchanging principle behind all of God's activities.

But what if the purpose for a command is not clearly revealed? May one deduce such an underlying principle from teaching that does not apply to us today? Just as in the case of historical passages, if clear parallels can be drawn from teaching that is universal, it may be proper to use the limited teaching as an illustration of God's will, but such an illustration does not have the authority of revealed truth any more than any other contemporary application of Scripture.

Consider passages of Scripture, particularly in the Old Testament, that are direct and clearly show the intent of the author but have been modified by subsequent revelation.

For example, war was explicitly and directly commanded in the Old Testament. Many throughout church history have taken that as authorization for justifiable, aggressive warfare. However, Jesus Christ taught nonresistance and explicitly taught that His kingdom was not of this world. Christians are not to fight with physical weaponry to defend or extend His kingdom. But whatever that teaching of Christ may mean for personal relations or international relations today, it is not legitimate to say that all physical warfare is against the will of God. Even if God commanded warfare only once, it shows there is nothing in physical warfare that is inherently, universally unacceptable to the will and character of God. Therefore, since some war is legitimate and some not, we are driven to seek a principle that lies behind the commands and resolves the apparent conflict between such teachings. So a general principle may be derived from a passage that does not directly apply to contemporary life: warfare is not always wrong.

We have considered four ways by which principles may be

derived from Scripture. When those principles are clearly the revealed will of God, they have equal authority with explicit declarations of doctrine or directives for life. Faith and obedience are the responses God expects to His revelation. And His revelation is replete with principles. I. Howard Marshall emphasizes that

> instead of arguing directly from a biblical situation to the modern situation, often by ignoring the differences between the two situations and by misapplying proof texts, we must work back from the biblical teaching in specific situations to the underlying biblical principles and then reapply them to our own situations and problems.[2]

A. Berkeley Mickelsen makes a similar point: "Personal application involves the working out from the passage a principle that is true for anyone who belongs to God or a principle for individuals in parallel situations."[3]

These are valuable insights provided they do not lead to disallowing the direct application of explicit declarations of Scripture. God awaits our response of faith and obedience, both to explicit declarations and to legitimately derived principles.

Note one further matter concerning principles. Although an explicitly revealed principle has full authority as the will of God, the application of that principle by the Christian or the church does not share in that infallibility. We may err in making application. But we are, nevertheless, responsible to constantly apply biblical principles to the best of our understanding of them and of their implications.

A Method for Using the Guidelines to Apply Scripture

To assist in using those guidelines for applying a Bible passage, the following flow chart (next page) might help. Consider these examples as I trace them through the chart, using Acts 2:44-45 as the sample passage.

Verses 44-45 read: "And all those who had believed were to-

2. I. Howard Marshall, "Is the Bible Our Supreme Authority?" *His,* March 1978, p. 12.
3. A. Berkeley Mickelsen, *Interpreting the Bible* (Grand Rapids: Eerdmans. 1963), p. 357.

FLOW CHART FOR APPLYING A BIBLE PASSAGE

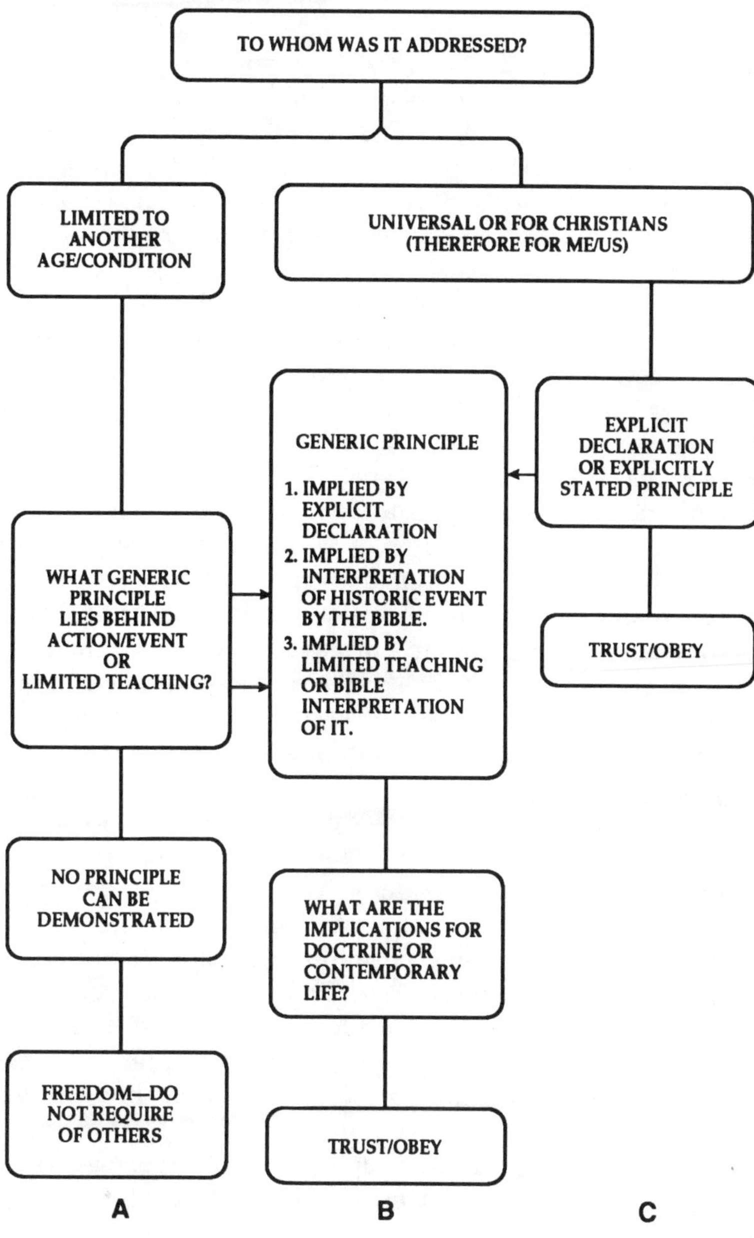
TO WHOM WAS IT ADDRESSED?
LIMITED TO ANOTHER AGE/CONDITION
UNIVERSAL OR FOR CHRISTIANS (THEREFORE FOR ME/US)
GENERIC PRINCIPLE
1. IMPLIED BY EXPLICIT DECLARATION
2. IMPLIED BY INTERPRETATION OF HISTORIC EVENT BY THE BIBLE.
3. IMPLIED BY LIMITED TEACHING OR BIBLE INTERPRETATION OF IT.
EXPLICIT DECLARATION OR EXPLICITLY STATED PRINCIPLE
WHAT GENERIC PRINCIPLE LIES BEHIND ACTION/EVENT OR LIMITED TEACHING?
TRUST/OBEY
NO PRINCIPLE CAN BE DEMONSTRATED
WHAT ARE THE IMPLICATIONS FOR DOCTRINE OR CONTEMPORARY LIFE?
FREEDOM—DO NOT REQUIRE OF OTHERS
TRUST/OBEY
A
B
C

gether, and had all things in common; and they began selling their property and possessions, and were sharing them with all, as anyone might have need."

To whom was it addressed? As a record of a historic event, this is *limited to another age/condition.* Notice the next question: *What generic principle lies behind the teaching/action?* Is that the way Christians in all ages and societies are to behave? Since this behavior is reported in a favorable light, both here and even more clearly in Acts 4:33–5:11, we can derive at least one principle: it is not wrong to have all things common in a Christian community or to sell one's possessions and give the proceeds to the needy. The only way that could be considered wrong would be if some limitation were set, or if condemnation were given in some other passage of Scripture. Since there is neither, we must accept that behavior as appropriate, at least, for some Christians at times.

But note that Luke does not give a clear-cut reason for the behavior. Because he does not spell out the principle, we cannot make that normative behavior to be required of all Christians; we cannot relegate it to the right side of the chart (column C) and treat it as an *explicitly stated principle.* In this case, we have even further evidence of limitation in the parallel passage (Acts 5:4). There was no rule that the early disciples had to sell or had to give all or even part of what they sold. Therefore, what positive principles may be derived from this praiseworthy action? Following the chart (column B), what are the *implications for doctrine or contemporary life*?

This example seems to depict generous and sacrificial giving as a way of life. Full responsibility for the physical care of church members seems to be considered the standard. There are no doubt other principles. Principles become much stronger when they are reinforced by explicit teaching elsewhere in Scripture. In fact, they become mandates. "Trust and obey" is one principle become mandate; trust God to care for your needs so that you are free to give, even to sell and give. We are to commit our lives to sacrificial living and to a fully responsible relationship with fellow church members (column B, generic principle 2).

Let's follow this process for applying a Bible passage with five other texts: Titus 1:5, 1:6; Psalm 121:3-5; Matthew 5:39; and Acts 1:8.

TITUS 1:5

> For this reason I left you in Crete, that you might set in order what remains, and appoint elders in every city as I directed you.

We start at the top of the flow chart: To whom was it addressed? It was addressed to a particular person (Titus) who bore a particular relationship to another particular person (Paul), so it is limited to another age/condition. Therefore, this passage cannot be made the rule for how elders are chosen. On the other hand, taken with a great number of explicit declarations, the implication for doctrine or contemporary life is that a Bible-study group or campus fellowship that does not have responsible, biblically ordained leadership is not an authentic church. The response required is for such a group to become a church or for each member to be joined to a church and not use the fellowship group as a substitute (column B, generic principle 3).

TITUS 1:6

> If any man be above reproach, the husband of one wife, having children who believe, not accused of dissipation or rebellion.

Again we begin with the question, "To whom was it addressed?" Note that there is a shift between verse 5 and 6. Verse 5 is a specific instruction for Titus as the apostle's assistant, but verse 6 sets standards for deciding who is eligible for eldership. Taken with the parallel passage (1 Tim.3:4), this is clearly for *me/us.* It is an *explicit declaration* and simply needs to be obeyed (column C). Those who do not meet this qualification should not be elders. Note that a word study is necessary to determine whether *faithful* in the King James Version should be translated "children who believe," as in the *New American Standard Bible.* That would be a much higher standard and would eliminate a large portion of contemporary elders! Nevertheless, once the meaning is established, the teaching must be accepted by faith and followed: *trust/obey.*

PSALM 121:3-5

> He will not allow your foot to slip;
> He who keeps you will not slumber.
> Behold, He who keeps Israel
> Will neither slumber nor sleep.
> The Lord is your keeper;
> The Lord is your shade on your right hand.

To whom was this passage addressed? The form was a song of praise or testimony addressed to God's people. Is it addressed only to Israel? If so, it should follow the chart through *limited to another age/condition* as far as non-Jews are concerned. As with most psalms of testimony, it was written for all God's people, including Israel. So through the Bible's own interpretation this limited teaching becomes a universal principle for all God's children (column B, generic principle 3). It is a wonderful truth about God and His children and should be fully trusted and acted on.

MATTHEW 5:39

> But I say to you, do not resist him who is evil; but whoever slaps you on your right cheek, turn to him the other also.

To whom was it addressed? Certainly to *me/us* (column C). If not, we are in trouble, for none of Christ's teaching could then be applied to us with confidence. And if He by His life and teachings does not reveal the response God desires, we are without hope of knowing God's will. It would seem to be an explicit declaration. And it is. But there are other teachings of Scripture that modify that. For example, the police officer is supposed to resist evil, and so are parents. In fact, Christ, when struck on one cheek, did not literally turn the other cheek (John 18:22-23). For that reason I would move the teaching from explicit declaration to generic principle 1: *implied by explicit declaration* (column B). In other words, nonresistance is clearly taught. That should be carefully related to all other Bible teaching that touches on the subject. The implications for doctrine and contemporary life should be faithfully worked out and fully obeyed, with confidence in the Lord to care for the consequences.

ACTS 1:8

> But you shall receive power when the Holy Spirit has come upon you; and you shall be My witnesses both in Jerusalem, and in all Judea and Samaria, and even to the remotest part of the earth.

To whom was it addressed? To *me/us* (column C). How do we know that? The section seems to be just as historical as Acts 2:44-45. But it is not limited to another age/condition for two reasons. Being filled with the Spirit is explicitly taught elsewhere as the norm for all Christians. World evangelization is taught and demonstrated as the responsibility of the whole church. On the flow chart, I would trace this through generic principle 2: *implied by biblical interpretation of historic events* (column B). The implications for doctrine or contemporary life are painfully obvious. When most congregations devote most of their people and monetary resources to their own "Jerusalem," the disobedience is nothing less than appalling.

In the above way, any passage of Scripture may be analyzed for its present-day application. I have used examples that would illustrate the various possibilities. But most of the major teachings of Scripture on what we are to believe (doctrine) and how we are to behave are not difficult to understand. The explicit teachings are enough to occupy us for a lifetime. Nevertheless, *all* Scripture is inspired and profitable, and though an application of a teaching may be difficult or disputed, it is our responsibility to study diligently to show ourselves approved with no need of being ashamed.

Biblical Authority for a Doctrine or Activity

But there is a further problem in applying Scripture. Much of the division in the church does not start at the point of some disputed passage of Scripture. Rather, someone states an idea, some accept it, others reject it without examining it carefully, and the church is divided. If we do not begin with a passage of Scripture (as in chart 1) but with a doctrine or activity, how do we evaluate its biblical authority for faith and contemporary living? Using guidelines we have studied, the following flow chart may help. Let us consider a few examples, tracing them through the chart.

FLOW CHART FOR EVALUATING THE BIBLICAL AUTHORITY FOR A DOCTRINE OR ACTIVITY

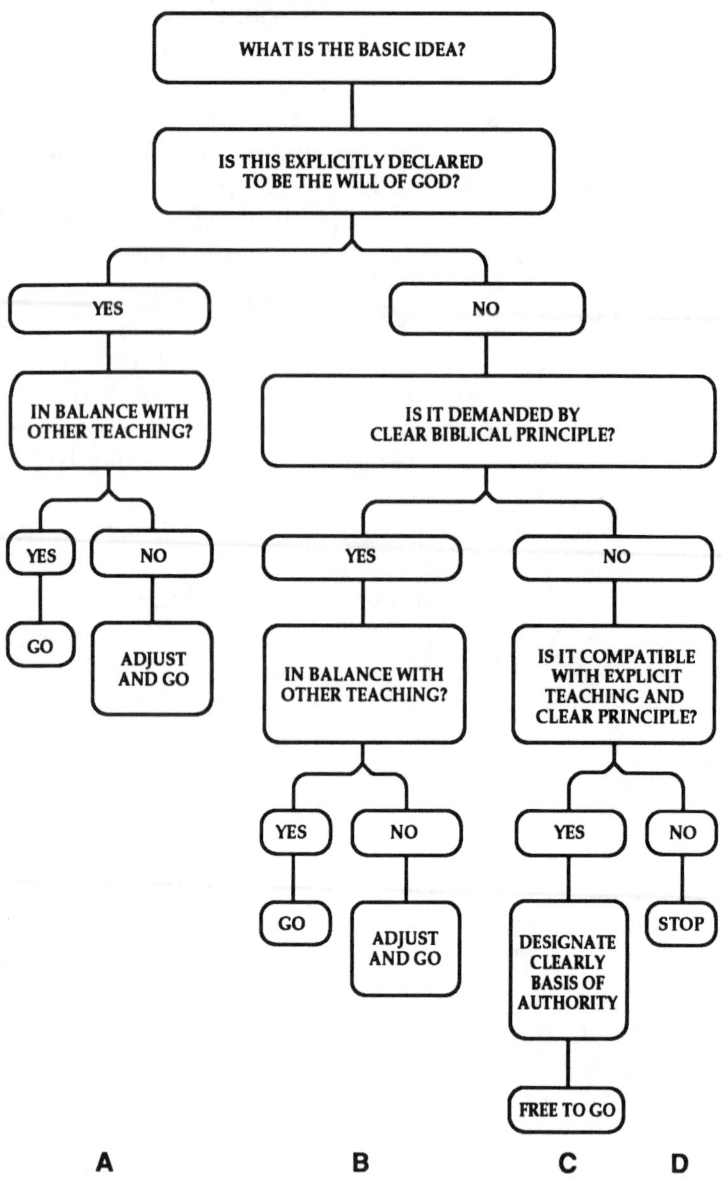

Some people advocate that evangelism is the primary purpose of the church. Before debating that assertion, we should insist on an answer to the first question the chart: *What is the basic idea?* Does the proponent mean evangelism is the *sole* purpose of the church? Then this would have to follow the chart through *no* (column D), because many other purposes are taught in Scripture. "Primary purpose" could mean that evangelism is the primary "responsibility" of the church toward the world. If so, I would say yes, it is *explicitly declared to be the will of God* (column A). Not all would agree, and so the debate can now go to the place it belongs: the specific passages of Scripture that deal with the issue. Once we get to a specific passage, we can use the former flow chart (chart 1).

But is that teaching in balance with other teaching? For example, does the advocate really feel that this is the *only* responsibility of the church toward the world? Does his church's activity indicate no responsible acceptance of the biblical mandate to seek justice and mercy in society? Then the explicitly declared will of God is not *in balance with other teaching* (column A) and must be adjusted. On the other hand, does "in balance with other teaching" mean equal emphasis? No, as we have seen earlier (chaps. 15-16), it means an emphasis similar to the Bible's emphasis. Does evangelistic zeal expend itself fully in one's own local witness, with no major effort for the unreached of the world? Does a missions program exhaust a church's energies so that it is not growing with new converts from its own community? In either case, the teaching is unbalanced and needs adjustment, followed by faith and obedience.

Consider the statement "The church should concentrate its energies on the people of the world who have never heard." First of all, *What is the basic idea?* If it means that no one has a right to hear the gospel twice until all have heard it once, it is not *explicitly declared to be the will of God,* it is not *demanded by clear biblical principle,* and it is not very *compatible with explicit teaching and clear principle* (column C). It probably should be rejected (column D). But if biblical evidence is given that proves it is in some way compatible with Scripture, though not required by it, the basis of authority should be clearly stated. It is one's personal conviction, not the revealed truth of God. On the other hand, if the basic idea is simply that the church should give top priority to seeing that every person on earth has an opportunity to hear the good news and that a church be established in every community, that is surely *explicitly declared to be the will of God* (column A).

Some might mean by that statement that we need a total realignment of people and resources to focus church activity on the dark half of the world, those who have no opportunity even to hear because there is no witnessing church among them. This cannot be proved from explicitly stated commands (column A). But it does seem to me to be demanded by clear biblical principle (column B), and if other responsibilities of the church are kept in balance, it would seem to be the most important and most neglected responsibility of the church today. If so, the call is to faith and obedience.

Should the church take the responsibility for arranging marriages for their unmarried? This is hardly the explicitly declared will of God (column A) or demanded by clear biblical principle (column B). Is it compatible with explicit teaching and clear principle? Certainly it is, and the practice should be permitted in societies where it is appropriate (column C).

What of the requirement that a call to confess Christ publicly be given at every church service? On the flow chart that would clearly come out as merely compatible, not biblically required (column C). Therefore, to invest the practice with absolute authority seems questionable.

Liberation theology is widespread. But what is its *basic idea?* That the gospel liberates those in bondage? Then it is *explicitly declared* (column A). Does it mean that the church should work toward justice and mercy in society at large? Then my conviction is that it is *demanded by clear biblical principle* (column B) and, if kept in biblical balance, must be obeyed. Does it mean that God is working in the violent revolutions of our time and that the church should be involved in the violence? Then it is not *compatible with explicit teaching and clear principle* and should be stopped (column D).

Those illustrations are intended to provide one possible way of highlighting and actually guiding the evaluation of biblical authority for a doctrine or activity. The responsibility for the Bible student is to identify the recipient intended and clarify the response God desires. How are faith and obedience to be expressed in light of a particular passage and teaching? Application to what we believe and how we live is the final goal of Bible study.

How does one make functional the authority of the Bible in his or her own life and in the life of the church? By allowing the Bible itself to control answers to the following questions: What did the author mean? For whom is this teaching intended? What response does God desire?

If the Bible is to actually function as the true authority in our lives, we must give ourselves to determining precisely what Scripture means (chaps. 8-18), what in Scripture is intended for faith and obedience today (chap. 19), what the generic principles are, and how God intends us to apply His revealed will (chap. 20). When we begin to do that in earnest, and with Spirit-given wisdom and faithfulness, the purpose of divine revelation in our obedience and faith will be more adequately fulfilled and God will be more fully satisfied.

Selected Bibliography for Further Study

Best, Ernest. *From Text to Sermon: Responsible Use of the New Testament in Preaching.* Atlanta: John Knox, 1978.

Greidanus, Sidney. *The Modern Preacher and the Ancient Text.* Grand Rapids: Eerdmans, 1988.

Henrichsen, Walter A., and Gayle M. Jackson. *Studying, Interpreting and Applying the Bible.* Grand Rapids: Zondervan, 1990.

Johnson, Elliot E. *Expository Hermeneutics: An Introduction.* Grand Rapids: Zondervan, 1990.

Kaiser, Walter C., Jr. *Toward an Exegetical Theology: Biblical Exegesis for Preaching and Teaching.* Grand Rapids: Baker, 1981.

Kuhatschek, Jack. *Taking the Guesswork Out of Applying the Bible.* Downers Grove, Ill.: InterVarsity, 1990.

Liefeld, Walter L. *New Testament Exposition: From Text to Sermon.* Grand Rapids: Zondervan, 1984.

Conclusion

We have come to the end of our study of how to understand and apply the Bible. Let us return to our initial questions:

1. How important is it to understand and apply Scripture?
2. Is it possible to understand and apply with confidence the teachings of the Bible?

Is it important to understand and apply Scripture correctly? The Bible is the only infallible revelation of God's will for man; therefore no human activity could be of greater importance.

> But evil men and impostors will keep on going from bad to worse, deceiving others and being deceived themselves. But as for you, continue in the truths that you were taught and firmly believe. You know who your teachers were, and you remember that ever since you were a child you have known the Holy Scriptures, which are able to give you the wisdom that leads to salvation through faith in Christ Jesus. All Scripture is inspired by God and is useful for teaching the truth, rebuking error, correcting faults, and giving instruction for right living, so that the man who serves God may be fully qualified and equipped to do every kind of good work. (2 Tim. 3:13-17, TEV)

Paul tells us clearly how important it is to understand Scripture. Whether it be salvation, doctrine, sanctification, or service, the Bible is the source. The Bible alone brings life and growth to maturity in all we were designed to be. Are you preaching the Word of God? Are you teaching the Bible to others? Or are you simply listening to sermons and reading Christian books and magazines? Certainly you are studying the Bible for yourself to understand what God wants you to know and do. Whatever your activity, how important it is to be skilled in digging out the meaning and significance of what the Bible authors intended.

Some of the illustrations from Scripture we have considered are not crucial for doctrine and contemporary living. But other issues, such as God's sovereignty and man's responsibility, and cultural factors in Scripture, reveal how critical it is to handle the Bible correctly.

We have seen from actual examples how crucial matters can be wholly distorted by failure to use basic guidelines for understanding the meaning of the biblical text. On the other hand we have seen how God's truth often shines out in beautiful clarity when the guidelines are used.

We cannot overemphasize the importance of mastering the principles and guidelines for understanding the meaning of Scripture. But can we understand and apply with confidence the teachings of the Bible?

If we are committed to the same view the Bible has of itself, we must stick to biblical principles and follow reasonable guidelines for understanding human communication. We *can* understand what the author had in mind.

The Bible treats itself both as a thoroughly human and uniquely divine communication. So must we, or we shall go far astray. And because it is from God, we must treat it as wholly trustworthy and fully authoritative. If we build on those presuppositions and stand by those principles, we will not go astray. Flowing from those principles are many specific guidelines that are crucial for clear understanding and authentic application. You have studied those tools and used them.

Perhaps you do not yet feel confident in their use. What should you do? Keep using them faithfully in your personal study, and the confidence will grow. When you are uncertain about the approach to a particular passage of Scripture or about some guideline, use this textbook as a reference work and check out the guideline and examples once again. Periodically review all the tools to be sure none has become rusty and dull. Do you plan to go on in your study of Bible interpretation, to study the original languages and the more complex problems? Do not forget the basics! They will keep you on a sure foundation.

The key to success in understanding and applying the Bible is constant sensitivity to the principles and constant use of the guidelines until they become second nature. Listen carefully when others teach from the Bible. Is what the teacher says really what the author intended? Is the application truly the response God intended when He inspired that particular passage? Read carefully when authors use Scripture. Is the author handling the Bible carefully, observing the guidelines you have studied, or does he ignore or violate them?

Listen and read with perception, but do so with charity and modesty. One result of this study should be the undercutting of all arrogant dogmatism. Not all Bible passages are easily understood, and our approach should be one of humility. Furthermore, we should be able to get spiritual nourishment from almost any sincere proclaimer of biblical truth. Sometimes it may be only from the negative: "Thank You, Lord, that You never meant *that.* Help me not to abuse Your Word that way." But usually there is positive blessing. Even if the preacher does not legitimately get his truth from the passage he is dealing with, what he says may still be true. It is amazing that God can bless to His people's benefit a misunderstanding of an obscure passage in a minor prophet! Nevertheless, that does not give us license to do careless work when we ourselves handle the glorious and majestic revelation of a holy and loving God.

No, we must be committed to study diligently. And when we do, we can be confident that truth is not hidden and that Bible interpretation is not the private preserve of learned scholars. We can understand its meaning and apply its teaching with confidence. If we study faithfully all the days of our lives, in the end we shall find ourselves approved by God with no need to be ashamed, because we have handled rightly His Word of truth.

Index of Subjects

Index of Scripture

Moody Press, a ministry of the Moody Bible Institute,
is designed for education, evangelization, and edification.
If we may assist you in knowing more about Christ
and the Christian life, please write us without obligation:
Moody Press, c/o MLM, Chicago, Illinois 60610.